Friends and Contemporaries

A. L. ROWSE

Friends
and
Contemporaries

METHUEN · LONDON

To Kenneth Rose
admirable historian
and recorder of our time

First published in Great Britain
by Methuen London Limited
Michelin House, 81 Fulham Road,
London SW3 6RB
Copyright © 1989 A.L. Rowse

Printed in Great Britain
by St Edmundsbury Press,
Bury St Edmunds, Suffolk

British Library Cataloguing in Publication Data

Rowse, A.L. (Alfred Leslie)
Friends and contemporaries.
1. Britons, 1900 – Biographies
920'.041

ISBN 0-413-18140-5

Contents

Lord David Cecil

I owe more to David Cecil than to anyone else – except, I suppose, my parents and my old Headmaster, who saw to it that I won scholarships to take me to Oxford. I learned more from David than from anyone else in my life – certainly than from any dons. For he had a marked didactic gift, he was a marvellous teacher, naturally and unconsciously, as well as professionally as tutor and then professor – even apart from his writing, though perhaps one shouldn't make a distinction.

He was my friend all through our long lives, and I came to know enough about him and his family, his interests and his work to fill a book. Indeed the family wanted me to write their history, and at one time I thought of doing it. I got as far as writing a research article about their origins, 'Altyrinnis and the Cecils', in the *English Historical Review*. This was to correct the view held in the 16th century that they were a *nouveau* family of upstarts. Even David's eldest sister, Lady Harlech, would say in grand aristocratic fashion, 'I thought we were descended from a pork-butcher at Stamford.' In fact they were descended from an ancient family of small Welsh gentry, who came out of Wales and made their fortune with the Tudors. David's brother, 'Bobb-ity' (Fifth Marquis of Salisbury), was the only member of the family who had the curiosity to track down the little old place, as I had done, in a remote corner of Herefordshire by the Monnow.

However, I did not write the family history. I fell for the

Churchills and wrote theirs: mainly because of the historic inspiration Winston Churchill gave in the darkest days of the country's history, but also because they were West Country by origin.

One day in my third year at Christ Church, 1924–5, there arrived in my rooms, Meadows VI. 6, an extraordinarily lanky pale young man, who looked very frail but was vibrant with nervous energy and talked so fast in a very idiosyncratic way, sputtering at the lips, that I couldn't make out all he was saying. Also, I knew only his name and wasn't very clear who he was, except that he was about eighteen months my senior and already living out of college. It may be that the dons had put him on to me as somebody interesting to know, though I was already writing and publishing poetry in *The Oxford Outlook* and *Oxford Poetry*, as he was. So we had a common interest in literature, and that was what we talked about. He then asked me to lunch in his rooms in Beaumont Street. I accepted rather timorously, for I feared that there would be something I couldn't cope with; there was – wine, and asparagus; I didn't know which was worse.

He had already sat for the All Souls Fellowship, which his famous grandfather, Lord Salisbury the Prime Minister, had won. His brilliant uncles, Robert, later Viscount Cecil (of the League of Nations) and Hugh (later Lord Quickswood and Provost of Eton), had sat in vain. When it came to David's turn to try, and he was faced by an assembly of inquisitive Fellows with a paper of foreign languages to translate from unseen, David fled from the room saying, 'I can't do it.' He was indeed of an incredibly nervous disposition. The year after, I scrambled through this horrible ordeal, not doing at all well, but got elected.

All Souls was rather grand in those days – with viceroys, archbishops and Cabinet ministers – and kept up something of the state of Victorian country-house life. David was kindness itself; he said, 'If you have any trouble with all those knives and forks and glasses, let me know and I'll tell you.' I hadn't any trouble that way, for my table manners were good; but I was afraid to be a teetotaller in that company, and couldn't bear the long sessions of dessert with

my seniors hanging on, sopping up port. Old Sir William
Holdsworth, for example, after these would go off to his
rooms and write hard till midnight; I used to think of his
History of English Law as solidified All Souls port. In a
lifetime I have never been able to bear those long sittings of
l'homme moyen sensuel, sip-sip-sip, sop-sop-sop. Ugh, and
the waste of time! That wasn't like David, nor was it like
me; we had much more in common.

By this time he was settled just up the road as tutor in
English literature at Wadham College, recruited thither by
his friend Maurice Bowra. Actually he had taken a First in
the History School; this gave him a far better background
and grounding than the (rather inferior) School of Eng. Lit.
He had a wider grasp, a sense of the society of which the
literature was an expression, gave it its character; this, along
with his sensibility and perception, made him an immeasurably better exponent of literature than the usual run of
academics and all too common media critics.

Thus I saw more of him than of anyone, except my
immediate companions in college. David would come along
to my rooms for talk, morning, noon or night; for his one
and only passion – like all the Cecils he was rather cool-
blooded – was conversation. We didn't exchange meals
much, but he would arrive after dinner and keep talking till
well after midnight (I didn't much care for late hours). Then,
out in the darkness of the quad, he would begin some verbal
game. What would be the worst thing to meet one in one's
bed, beginning with a B? I suggested a Butcher; David
thought, a Boy. As we came to the step into the street, I said
'A Bishop', and then 'Step up!' 'Oh, I quite see it would be a
step up', and he went off giggling into the dark.

He had a natural quick wit, which sparkles, if in subdued
fashion, in his books. I can't remember many of his jokes
now: the apt description of 'the little bicycling colleges in the
Turl'; the 'Witches of Macbeth of North Oxford'. When
there was question of returning the Colonies to Germany,
it was he who suggested that we might give them the
Connollys. Anything for a laugh – simplest of jokes. I think
of him now coming into my room, giggling and sputtering

with fun. Someone had said, 'My grandfather was killed at Waterloo.' 'I'm so sorry – which platform?' And he was no prig. There was an enormously fat peer who was a well-known journalist, carrying a pregnant belly before him. Nancy Astor was supposed to have said, 'If that were on a woman we should all know what it means.' 'Last night it *was* on a woman: what does it mean?'

As for absent-mindedness – he was to give a talk on George Eliot at Mansfield College one evening, only five minutes' walk from Holywell where he and Rachel then lived. After the fixed time had passed the Warden rang up to know if Lord David had forgotten. The evening passed; after some hours he returned, quite pleased; all had gone well, 'only they did seem as if they hadn't expected me.' He had been and given his talk to the Cowley Fathers. It reminds me of G.K. Chesterton's telegram to his wife when away lecturing: 'Am at Market Harborough. Where *should* I be?'

Once married, he became utterly dependent on Rachel. He came down to stay with me in Cornwall for a few days, when I got him to lecture for King's School, Canterbury, evacuated to Carlyon Bay. Every evening he had to telephone her to say that he was all right. My house then was in full view of the Bay, and subject to wartime regulations about blackout: I had to rush round after him to see that the lights were not left blazing away in the windows, or the police would be upon us.

In earlier days when he was at Wadham we kept pace in our reading. One vacation we both read Wordsworth's *Prelude*, and compared notes when we got back to Oxford, each of us having thought how Proustian it was – experience transformed by memory into art. Reading Proust was all the rage in the late Twenties; we discussed it as we did all our reading. It was from David that this *ingénu* first learned that Proust's Albertine was really an Albert, and that it was the Baron de Charlus' conspicuous socks that gave him away as a homosexual, with the comic episode of the Baron getting into a suburban train with a likely young man – to find, when they got out, that he was met by wife and kids, already a *père de famille*.

Another vacation we were reading Flaubert. I read *L'Education Sentimentale* alongside *Middlemarch*, and had an unexpectedly paradoxical experience. George Eliot was heavily ethical; Flaubert not at all, much the reverse, rather scabrous. But the aesthetic effect was that the atmosphere of *Middlemarch* was cloudy, even muddied; where that of Flaubert was transparently limpid and clear.

We discussed everything in those days – the best way of educating ourselves, forming our minds. I was on my way to concentrating on the Tudor period, always of interest to him. We discussed Elizabeth I – a living presence to him at Hatfield; and constantly Shakespeare. We were under the common misapprehension that the Sonnets were homo-erotic – I more strongly than David; and neither of us could make out who 'Mr W.H.' could possibly be. We thought that we should never know. It was many years before I began to work out the problems, and suddenly tumbled to the significance of the fact that Mr W.H. was Thorp, the publisher's man, not the young Lord of the Sonnets at all. To think that nobody had ever noticed the obvious fact hitherto!

Then too David elicited jokes from others. He announced that the subject of his inaugural lecture as professor was to be 'Reading'. On the day he brought me a pretty little package he had received by post, which proved to be *Reading:* a Victorian topographical guide, from John Betjeman.

Here I should pause to give the reader a few biographical facts. Lord (Edward Christian) David Gascoyne Cecil was born 9 April 1902; his grandfather died in 1903. So perhaps David's joke on meeting Margaret Thatcher – 'First time I've been kissed by a Prime Minister' – was not strictly true. Grandfather had made a middle-class marriage to Georgina Alderson. David told me a lot about this remarkable woman. She was a powerful personality, who made a man of her husband, hitherto an over-bred, clever, but highly nervous type, and revivified the stock. She was evidently rather a dragon who, when Eton didn't provide weekly communion for her sons, swept down on the school and saw to it that it did. These same four sons she would not send to the family college, Christ Church, on account of the matrimonial proclivities of Dean Liddell's wife (mother of Alice in Wonderland). They all went to University College, where there is a conversation piece of them gabbling together in the hall at Hatfield. That Lady Salisbury was without fear or favour. Edward VII couldn't bear ill-dressed women; when he said to her, 'Lady Salisbury, I've seen that dress before', she put him in his place with, 'Yes, sir, and you'll see it again.'

She produced a remarkable brood of children, who were usually known by their nicknames. James (Jem), the eldest, was probably the most practical of the bunch. Robert might have become leader of the Conservative Party and Prime Minister, if he had not been too angular and independent. Hugh (Linky) was the cleverest, and should have gone into the Church as he wished, except that his mother was too ambitious for him – he was a brilliant speaker – and determined him for politics. William (Fish) was the most eccentric, yet sensible of the lot, really loved being Rector of Hatfield, pedalling away on his bicycle, visiting parishioners, and hated being a bishop. He became Bishop of Exeter, memorable and loved for his eccentricities – he had the family absent-mindedness to an extreme degree. Edward married a celebrated reactionary in her own right, Violet Maxse, who edited some journal of that character; I remember meeting her, and getting on rather well with her – as I met most of them through David.

Of the two daughters Maud married Lord Selborne, who was sent out to govern South Africa during the Boer War – she was hardly less well known for the family neglect of dress and goodness of heart. Gwendolen, of a masculine disposition and ability, served her father well as a confidential secretary and, never marrying, wrote his biography in four volumes. David was expected to finish it with a fifth, but had other things a-plenty to do. His grandfather's sister had married a Balfour and become the mother of Arthur Balfour, who succeeded his uncle as Prime Minister in 1902. No wonder the governing group in Britain was known at the turn of the century as 'the Hotel Cecil'. (This had existed on the Embankment on the site of the first Robert Cecil's – Elizabeth I's minister's – big house.)

Why did not this exceptional galaxy of talent, of undoubted brilliance and public spirit, with their passion for politics, achieve more and continue something of the old Marquis's ascendancy? This was partly due to historic circumstances, the movement of the age away from aristocracy to the middle classes (Chamberlains, that disastrous family whom the Cecils could not abide, and rightly). Still more it was due to the too great independence of mind, the over-scrupulous conscience, the positive pernickitiness of the brothers, the way they were brought up – away from life in the splendid isolation of Hatfield and Cranborne. David's brother, Bobbity, who had no small share of the family temperament, called them 'my harlequin uncles' – this was to Clem Attlee, who appreciated the description. David himself summed up, in his fine book, *The Cecils of Hatfield House*: 'To influence one's age one must, for good or ill, be more in tune with it than they were.'

Though I was a strong Labour Party man in the Thirties, we shared a dislike of Neville Chamberlain, and I had the advantage of hearing from David what went on among the leading Tories. David's grandfather, the Prime Minister, failing in health, used to call the South African war, which left such a fatal legacy, 'Joe's War', i.e. Joe Chamberlain's. His son, Neville, in sucking up to Mussolini, used his ambassador, the Fascist Grandi, to score off his own Foreign Secretary, Anthony Eden. When Chamberlain rejected President Roosevelt's proposal to call the Dictators into conference with the other powers – a crucial intervention on the part of the United States, a last chance not to lose – Eden at last resigned. But the will-power behind him was Bobbity Cecil, his Under-Secretary. Eden should have come out in open opposition to Chamberlain's hopeless course, and allied himself from that moment with Churchill; but, a weak man, he was afraid to risk his popularity with the Tory Party, going the whole hog with Chamberlain to the precipice.

When they got there, and the bankruptcy of Appeasement was brought home to them, with the war Chamberlain was forced to bring back Eden and Bobbity into his government. He never said one word of welcome or recognition that he had been wrong. As David said to me, Hitler's triumphs one after the other were hardly surprising, considering the feeble lot he had to deal with on our side. However, David did make one mistake himself, which he recognised as such and repented: he wrote a *Times* letter suggesting the return of the German colonies. No concession whatever should have been made to Hitler's Germany, as his opponents within Germany realised: only resistance was any good with him, as Churchill saw and they recognised.

There was a vein of common sense and realism in David, for all his Cecilian temperament and appearance. He was indeed markedly a Cecil. At a lunch-party I gave for my friend Rouben Mamoulian, the film producer, on the dais in hall at All Souls, I placed David immediately beneath the portrait of his grandfather. The likeness was striking: the dominant brooding forehead, pallor of skin, line of nose, the long, sensitive fingers. Rouben, with his visual sense, creator of those historic films, 'Queen Christina' and 'Becky Sharp', appreciated the joke.

David got his common sense and *engouement* for life from his mother. She brought in again an entirely different strain. A Gore (cousin of the famous High Church Bishop Gore), she was descended from the Grand Whiggery, Ponsonbys and Bessboroughs and (I think) Lambs, for she possessed Lamb papers which helped her son's book, *The Young Melbourne*. This was a totally different stock from the old, countrified Tory Cecils, not much given to society. Alice Salisbury was wise and warm-hearted, not only sociable but with a real gift for understanding people, deeply interested in them and in helping them. This was where David got his sociability and understanding of character from. It was understandable that she should marry her children into the Grand Whiggery: her elder son to a Cavendish and her daughter Mary ('Mowcher') to the heir to the dukedom of Devonshire. David had inborn feeling and admiration for the Whig society of the 18th century – it enters into his books on Melbourne – its cultivation and sparkle, their splendid houses and taste (though not uncritical of the last, for he had even better taste). He would like to have been a member of their historic club, Brooks's (haunt of feckless Charles James Fox, aristocratic irresponsible as *he* was – how much I prefer the younger Pitt!). However, a scion of so Tory a family, David's father would not have approved: if a club, it would have to be the Carlton.

David stood too much in awe of his father, and that entered into his character. This Lord Salisbury was kind-hearted and considerate, but burdened with conscience to a degree that bordered on religious melancholia. He would have been a sad man indeed without the help of his wife; even so he regarded life as an ordeal, no enjoyment of it. A remote and withdrawn man, David saw little of him; he watched him walking down the grand staircase at Hatfield muttering to himself, overburdened with the responsibilities and duties he had inherited, not feeling up to the big boots his father had left him. Once the young David was sum-moned to his study. He went, trembling like a leaf. All his father had to say, quite kindly, was that he wished him to get up in the mornings in time for daily chapel; but the boy was unnerved.

A comic example of his lack of nerve was provided by an early visit to Germany. In Munich he ran into Elizabeth Bibesco, Asquith's daughter, in his hotel. She, a relentless talker, kept him up to the early hours of the morning. He couldn't face another session of that; so, a few hours later, before she was up and about, he packed, took off his shoes as he stole by her bedroom, and fled to Berlin.

There the chief feature he noticed was an invitation to an Exhibition of Sadismus and Masochismus – I don't suppose he went; for Berlin under the Weimar Republic was very much the capital of that sort of thing.

An occasion when he did nerve himself to take a high line was an artistic one, over the Reynolds window in New College Chapel. Warden Smith, who hated it, had had it stowed away 'for safety' during the war, hoping to keep it in perpetual storage. David spoke up with real feeling about this – and the window was replaced.

This brings us to the inner side of his life, which was deeply religious. Here was the source of his perfection of character – at least I have never known anyone who came closer to it, except Arthur Quiller Couch, dear Q., who was even more high-minded (I am low-minded, as befits a son of the people). David did not talk about it; only once did he mention to me that, when young, he had undergone an experience like religious conversion. He held to that all his life. I have watched him unaware, at prayer at evensong in New College Chapel, utterly absorbed in devotion, in contact with the unseen world by which he regulated his life. An attentive reader can occasionally catch something of it in his books: he thought that the earthly beauty to which he was devoted – in nature and art, in poetry and painting – was a shadow of another world, where perfection was only to be found.

For he too shared his father's view of life without illusions. He thought that Christianity, rightly understood, had a tragic understanding of life, that only through suffering could the soul be perfected, or perhaps achieve fulfilment. I do not pretend to understand this, the deepest side of his nature; at least it means that he was no mere literary critic.

It equipped him remarkably to write the life of the poet Cowper, with his religious melancholia, which David wrote while a tutor at Wadham. Here he was teaching both history and literature (among his history pupils a Cornish *protégé* of mine – one of what Richard Pares at All Souls used to call my 'Cornish *clientèle*'). Hence the writing went slowly; he used to read me bits of it to criticise, and I feared it would never get finished.

Actually I had not much sympathy with the subject. With the struggle I had had to get to Oxford, I had no patience with a man like Cowper who – rather than face an easy interview for a promising job in life – preferred to attempt suicide. Then there were the successive breakdowns and madnesses, the depression of spirits and self-pity. Decidedly 'the stricken deer' – Cowper's name for himself and the title of the book (Lady Salisbury used to get it wrong and call it 'The Wounded Stag', as she used to change Carlyle's description of Robespierre, 'the sea-green incorruptible' into 'the pea-green insupportable') – no, the poet Cowper was not my cup of tea, and I underrated the book. When it came out, in 1929, Dougie (Sir Dougal) Malcolm at All Souls said to me that he hoped my young friend did not know from experience the melancholia he so well described.

The fact is that David did understand it; and when I read the book today I am struck by its maturity and comprehension of that side to Cowper, the patience and sympathy with which he deals with it. On his mother's side Cowper could trace himself back to the poet Donne. David has a perceptive comment: 'It is a whimsical thought that this eccentric 16th-century divine, alone of Cowper's family, could have truly understood and expressed the pity and terror of such a spiritual tragedy.'

Whatever made David undertake such a subject when young for his first book? One can recognise a good deal of him already in it, particularly his fascination for the Whig society in the background. Horace Walpole had lived in Arlington Street, where was the Cecils' big town house. David looked on Mayfair as his local township; I remember there was some vulgar millionairess who bought the house next door, hoping to get to know the Cecils. She never did. Then there was the Hertfordshire countryside – not so much of it left in David's time as in Cowper's, but more than is left today. One recognises the affinity too in the hatred of taking decisions.

But school? Cowper had a hellish time at his first school – it helped to destroy his nerve – as David's grandfather had had at Eton. He had been so bullied and beaten there that, when a grown man, rather than meet a former schoolfellow in the purlieus of Mayfair he would slink down a back-alley. Result – the Cecil family tradition that school was hell.

Once more David was the exception. When his father took him down to Eton he said, 'Of course, you can't expect to be happy here.' In fact he was; he enjoyed Eton. No doubt it helped that his mother made time to come down for an hour each week to see that all was well. He looked on Eton as offering more the freedom of a university than the rigour of a school, and he made friends there – very much more mother's boy than his abstracted father's. One notes this in the book when he suddenly comes out with, 'friendship without intimacy meant nothing.'

There are deeper touches that reveal him. 'It is over religion, above all, that people nowadays so often fail to understand a past age. Their historical imagination fails them.' Again his historical imagination marks him off from the usual literary critic. His lively sense of humour relieves the gloom of Cowper's excessive religiosity. He was doubtful about making friends with some neighbours; he had to admit that they were very amiable people, though they did not have family prayers.

Here and there one can sleuth the author himself thus early. 'Nothing is more wearing than living alone': the remedy for that is to marry and have a family of one's own. Characteristic shafts of fun. 'Of course the Evangelicals were highly ridiculous. They had rejected reason, and reason soon rejected them.' Cowper led the Evangelical Newton to speak from Hebrews XI. 10, but he did not feel any the better for it. David: 'When Hebrews XI. 10 failed, what was one to do?' Then Cowper's friend Lady Hesketh 'actually got to know the King and Queen. One would have thought that to meet George III and Queen Charlotte in their unlovely old age must have damped any loyalty, however ardent.'

Cecils, David says, 'though loyal, were not servile'. Actually as a boy he fancied himself in love with a neighbour, a charming girl from St Paul's Walden who was often at Hatfield, and became Queen as wife of George VI. They remained friends all through their long lives.

An eloquent comment from early Oxford days appears in 'a wise distrust of the discretion of undergraduates'. He evidently trusted mine; for when his brother decided that younger brothers were apt to be inadequately provided for, handing over a large wad of investments, David called on me to go through them and witness them. Though not extravagant, he hadn't much money sense. When he married, Rachel used to go comically to the waste-paper basket to rescue cheques he had inadvertently thrown away. And, of course, he had been brought up so grandly, a valet to wait on him, that he never thought of putting clothes away; her epitaph for him was: 'He never shut a drawer.' He shared the family absent-mindedness, always leaving things on one. As I write, I am wearing the red check scarf ('New and Lingwood, 56 Jermyn St, and at Eton'), which he left on me and then gave me, sixty years ago when we were young.

'Why don't you keep a bottle of sherry in your rooms?', he suggested. It had never occurred to me – sherry had never been seen in our teetotal frugal house at home. After that I have always kept a bottle of sherry available for my friends (not for me). Similarly when I went along to David's rooms and he was out, leaving the electric fire on, I used to turn it out to save him expense.

Wadham is a Jacobean quadrangle, built by Somerset builders – rather like Cranborne, he used to say, and was at home there, in those attractive panelled rooms, second staircase on the left hand as you go in at the gate. At one time he had them painted a very modern scheme, pale pink and primrose – a suggestion from Cocteau. Another piece of bravery was when the income-tax inspector came to call, David kept him waiting outside on the mat. Think of it today! – no one would dare to affront one of those penalising bureaucrats who make our lives miserable. In those days the man waited patiently on the doorstep until admitted.

David was generous with his friends, and introduced me to a number of them. He had been at Eton with Eddie Sackville-West, talented but hypochondriac. I came to know him better in his BBC days. He was a good writer, but defeated by life, gave up Knole (think of it!), went to live in Ireland to be near Elizabeth Bowen, and found a more welcoming bosom in the Roman Church. Puffin Asquith became a gifted film producer – had been a friend of Richard Pares. I don't remember meeting Leslie Hartley, the novelist, who remained a lifelong friend of David's; ingenuous as I was, I had no difficulty in recognising his affair with his gondolier in Venice in his first novel, and himself as Simon-etta in *Simonetta Perkins*.

It was David who took me one evening out to Garsington to be presented to Lady Ottoline Morrell. I felt abashed in so exotic an atmosphere, the panelled drawing room painted coral colour as a background to her ladyship's Venetian-dyed hair, her extraordinary appearance, the out-thrust Habsburg jaw, the trailing, swishing silks, the heavy scents and that extraordinary way of talking English as if it were Italian – so recognisably reproduced in D.H. Lawrence's Hermione in *Women in Love*.

Ottoline was kindness itself to me – underneath everything she had a good heart and (surprisingly) religious faith. But I couldn't bear the company of all those malicious intellectuals at gatherings at her too hospitable table – and the things they said about her too behind her back! When she left Garsington for Gower Street, she swore me to come and see her, after my return from Germany. But I took the opportunity to break away and never visited there – I should think the only person in the world to drop Ottoline. The simple fact was that I was a bit frightened of her and, put off by that malicious milieu, couldn't cope with it. However, it was something to have seen what it was, (as usual) without committing myself.

It was not through David that I came to know Elizabeth Bowen (much better later, on my own). He kept her to himself, for it was a real *amitié amoureuse*, Platonic on his part – I doubt if it was on hers. After David's marriage it turned into a lasting friendship – though towards the end there was, sadly, a *froideur*: Elizabeth seemed to resent something, perhaps felt excluded. The fact was that there was no passion in that cool Cecilian nature: the only passion was for talk. And, when we talked – as we did all the time we met – it was always about subjects: literature and history, Shake-speare and the Elizabethan Age, Queen Elizabeth I, politics.

He put up with my increasing fixation on the whole corpus of Marxist thought, and was quite ready to discuss it; I think that it had some (slight) influence with him, for of course he already knew from experience the importance of

class-categories and class-conflicts in history. He thought
that I was excessively class-conscious – but what wonder,
with the extreme contrasts in my life (like D.H. Lawrence,
similar raw nerves and touchiness)? And anyway, all the
Cecils were anti-middle-class – Lord Robert vehemently so
– and thought, like Lord Melbourne, that there was more in
common between upper and lower classes, especially in the
countryside.

One sees something of this in Virginia Woolf's attitude
when she came to know David. She was always quizzing
him, in her usual manner, to know how grandly his aunt
Gwendolen lived at Hatfield. If she could only see her, David
would say, traipsing around in her old tweeds and mannish
boots – then changing off properly for dinner.

Later on, he got me to take on his nephew, Dicky,
cleverest of that bunch, as a private pupil. Dicky had been
bored at Eton and was not doing as well as his wits
warranted, especially in his writing, as he found when he
came to write essays for me. He was passionately interested
in politics, and very keen to gather all he could about
Marxism. I didn't want to make a convert of him to my
fanaticism, and asked David if this was all right.

'Of course,' he said, 'this is the world he has to grow up
in: he ought to know all about it.' I registered then how
different this was from a conventional middle-class point of
view, afraid of having their lambs corrupted by my Leftist
views. Not so the Cecils – here again was their vein of
commonsense realism. Dear Dicky in the RAF did not
survive the war; like another of David's nephews, Billy
Hartington (married to Kathleen Kennedy – and what a fuss
was made by her fanatically Irish-Catholic mother, old Rose
Kennedy!). Two victims of the German mania that ruined
the 20th century for us.

At that time I had a window into the German mind and
soul thrugh my intense friendship with Adam von Trott. It
was indeed a (Platonic) love affair. David was not impressed
by Adam, as everybody else was – David Astor included;
looking back on it now, I think he was right. Adam was *too*
German, too ambivalent and muddle-headed. David thought

my love for him 'callow': it certainly was obsessive. (However, it gave me poetry – which David had ceased to write.)

The Stricken Deer was awarded the Hawthornden Prize, and that launched David as a writer. At the time I was doubtful, but I was wrong: the book was a remarkable achievement for a young man. Its author looked increasingly to London literary life, and gave up his tutorship at Wadham – to Maurice Bowra's chagrin. An essentially Oxford figure, he was always rather jealous of London literary life, where he made no such impression.

David took a pretty house in Edwardes Square, Kensington and took the plunge. He became a friend of the Bloomsberries, without being one of them – in particular of Virginia Woolf and of Desmond MacCarthy. One can read about the impression he made in her Diaries, and of course he was entranced, as everybody was, by Desmond's talk. This was a real bond. David, however, did not talk it all away, as the Irish *littérateur* did, never writing the books he projected. Still, David learned much from this *promeneur* in literary life, who knew everybody, and had width of sympathy, a comprehensive catholic mind, unlike the true Bloomsberries.

Thus it was that I learned, through David, of the exotic goings-on in that exclusive circle, Lytton Strachey's love-affairs (David was conventionally anti-homo), and the extraordinary story of his death, Carrington's crowning him with a wreath of laurel and killing herself. Well known now, it was not widely known then: David thought it was like a Jacobean tragedy. He also foretold that this would become one of the best-known circles in literature, for they all wrote to and about each other like mad. He regarded the strains and stresses they endured as partly owing to their departure from the straight and narrow path of conventional morals, indeed openly challenging them.

Meanwhile he had fallen in love with Desmond's charming daughter, Rachel – and reported to me on the progress of his courtship. In fact so intimately that I do not feel at liberty to go into detail. One motive in fixing him was that he was afraid of becoming a flirt – there were so many attractive young women about him: *The Stricken Deer* was dedicated to Irene Plymouth. The beautiful bronze-haired Lady Cynthia Asquith, of Lawrence's Letters, to whom he introduced me, had been Barrie's secretary and legatee. A tremendous authority on Jane Austen, she got all sixty-four questions in a quiz faultlessly right, and won a lot more cash. Then there was the affair with Elizabeth Bowen. All were married women.

David *wanted* to get married – to me incomprehensible: I agreed with his uncle, Arthur Balfour, 'I rather fancy a career for myself.' For David the marriage turned out blissfully happy and the best stroke of fortune. They were ideally suited: I used to think of them as two Babes in the Wood, neither of them very practical. But it was brave of him to break away from family tradition and make a middle-class marriage. Not all the younger Cecils approved: some of them used to call Rachel 'the watch-maker's daughter'. She was rather small, but with beautiful expressive eyes, and more open-minded than David was about sex.

His account to me of his courtship is completely corroborated from the other side by Rachel's novel, *Theresa's Choice*. I did not read it when it came out in the 1950s; now I see what a clever girl she was – I always found her sympathetic and sweet, but did not really know her. What emerges is that he was put off by the pressure put on him by other girls, who fancied him as a good catch. 'You do understand, don't you?' Rachel did, and was prepared to wait for him to make up his mind. Her one and only novel is an accomplished piece of work.

The picture that emerges is one of no passionate affair, but one of total sympathy of mind and tastes – a more lasting foundation for marriage. It is also clear that David's wise mother was behind it, as I thought. Ottoline, as he told me, tried to prevent it – imparted to Rachel's mother that he would be no good at it. (Ottoline was a notorious interferer in other people's affairs: perhaps my instinct to steer clear of that quarter was, regrettably, right.)

The marriage confirmed that the future for David would be more literary. Dicky and others hoped that he would write about politics; he was well qualified, as interested as ever, and had a vital source of information in Bobbity, whose career it was. This was not to be. The whole tone of the MacCarthy circle was literary. David recommended to me his mother-in-law Molly MacCarthy's *A Nineteenth-Century Childhood* as the good book it was. And Rachel had her quiet influence. When one of the papers, the *Observer*, wanted him to become a regular reviewer like her father for the *Sunday Times*, she put the damper on that: she knew what agony Desmond endured in writing his articles to time. (Cyril Connolly, another Irishman, was not much better.)

For quite a time there were no children; though David was enormously equipped for sex, his was a cool temperament. Augustus John, their neighbour down in the country – who painted a portrait of David not much like and entirely failed with Rachel – told her, 'If he doesn't give you a baby, come to me, and I will.' 'He would have done, too', said David, rather amused. Later on, Augustus wanted to do a portrait of me; but I couldn't face going down to Fordingbridge, that mixed-up household, Augustus's two families, and all the drinking.

With David away from Oxford and now living down in Dorset at Rockbourne, going in for the joys (and burdens) of family life, I saw little of him. One sees a charming picture of him and Rachel in fancy dress skipping at one of Cecil Beaton's entertainments at Ashbourne. In 1934 he brought out a volume on *Early Victorian Novelists*, based on lectures he had given at Oxford.

Barbara Pym probably went to them; for in her delicious *Jane and Prudence*, Jane's daughter and her friend Penelope 'were to go to Lord Edgar Ravenswood for tutorials, which would be most stimulating – imagine doing *Paradise Lost* with Lord Edgar!' In those days the girls were not allowed to go to tutorials with male dons alone. There follows the exchange: 'I'd hoped that Lord Edgar might fall in love with her – when they were at tutorials, you know.' One sees what targets we were (I was supposed to fall in love with one of my women pupils, who rose to fame instead).

'But he hates women, surely?', Prudence asked.

'I know, that's the point. I'd imagined Flora breaking through all that.' As we know, that was far from the case with him.

The Preface treats the reader with the tactful excuses he regularly used (like William Shakespeare with his auditors, unlike bluff Ben Jonson). 'I cannot pretend that they treat their subject exhaustively. An exhaustive treatment of these novelists would involve a consideration, not only of their literary, but also of their social, historical, and personal aspect.' That was clean contrary to the gospel according to the Leavises at Cambridge, and the book was attacked by the insufferable Queenie, who had taken the Art of Fiction as the province over which she reigned.

I sent her a postcard suggesting that she confined herself to the kitchen. (She was a notoriously bad cook. When her crank of a husband came to All Souls years later, he claimed that he had not eaten for forty years. Sweating with sincerity and inaudibility, he confined himself to asserting the greatness of Dickens – himself having laid down the Great Tradition, who belonged to it and who did not.)

Desmond MacCarthy, a Cambridge man, used to have fun with Leavis's fatuous statement that it was 'with singularly little fuss' that Mr Eliot had with a single essay dethroned Milton from his place in English literature. Desmond used to quote this from time to time, like tying this piece of nonsense to a dog's tail, and of course it drove Leavis mad.

The book is dedicated to novelist L.P. Hartley, who is thanked along with Desmond and Eddie Marsh for 'judicious and sympathetic criticism' – hardly the words for *Scrutiny* and the Leavises.

During the appalling Thirties I saw David occasionally, but it was politics now that we talked chiefly about. Hitler dominated our minds, and I was much in touch with what was going on in Germany, through Adam von Trott, with whom I stayed in Berlin. Also I was an active Labour Party candidate. David's brother, then Lord Cranborne, was in government, but as much opposed to Neville Chamberlain's hopeless policy of Appeasement as I was. Through David I had inside information as to what went on in the dreadful 'National' government that brought Germany down upon us again, in the worst possible circumstances – without an ally, totally unlike 1914.

One thing I learned was that Bobbity Cranborne was the force behind Anthony Eden when he resigned as Foreign Secretary, in opposition to Chamberlain's sucking up to Mussolini, aided and abetted by Austen Chamberlain's widow in Rome and our ambassador there, Perth, a pro-Fascist Catholic, like Pius XII. Eden should have come out in open opposition and given a lead to the country. But let us not forget that that unspeakable assembly, the House of Commons, upheld Chamberlain all the way along and shouted Churchill down when he protested against Munich as the humiliating defeat it was.

David did recognise the mistake of his *Times* letter advocating the return of the German colonies, as against my view that no concession whatever should be made to a Germany under Hitler's criminal régime. I initiated a *Times* controversy with the muddle-headed Philip Lothian, who had made himself a foremost proponent of Appeasing Hitler; I had no reason to fear publishing it all in *The End of an Epoch* for the historical record afterwards.

So David and I were together again on the crucial issue of Appeasement (it was chiefly the grievous record of the Tories between the wars that kept me a Labour man). The old aristocrats, Cecils, Churchills, Edens were with staunch working-class types like Bevin – *my* leader – against the spineless middle classes thick on the benches of the Commons, a Chamberlain their *beau idéal*, with his corvine rather than aquiline features and his inseparable umbrella.

In 1939, with the oncoming of war, David came back to Oxford as a full-time tutor in English literature at New College. He had large, rather lugubrious rooms in the old quadrangle looking towards Queen's – as my beautiful rooms in All Souls did, across New College Lane and the Warden's garden. He took a house in North Oxford, where, with a young family – two boys and a girl – people were not much invited (and I was not one for family life anyway).

Before I went into hospital for two critical operations – the accumulation of years of duodenal ulcer, overwork, endless strain to which I had subjected myself – it occurred to me that Cornwall ought to have a portrait of our leading writer, Q. I consulted David; he suggested his friend Henry Lamb, who had done enchanting drawings of the Cecil children, and I duly got Lamb to do the characteristic portrait now in our County Museum.

Meanwhile David had written *The Young Melbourne* (1939), dedicated to Rachel. Historians thought it rather a slight book; but really there was not much in Melbourne's earlier career to make it a heavy one. He was rather an amateur and, though a clever man, did not enter the Cabinet until he was forty-six. (And then, 'What I like about the Order of the Garter is that there is no damned merit about it.' Today, it decorates the leg of the meritorious Harold Wilson.)

Once more David forestalls criticism by his subtitle, 'And the Story of his Marriage with Caroline Lamb.' He calls the book a conversation piece, and it offers a portrait of that Whig society which fascinated him – that aristocracy which was 'a unique product of English civilisation'. What a high old time they had in their splendid houses, the English countryside laid out around them, the parks and plantations they made, the fox-hunting interspersed with reading the classics! Melbourne was an omnivorous reader, Pitt a good classic; Fox and Palmerston had languages at command. 'Politics were not then the life sentence to hard labour that in our iron age they have become.'

Those English grandees despised the (German) royal family, and even David is too hard on poor conscientious George III. And much too soft on Lady Caroline Lamb, with her tantrums and her exhibitionism, who drove Byron frantic and gave Melbourne such a devil of a life. He should have spanked her pretty little bottom every morning at 8 a.m. – but perhaps that is a proletarian option. David is astonishingly patient with her, even sympathetic: I wouldn't have put up with her in the house for a second.

In grand Whig society so many of the children were not those of their supposed fathers. David suggests, what was apparently the case, that Melbourne was not the son of a boring Lord Melbourne, but of clever Lord Egremont, patron of the painter Turner. He told me the story of Melbourne, when famous as Prime Minister, looking at a portrait of Egremont one day, and noticing that his companion was observing a likeness. Melbourne said, 'People say he was my father; of course, he wasn't.' Then, *sotto voce* to himself – 'But who the devil knows who his father was anyway?'

Comments along the way reveal the author, some of them rather grand. 'Children brought up in gay and patrician surroundings seldom react against them with the violence common in more circumscribed lives.' No, indeed, I may say. 'And they were free from the tiresome inhibitions that are induced by a sense of inferiority.' *Touché*, once more. They had 'that delightful unassertive confidence only possible to people who have never had cause to doubt their social position'. That spoke for David: naturally not for me. And 'then, as now, London society was disposed to look kindly on the literary efforts of handsome young men of good family.' Naturally, again, I had not found that. On the other hand, 'the advantages of living in the thick of things' taught one to relate thought to experience, to estimate theory by practical working. Living at All Souls in term-time, with its immersion in public affairs, alternating with my working-class folk in vacations, did give me that advantage, as against political theorists. And I was pleased to see him putting the 'stiff upper lip of the Public School Englishman' in its place – one for the middle-classes again.

Over *Hardy the Novelist* we had much more in common, for he was a frequent subject of conversation between us. He was an intimate admiration of mine, for I had read *Jude the Obscure* during my own struggle to get to Oxford, and 'identified' with him (except, of course, for his fatal marriage). Hardy's sombre outlook on life had deeply entered into my own, perhaps unfortunately. David had had none of that experience, and so was able to pin-point Hardy's greatest defect, the lack of balance, 'the violent oscillations of his genius'. Perhaps imbalance goes with genius struggling from such beginnings, as with D.H. Lawrence whose 'oscillations' are no less notable. David had none of them; he always exhibited a cool, Cecilian balance – though he had a touch of genius of his own.

He had also the love of the Dorset countryside – I am sure that the background to Cranborne meant more to him than that of Hertfordshire, with suburbia creeping up to the gates of Hatfield (very profitably to the Cecils). This book, dedicated to Elizabeth Bowen, consisted of the Clark Lectures at Cambridge – once more a tactful apology for their conversational tone. An essay in pure literary criticism, it begins with a question: 'How far did all this erudition and industry *and ill-temper* make any difference to one's appreciation of letters?' There was a poser for Leavis on his own home-ground. 'Erudition' did not apply, for Leavis knew hardly any language other than English, and that not well. 'Industry' of a kind, perhaps: what Victor Pritchett called that 'pedalling away on his Nonconformist organ', and in a way which the light-hearted, light-weight Alan Pryce Jones described as 'neither high-brow, nor low-brow, nor middle-brow but flat-brow, and in a style having the consistency of coke'.

David spoke out straight against *inept* criticism, forgetting that 'a work of art is the expression of a personal vision and so, to a certain extent, must create its own appropriate form'. And had one ever noticed that in a photograph taken twenty years ago it is impossible to tell which women were well dressed – all the clothes looked equally grotesque – yet, in a group of forty years ago, some were clearly charming? Here is the perspective of time, not only visual sense: to judge properly one needs also historical sense. Hardy was one of the most historically inclined of novelists – another reason why I loved him so much. Then, too, with him Nature played a larger part than in any other English novelist.

More generally, our novel descended directly from the English drama, an unrealistic tradition: Shakespearean drama did not have to have realistic plots. Hence the enduring conflict in the novel between a dramatic story and realism. Hardy himself said uncompromisingly that a great deal of life was *not* worth telling: 'A story must be exceptional enough to justify its telling.' I much agree with him there, for in my own short stories I am interested only in the exceptional, the strange and odd, the abnormal, even the extra-sensory. One reason for thinking that the kitchen-sink style, the every-day kind of all too commonplace life, will have no permanence.

One notes a familiar comment – that it is only the type of life and character to which they are brought up that writers understand instinctively. Hardy's aristocrats are as unreal as Henry James's lower-class characters – as in *The Princess Casamassima*, I noticed. It makes one wonder what kind of novel David might have written – of Dorset, or of Hatfield life. He had written no verse since those early days at Oxford. I don't think he was wanting in imagination, certainly not in sympathy; but his was a discursive, descriptive talent, perfectly appropriate for biography and literary criticism, both of which he excelled at.

In 1948 he produced *Two Quiet Lives* – one of them a delicate portrait of Dorothy Osborne, the letter writer – and *Poets and Story-Tellers: A Book of Critical Essays*. Both these books exemplify his equal gift of historical evocation and critical sensibility. How lucky we were to have taken the History School, instead of Eng. Lit.! – Auden did not do well in the latter, Barbara Pym much better; indeed she made the best of it, better than any.

David gave me both books, inscribed 'with love'. Historical sense is apparent all through. He saw that *Antony and Cleopatra*, which he discussed with me, was at least as much about the political feuding at the end of Elizabeth I's reign as it was about love. Ordinary literary critics see it only in terms of the latter. The appreciation of the past is no less evident in his treatment of the poet Gray, who was deeply interested in and influenced by it. 'England in the 18th century was an integrated society, in which people agreed to respect each other's interest and united to accept similar standards of value.' This applies to the governing class, rather than to society in general, though the ruling class gave it integration and imposed what unity there was.

'Why the sense of the past came to birth in the 18th century is not certainly known. But I would suggest that the sober rationalism which permeated the general outlook of the age led its more poetic spirits to find contemporary life intolerably prosaic.' He was not a pure scholar, and here he overlooks the sense of the past that was already so conscious in the Elizabethan age, not only with the antiquaries, Camden and his fellows, but with Spenser, Shakespeare and the prolific historical drama. Still, he does draw attention to the way in which, in Gray's descriptive passages, both prose and verse, his 'aesthetic response to the beauty of the scene mingles inextricably with his response to its historic appeal'.

His friendship with Virginia Woolf does not impair his literary judgment – and justice of mind is the rarest of qualities among critics: they usually judge from their prejudices. 'A novel without drama, without moral values, and without character or strong personal emotion – it is a hard thing to write: and it cannot be said that Virginia Woolf is always successful.' I have never thought of her as a novelist *pur sang*, but a poet, a poet in exquisite prose.

'Justice of mind' – 'the critic may well hesitate before passing judgment on an author less than thirty years older than himself. Consider the shocking blunders committed by those who have tried to do it. Matthew Arnold thought poorly of Tennyson; Sainte-Beuve spoke in slighting terms of Flaubert; Dr Johnson said that the taste for Sterne was a fashion that would soon pass, etc, etc.' I have long wanted to write an essay on 'The Silliness of Critics'. 'A vital writer generally represents a strongly defined and controversial attitude to the life and thought of his time.' Perhaps that is why I get into so much trouble: I rather fear that my own name may be writ in hot water.

I find him too generous to E.M. Forster. He allows him humour, and that he can tell a story as well as anyone. He is

both 'tender-hearted and unattached'. But is he? David
knows the score well enough, without telling us.

> Unattached congenitally: he feels himself part of no
> corporate unit, seems temperamentally unresponsive to
> those instinctive, irrational, magnetic forces that draw
> the individual into a group: national feeling, class feel-
> ing, comradely feeling. Even the more primitive animal
> emotions, which link people otherwise diverse, do not
> mean much to him, *if we are to judge by his account of
> them*. Sex in his stories is a curiously bloodless and
> uncompelling affair.

I have italicised that saving clause, for we all know now
that Forster was not the least interested in normal hetero-
sexual sex. He has told us that he was bored having to
pretend – that was why he gave up novel-writing, and took
to homosexual stories which, as a moral *guru*, he could not
then publish. 'Only connect,' he adjured us solemnly; we
know now what he longed to connect. David knew quite
well at the time, and used to tell me about Forster's police-
man friend, 'my boy in blue', as he called him. I have no
objection: I am all in favour of people finding their own way
to happiness. But E.M. Forster is not my moral *guru*: I have
never taken seriously his middle-class ethical pretensions,
unlike his Cambridge claque. I much prefer his naughty
short stories.

And where do we find David in these matters, as to ethics?

> If I were in doubt as to the wisdom of my actions I
> should not consult Flaubert or Dostoevsky. The opinion
> of Balzac or Dickens would carry little weight with me.
> Were Stendhal to rebuke me, it would only convince
> me I had done right. Even in the judgment of Tolstoy I
> should not put complete confidence. Certainly not! But
> I should be seriously upset, I should worry for weeks
> and weeks, if I incurred the disapproval of Jane Austen.

Dear Jane was a moral perfectionist.

★

In 1948 he was elected Goldsmiths' Professor of English Literature at Oxford, the chair which he held for the next twenty-one years, until his retirement in 1969. In the course of it he examined for the Final School of Eng. Lit. some thirteen times. I remember being surprised at his willingness to undertake these chores. Surely, by this time, with his position as a writer assured and an independent income, he could have left that sort of thing to run-of-the-mill academics? No – it was what his family expected of him, he said; and that was that.

Lord M., or the Later Life of Lord Melbourne came out in October 1954, and immediately went into a second impression. It was dedicated to his mother, 'who first told me about Lord Melbourne'. He had lived at Brocket, the big Georgian mansion with a sumptuous interior and splendid library, not far from Hatfield. A not at all congenial interior to the Cecils at the time, for it was owned by the brewing Lord Brocket, a notorious Appeaser and pro-German they strongly disapproved of.

This second volume was not highly regarded as research by the school of heavy academic researchers; but it is a distinguished historical biography, with quite enough of it to suit any normal digestion. It was proclaimed his favourite book by President Kennedy, no doubt partly owing to the family connection. Since Kennedy had his book, President Nixon, not to be out-done, announced his – Robert Blake's *Disraeli*. (No family connection.)

The author shows a surprising amount of sympathy with the sufferings of the poor in those days of the new Poor Law (they should have controlled their breeding). Especially with the Dorset agricultural labourers, the Tolpuddle Martyrs, sentenced to transportation for forming a trade union. (We have had our belly-full of trade unions today.) 'Surely so kind a man [as Melbourne] should have had more qualms about applying, however moderately, a criminal code of this ferocity.' Melbourne was a notably kind man, who treated the appalling Lady Caroline with tenderness, when a good smacking might have done her good. But he was a sceptic and an indifferentist, who did not believe in action – let things take their course. Education? He believed in it only for those who could profit by it. One cannot but sympathise.

Since Melbourne was a clever, well-educated man, dealing with other clever men in that *élite* society, there are plenty of jokes. Disraeli, on the Whig diarist who recorded it, Charles Greville: 'the most conceited man I have ever known, though I have read Cicero and known Bulwer Lytton'. Dizzy had a very good conceit himself – but rightly: in a different class from Greville. And there are rollicking portraits of those originals: the insufferable Brougham, and Lord Durham, who could 'jog along very well on £40,000 a year'. (Multiply by fifty or a hundred for today.) They were, however, unpopular: 'intellectual originality does not make for popularity in English politics'. So David's 'harlequin uncles' had found.

The least original of them was his uncle William, Bishop of Exeter. This dear old man had lost all three of his sons, killed by the Germans in the first war, 1914–18. David arranged for me to stay with him on my way home to Cornwall. This humble-minded prelate wouldn't live in the Bishop's Palace there; he and Lady Florence occupied a charming Jane Austeny house, now swallowed up in the proliferating campus of the university.

They couldn't have been kinder to their nervous guest – a bouquet of flowers in my bedroom; the Bishop in long purple cassock at dinner in the evenings. But what was he reading? Füllop-Müller's enormous tomes on *The Mind and Face of Bolshevism*; and that was what he wanted to talk to me about. There was the independent Cecilian mind – how many bishops would have taken the trouble to undertake such reading?

Privately, gently, he put in a word against engaging myself in politics – one had to make so many compromises with one's conscience. I wonder a little now whether David might not have been behind that, hoping to sheer me off from wasting time, energy and health on politics. But that was quite early on. As the confusion of British policy unfolded in the Thirties one could not but engage oneself in the struggle, hopeless as it turned out to be. For it was the last period, an historian sees, in which Britain still had some primacy and might have influenced the course of events. Churchill saw that. The time has now gone. I wasted no more time on it, once Britain's great days went out in flames in the Second German War, which might have been avoided if the right course had been pursued. Churchill called it 'the Unnecessary War'.

In the book I appreciate the recognisable touches of humour – and of Cecilian realism, striking when one thinks of the improbable source. 'When did unpopularity ever bring a government down?' I remember the slight feeling of shock one day when David, holding forth from the fender in front of my fireplace, came out with – 'Nothing is easier to eat than words.' Experience of politics and politicians spoke in that. Also in 'earnest well-informed persons with liberal ideals and Nonconformist consciences are always powerful stimulants to the comic spirit'. There again we were together: neither of us liked Liberals or Nonconformists, the Simons and Foots, the Kingsley Woods and loud-mouthed Ernest Browns. Only, where he saw them as asses, I saw them as nuisances, cluttering up the path with their corpses. In contemporary conditions one was either a Tory or a Labour man – anything else was irrelevant. Why go on with a Liberal Party, dead since 1924?

He was no more sycophantic about William IV than about George III: indeed, 'on the throne of England a buffoon is no laughing matter'. (Edward VIII was not a buffoon, but he wasn't up to the job; David used to tell me the inside story of the goings-on with Mrs Simpson, 'a tough little tart' – Lord Alington on that *belle bouche*.) I suppose Queen Victoria saved the monarchy – today we couldn't do without it. Lord Melbourne educated her to the job, until the Prince Consort took over: a good German, as opposed to the bad, Bismarck & Co. (as even Adenauer thought).

The author himself speaks in – 'We are happy in proportion as we believe ourselves and our life to be of value; and few people are so disinterested or so conceited as to trust wholly to their own judgment in this matter.' Here is a measure of genuine modesty, to set against the occasional flashes of superciliousness, however much justified.

In 1959 came an admirable volume of literary essays, *The Fine Art of Reading*, which included his inaugural lecture as professor. He tried it out on me – privately I didn't think much of it as a subject. I thought it a soft option, and didn't attend – too busy with my own historical writing, the Elizabethan Age, the Churchills, etc. But I was wrong: the lecture is a clear statement of principles and beliefs, even a challenging one in the critical confusion of the time, when the discreditable *Times Literary Supplement* was then making a cult of Leavis. Contrary to his gospel of 'Ev*a*aluation' David put the view that the aim of all art was not truth (for that one looks to history), but delight; and what the critic needs is a combination of common sense and uncommon sensibility. How many contemporary critics have just that? Look at their literary media, and see how many are lacking in both.

Pace Kingsley Amis, one of the auditory, David was not afraid to confront the obvious. He will tell you, said this bright undergraduate, that Swift wrote with savage indignation, and that Wordsworth put an end to the poetic style of the 18th century. Well, why not? This was what was primary about them: first things first, then the rest follows. One should never be intimidated by undergraduates like Amis and Larkin proclaiming to prefer Duke Ellington's Jazz to Beethoven.

David put that kind of thing on a par with the muff of a reviewer who had rebuked a poet for not employing 'what he hideously calls a contemporary vocabulary'. I suspect that speaking out thus was partly responsible for his being overlooked by these same media-men in the *TLS* and such places: since they couldn't answer him, they thought better to ignore him. Of course he had no respect for their theorising: systematic aesthetics are only tentative generalisations from the works themselves. Even Pater's aesthetics are *obvious* enough – only the experts seem to be ignorant of them. A usual enough situation.

Once more common sense and observation speak in his comment on 'the curious modern prudery about mentioning social distinctions which everybody knows to exist and which in fact most people set store by'. Here I should say self-consciousness, rather than prudery, accounts for it: the desire in a demotic society to level everybody down to their level, the wish to lop the tallest, to reduce the first-rate to their rating of second- and third-rate.

À propos of Jane Austen he makes the obvious point that some knowledge of history is an essential preliminary to appreciating her. Then follows the *un*obvious point that Lady Catherine de Bourgh in *Pride and Prejudice* is not a caricature. There are, or were, such examples of aristocratic insolence (Lord Curzon was one in our time). I find David a more *just* critic than Eliot, more illuminating on the Elizabethan dramatist, John Ford.

> Ford, in Eliot's opinion, was a man of shallow superficial mind with a talent for achieving certain musical effects of his own in blank verse. Surely this is a confused judgment. A verse form is beautiful and moving because it effectively conveys certain meanings. Ford's rhythms move us because they are so truly the voice of his strange, subtle and tender spirit.

This inspires me to read Ford, which is what a better critic should do, not put one off. Eliot's earlier judgments were apt to be mistaken, like those on Milton and Shelley, or Gilbert Murray.

On a deeper level is David's conviction that art is to be seen in an other-worldly perspective. The epigraph of the book reads, 'For the earthly beauty is a shadow and image of the heavenly beauty.' The conclusion of his lecture must have been an unwelcome surprise to the Amises and Larkins, though not to Miss Pym. Myself, I am not certain what to think about it, except in Hardy's terms, 'If only it might be true.' 'In so far as they are artists, writers have expressed their spirit in the harmony of a true work of art, they have opened the eyes of the soul to a sight of that divine and flawless essence whence it springs and for which, while its unquiet exile on earth endures, it is immedicably homesick.'

This is so strangely worded as to confirm conviction – it makes the Amises and Larkins look common. It also has that true Cecilian touch of melancholy, no illusions about life.

The book is dedicated to Cynthia Asquith, Elizabeth Bowen's friend – I remember staying with them at vanished Bowen's Court – with the famous lines of Henry Wotton's to the Winter Queen:

> You common people of the skies,
> What are you when the moon shall rise!

I expect that that also irritated literary journalists with a social inferiority-complex.

In 1964 he came out with quite a fat biography of Beerbohm, *Max*, who had nominated David as his choice for author. Bobbity told me this, regarding it as the compliment it was. I think the Cecils were proud of having produced a distinguished writer, an exception in all that long line of politicians. Lady Donaldson writes that he was every inch a Cecil; that is true, but I suspect that his gift for writing may have owed more to the feminine strain in him, through his mother.

He did not give me this book – Max Beerbohm was not my pigeon, though very much his. Here was the comic spirit, the sense of fun, in his make-up. I had a score against Beerbohm – his hatred of Kipling, whom he pursued with a vendetta for years, with his caricatures and parodies. Kipling – an original genius, as he recognised – had far too much of that to put up with from lesser people. Beerbohm hated the prophetic side to Kipling, who was more far-seeing about the horror and terror of modern society, civilisation on the edge of breakdown (India!), than ever his liberal critics were, with their superficial view of humans.

Actually, their views on the Germans, responsible for so much of the disaster, should have narrowed the gap; for Beerbohm, being half-German, knew what to expect from *them*. 'As early as October 1914 Max had prophesied that

Germany, if defeated, would want to start another war in revenge.' And Beerbohm regretted the muddled quarrel with Italy over Abyssinia, which might 'throw them into the arms of the sinister Germans, waiting under Hitler for another chance to plunge the world into bloodshed'. This was exactly what happened. No wonder that Beerbohm was 'implacable about the Germans, more so than Rothenstein himself was', who as a Jew had grievous reason never to forgive them for what they did to a whole people. And that a most distinguished among ancient peoples – along with the Greeks and Romans, a main source of European civilisation.

The book is interesting for its portrait of the literary 'decadents' of the Nineties, out of whom Max sprang, in particular of Oscar Wilde, for whom there is less than no sympathy: 'a genial, brilliant, spirited Irish buccaneer, with a thirst for self-advertisement, incurably crude taste and a strong streak of sentimental vulgarity'. On the other hand, David saw the whole episode in historical perspective.

> The story of Oscar's downfall, looked at in the cold light of subsequent history, is a mean and miserable tale of weakness and sordid folly on Oscar's part, of hypocrisy and sordid spite on that of his enemies. Yet everyone concerned, and the rest of England too, combined to inflate it to the proportions of a dark and tremendous tragedy. . . . England reacted to the whole story with a preposterous and hysterical horror.

That is about right. It was also infantile and silly.

Wilde and the whole affair have been absurdly overwritten-up. I remember a conversation between David and Somerset Maugham on the subject, under the summer sycamores in the Warden's garden at All Souls. Maugham, who knew Wilde, put the whole blame on naughty Lord Alfred; said that Oscar had a golden nature, never mean or malicious. No doubt true. But, David answered, he was a middle-aged man, who should not have allowed himself to be led by the nose (if that is the word for it) by a bad boy.

I agree with him. Wilde's vulgar, Irish exhibitionism,

challenging ordinary folks' conventionalism at its tenderest
spot, created more unnecessary suffering and ruined more
lives than perhaps even Calvin, that 'enemy of the human
race', as Maurice Bowra called him. Fancy making such fuss
about homosexuality, just one more variation in the human
spectrum, common enough, any more than about the nonsense of Predestination. People are as they are made.

I do not think David felt passionately about these things –
this was about as near as he got to it. All that he would say
to me about the Germans was that they were 'charmless'.
Charmless! How about that for meiosis?

We encounter an interesting comment about Lytton
Strachey, to whom again David was not sympathetic. He
considered that Max overrated Strachey's art, 'which,
though deft and lively, is a crude affair compared to that of
Max. Max overrated it as he had overrated Oscar Wilde's.'
And, as I think, David overrated Max Beerbohm. I cannot
forgive a man for depreciating Kipling and Yeats and Shaw,
and also Housman and Bridges. There is a general point to
make here. These were all men of genius; Max Beerbohm
was a man of taste. Taste after all is a secondary matter
compared with genius – as even Leavis saw. It is only fair to
say that Max Beerbohm saw it too.

Asked to give the Mellon Lectures on Art in Washington,
David chose to speak about Samuel Palmer and Burne-Jones,
for which he was well qualified. Still, it is one more
remarkable evidence of his range and response – Strachey
had no such width. Even apart from visual sense and love of
painting, David had deep religious feeling in common with
Palmer; and he had always been interested in the Pre-
Raphaelites. Quite early on at Wadham he was buying red-
chalk drawings by Burne-Jones at four or five pounds apiece
– think of it today! Or he would burst into my rooms
sputtering lines of Rossetti:

> Look in my face: my name is Might-have-been;
> I am also called No-more, Too-late, Farewell . . .

The Lectures came out in book form as *Visionary and Dreamer* in 1969: I find it full of insight and illumination of the subjects – and he had put a good deal of work into it. Once more a tactful alibi is provided: the lectures were intended to be 'portraits in words not essays in criticism'. And a good thing too: there is far too much of the latter, whether literary or artistic, and rarely illuminating. I learned a lot from this book – so could the art critics.

For one thing one understands these artists better for their being seen in the perspective of their time – the acute, and essential, reaction of each to an age uncongenial to their spirit: Palmer's hatred, like Blake's, of the materialism of the Industrial Revolution, while Burne-Jones's problem was 'how to be a poetic artist in a prosaic age'.

Nor does the author fail to plant a few shafts into our own vulnerable time. Literature had provided inspiration for artists in the 19th century, and among the greatest: what about Turner or Delacroix, even apart from the Pre-Raphaelites? Today, absurdly regarded as anathema. But literature provides inspiration for contemporary music – look at Britten! Then, 'it may be that modern painting would also be enriched if it sought inspiration from poetry'. This is a moderate way of putting it – when one thinks of modish Modernist painting, mainly abstract, mostly subjectless and formless.

And Education? Palmer's mother was 'a living proof that we have not advanced so far beyond our 18th-century forebears as our efforts to do so might lead us to hope. Education was harder to come by for them, but there was a more widespread feeling for true culture.' Again, 'Artists in general are as inept about politics as politicians are about art.' David, remarkably, understood both.

I find him grasping as well the essence of each artist's work. Palmer was inspired only when he could see nature as revealing a 'spiritual vision'. Burne-Jones's was a divided life, in contemporary jargon, a split personality: his art reflected only his inner dream, he could not fuse it with what he observed in the actual, external world – though his caricatures, oddly, released it. Illuminating too about Morris, who repressed, under that massive, masculine personality, a hypersensitive inner strain, so that he became incapable of an intimate relation with anyone. Then, 'who understands altogether the workings of his inner mind?'

This beautifully written and instructive book has been overlooked by the art people, in the way things are in the over-specialisation of our time. Just as my Shakespeare discoveries have been by the Eng. Lit. Trade Union: 'I don't read his books, you see he is not in the field,' said one youthful lecturer at McGill. Similarly, David's book was nastily – and characteristically – attacked by Geoffrey Grigson, who had also written a book about Palmer. (Had he David's understanding of Palmer's religious experience?) Joe Ackerley, as literary editor of *The Listener*, said that to send a book to Grigson for review was to declare war on the author. Both his friend John Betjeman and I had that experience; John, though a Christian, did not forgive it. Neither did I. David, more grandly, took no notice.

In 1973 came *The Cecils of Hatfield House*, a splendid book he was born to write. Over this he came down to All Souls for my advice. The historical point was this. Everybody knew the importance of the great Lord Burghley, who ran England with such success, under Elizabeth I, for half-a-century. But few people appreciated that his son Robert was almost equally influential; I had earlier had some success in persuading Sir John Neale, who had underrated him, of that. And over the years I had occasionally urged the point upon David, willing enough to listen.

In thinking of their historic family most people think of the Hatfield lot; but they are the junior branch. The senior branch of the clan are the Cecils of Burghley House, Stamford, descended from Lord Burghley's elder son, represented by the Marquis of Exeter. An amusing family custom is that, when a member of the junior branch marries, it is reported in due form to the head of the senior branch – and when David married Rachel the tradition was observed.

He has a nostalgic evocation of that marvellous house (Burghley is hardly less so, but hasn't been written about

like this). There is a Proustian passage about the scent of it:
'a complex, pervading and, to me, infinitely evocative smell
compounded of washed stone and varnished panelling and
floors polished with beeswax and smoke from generations of
wood fires'. I remember his telling me about going back
there for a grand ball, some family celebration under his
nephew Robert, when the whole palace was lighted up and
full of people: 'one saw again how it ought to be'.

The place is a treasure-house, dominated by the personality and portraits of Elizabeth I – to whom the Cecils owe
everything; and the book is dedicated to her memory, as I
had earlier dedicated my book, *The England of Elizabeth I*.

Hatfield had its verbal traditions, serious as well as comic,
some of which may well be authentic. David told me one of
Robert Cecil which is likely enough. In the last days of
Elizabeth I he was in correspondence with King James of
Scotland. The Queen had no liking for Mary Stuart's son,
who was to take her place on the throne. One day a
messenger brought a letter from him to Cecil while in her
presence. Suspicious as ever, she demanded sharply to know
what it was. Cecil, knowing her dislike of any ill smell, said,
'Faugh, it smells vilely', and put it out of sight. A narrow
shave for him.

The top courtiers around the Queen were, like her, heavily
scented, for baths were few and far between. The Hatfield
tradition was that 'the Queen taketh a bath once in three
months, whether she needeth it or no'. There may be
something in this; for, as I know from the documents, it was
rather an occasion when she did take a bath. It was elabor-
ately prepared with herbs, etc. and occasionally after the
infrequent experience she caught a cold.

He had not absorbed my research into the earlier Welsh
ancestry – too technical, and lost in the unreadable pages of
the *EHR*. His ancestor David had come out of Wales with
Henry VII and made their fortune with the Tudors. But he
gets the essential historical point that only Burghley and his
son Robert completely understood the complex character of
the Queen: those three alone thought always of the essential
interest of the state and adhered to it. David has a fine phrase

about Robert Cecil's 'isolation of spirit' – like the younger Pitt, burdened with responsibility so young, worn out by middle age. Burghley lived to be a very old man – one reason why he looms so much larger in the history books. Neither of them had any illusions – unless about religion; both of them were religious, Burghley more of a Protestant, Robert a real Anglican.

Hatfield House

> may represent the past, but not the dead past. Like the plays of Shakespeare, this massive architectural monument of Shakespeare's age somehow still manages to speak to us with a living voice . . . Who should recognise this voice better than I? I spent my childhood there and, because I was the youngest of my family by seven years, my relation to the house was close and private . . . Thus, in company or in solitude, gradually I was penetrated by the spirit of the place; thus I grew intimate with its changing moods and the varied aspects of its complex personality.

Thus too, though the book is a lively history of the family, it may stand partly for an autobiography: his main concern was to give a portrait of the family life he had known from the time of his grandfather. We find the regular touches of humour, not only the Cecilian wit but from his mother: 'Learn to laugh at nothing, because very often there is nothing to laugh at.' And the vein of realism that is so surprising, coming from that odd background.

> It is one of the ironies of history that the English aristocracy maintained its power and position longer than foreign aristocracies mainly because, unlike them, it did not believe in noble birth as such. Whereas foreign aristocrats were permitted only to marry other aristocrats, the English could marry whom they chose, so that their blue blood was always being refreshed and invigorated by the infusion of red blood drawn from the veins of other ranks of society.

His own marriage was a case in point. As he says of his grandfather's, 'Though his view of human existence remained to the end on the sad side, he himself knew happiness in its most secure and lasting form – that of a happy family life. This immeasurably improved his morale.' So, too, for David: Rachel, who looked the weaker vessel and always subordinated her own to David's interests (she never wrote another novel), was really the family's strong pillar.

One hardly needs to repeat the so characteristic touches – 'One of the difficulties about great thinkers is that they so often think wrong.' What about the utter nonsense that the ducal Bertrand Russell thought; or the tragic confusion of Tolstoy? It is a curious thing that much of what men of genius *think* is often nonsense, for example, Milton, or Shelley; Yeats or Pound or Shaw; Sartre, Beckett or Brecht; Waugh or Greene. As to his own family David concludes:

> This apparent failure, if indeed they ever thought about it, did not ultimately dishearten these latter-day Cecils. They saw their lives, as they saw the lives of all men, in the light of their faith in a Divine Reality, whose creatures they were; and in relation to whose being – timeless, changeless, all-powerful, benignant – all that happened in this dimension of fleeting time was, when all was said and done, insignificant.

Alas, ungratefully perhaps, I cannot follow him there.

I can follow him entirely in his last, enchanting little book on *Dorset Country Houses*. Here he was able to do justice to that other Cecil House, Cranborne, transformed into beauty from a small hunting lodge by the original Robert Cecil, who was something of an aesthete. 'For me, Cranborne Manor is the first of Dorset country houses. No doubt I am biased in its favour because I was so happy there during the "long blessed eventless days" of childhood.' What splendid advantages he had, to be sure; but it must be said that, unlike so many, he made the most of them, fulfilled them to a degree accomplished by few.

> From very early years the arts, including the art of architecture, had been my chief source of pleasure. I am also by nature particularly susceptible to the imaginative appeal of the past and deeply concerned to note and analyse what were the elements that gave any particular period its distinctive atmosphere and character. . . . The country house, especially the small country house, is one of the most characteristic expressions of the English artistic genius.

He tells us why. It is partly 'their power to stir in us the sense of history. They are records written in stone and brick and wood of the varied and successive phases of their past.' But also there is the relation to nature, which they do not dominate, like grander mansions: they are 'more subservient to natural surroundings and more intimately related to them. The character of these houses is coloured by the hills and valleys and woods and downs in which each finds itself.'

As an historian I have always regarded English country-house life as the best way of life that history has anywhere to show – in its balance between country and town, its mixture of culture within and responsibilities out-of-doors, social obligations to people and countryside. Alas, this is being ended by the squalid demotic society of today – the houses being turned into agricultural or police training colleges, nursing homes or schools, or being pulled down in hundreds. He takes this more for granted than I do. No servants:

> When the older servants died or retired, no younger ones appeared to replace them. This was not for political reasons – as a result of solemn democratic convictions – but simply because they preferred to live more independent lives. This social change was far more important and significant than the political change; for social changes represent an alteration in people's conception of what they want their life to be, and are likely to be fundamental and irreversible in a way that changes of political opinion are not.

This sounds very reasonable, and he didn't resent the social changes as I have done, curiously enough, who was not brought up with his advantages (I have had to create them for myself, and so resent the frustrations the more). Everywhere he went to study the country houses that linger on, the hostess cooked the lunch and the host clipped the hedges and kept the garden trim. Why shouldn't there be servants to do it? What else are ordinary talents *for*? As an aristocrat, he couldn't, or wouldn't, say that sort of thing; as a man of the people, knowing them quite as well as a Scargill (with his thousands a year for misdirecting them), I can, and do.

In 1958 Rachel produced a novel, *Theresa's Choice*, which gives her side of David's courtship, as I had heard it. It is all very veracious and recognisable, David's personality and characteristics – I had not known hers, or what a clever woman she was, as she should have been with such parents, Desmond and Molly MacCarthy. I knew her charm, and her reserve, beautiful eloquent brown eyes and clear, bell-like voice: but the novel, a most accomplished piece of work, enables one to descry her inner life – delicately feminine, all for love.

It was not a passionate affair, the marriage was based on affinity, of tastes and principles, a firmer foundation. One sees that she had had to bring David to the sticking point, and that his mother was in favour of his marrying, rather improbably, outside their circle. All his characteristics are there: the absent-mindedness, the physical clumsiness along with a certain grace, knocking a wine glass over or spilling soup and not noticing; going about with shoe-laces undone, leaving his coat behind, a kind of elegance in disarray. She notes his spidery writing – it always reminded me of the Elizabethan Lord Burghley's, familiar to me from research among the manuscripts. Again, there was his way of driving a car, talking all the time and apt to turn round. When I had belatedly to learn to drive, I used to console myself for my ineptitude and boredom by thinking, 'if David can drive a car, I certainly should be able to'.

Above all is the extreme sensibility, which made her wonder whether he would ever marry. (His favourite uncle Hugh never had.) And Ottoline interfered, as she would, telling Rachel's mother that he wouldn't be any good in bed (she was wrong about that). He delayed long before making up his mind, and at the end stayed away to make sure – just as in the novel, where something happened to precipitate things. He described to me how it all came about, how after his absence he returned, to call up the stairs. Rachel's voice came down, clear and unclouded – 'David!' and 'I knew it was all right.'

He only once mentioned the novel to me, rather casually, for he knew I was not interested in family life, nor much in novels. So I do not know what he thought of it, and I had never read it until now. Written more than twenty years after, with hindsight, the children growing up, it has maturity and a perceptive understanding that must always have been there. Rachel was the tower of strength in the family, perfect at looking after him, to leave him free for his work – he managed to accomplish much more after his marriage than during his bachelor freedom.

The background is all there: Rachel's relation to Bloomsbury: they appear as 'the Planets', broad-minded about sex, narrow-minded about religion, with their fixation against worldliness, their own snobbishness. Virginia Woolf appears as Miriam Frost, with her habit of quizzing, her ethereal looks (her malice was far from ethereal), her way of holding out her long hands to the fire. David appears now and again in her Diaries, talking about Hardy, disapproving of *Jude the Obscure*, and sneezing across the table. Edward Clare's elegant little Georgian house in Brompton Square is David's house in Edwardes Square, where I visited him. Out he came from his dressing room stark naked, to warm himself in front of the fire, quite unconscious of the oddity. (Just like Shelley walking through the drawing room at Spezzia, oblivious of everything.)

In the novel somebody says, 'aristocratic sculptors or painters have their confidence taken away by real artists, and they have an awful time trying to get their work recognised'.

Something of that holds for writers too (though the Paken-hams manage very well). I notice that David early on dropped his title from his title pages and book jackets, so he must evidently have thought it a disadvantage (critics, *pace* Connolly, are much motivated by envy).

Rachel was the perfect wife for him, she built up his confidence and steadied his nerves. He was so dependent on her – I thought, like a child – and yet intellectually so adult, even *désabusé*. When she died, he wrote me a most touching letter saying that his marriage had been the happiest he had ever known of, or even read about. He was rather lost without her – and invited me to come and see him at Cranborne, whither he had retired. How I wish now I had gone – but have never been one for going about visiting. He would never have achieved what he did without her: she fulfilled the rôle his mother had done for his over-wrought, over-burdened father. Rachel bore more than half the burden.

When I look back over his work as a whole I am more impressed than I expected to be. I have not reckoned up the full tale even of his writing. There were a couple of books about Jane Austen, a Portrait of Charles Lamb; various volumes of selections from Tennyson, Max Beerbohm, and Desmond MacCarthy, with a perceptive and kindly account of the man and the writer. Perception and sympathy, justice of mind and personal charm, such were keynotes of his contribution to literature. No doubt he had less originality than Lytton Strachey, but he was a better writer, with altogether more justice of mind – Strachey had none – a truer biographer and a subtler critic.

Then too, besides his full-time professorship, lecturing, teaching, examining at Oxford, he took on various public duties, as a Trustee of the National Portrait Gallery from 1937 to 1951, and President of the Jane Austen Society for many years. He had a sense of duty towards contemporary literature, speaking up for writers he thought neglected. He saw to it that the poet Ruth Pitter, for example, was awarded a Hawthornden Prize; and he was mainly responsible, along with Philip Larkin, for seeing that Barbara Pym – shockingly droppd by her publishers – eventually got re-published, to become a bestseller, a modern classic.

Lest I be thought incapable of criticism, possibly sycophantic, let me say outright that he never once spoke up for me. He was keen enough to get me to review his books – which I loyally did; he never once reviewed a book of mine. He never said a word about my poetry, or spoke up for my (unanswerable) discoveries about Shakespeare. When we were young we were mystified, like everybody else, by Mr W.H. and wondered who it could possibly be. When, as a leading authority on the age, I had cleared up all these confusions and at last reduced the career of our greatest writer to common sense, David never troubled to go into the matter; he merely thought that I 'might be right'.

It is true that he was not a pure scholar, but at least he should have tried to go into the matter – it was his duty. I understood him very well, that he hadn't much backbone and always avoided controversy. Actually, I do not like wasting time on controversy either, but an historian regards it as an absolute duty to get things right. I suppose he thought, as most of my friends apparently do, that I am capable of looking after myself; but it has been a lonely campaign, and I much resent it. As *my* mentor, A.E. Housman, said, the concern for truth is the least of human emotions. I despise that in them – the truth at all costs, and in spite of any inconvenience it may cost. David always wanted to avoid unpleasantness; but one can't avoid it in pursuit of what is true, humans being what they are, not even caring to know and resenting being told.

One thing more: David Cecil, almost as much as Philip Larkin, was careful about the image he presented to the public. Fancy anybody caring what people think in a society such as this, with no standards! I doubt if D.H. Lawrence cared any more than I – but then we did not belong to the *bourgeois* establishment, we are Outsiders. Even John Betjeman's real nature was misunderstood by his vast, sentimental TV public, D.H. Lawrence maddened, and I misrepresented. What matter? As for me, I write to please myself alone.

Lytton Strachey, who didn't care whether what he said was true or not, had much more *réclame* than David, more recognition and popular success. David got a certain amount, was made a Companion of Honour in 1949, along with a Trade Unionist who committed some financial finagling or other. A friend congratulated David 'on the Companion – not so sure about the Honour'. And he collected various honorary doctorates, for what those are worth in the inflation of such things today. Altogether, when one considers the range and quality of his work, it merited an OM, instead of a run-of-the-mill historian at Cambridge, or a mere editor of historical documents in New Zealand; or others who have made no original contributions to scholarship or discoveries in science. But, of course, in the decline of standards today, few people can tell the difference between what is first-rate and what is second-rate, or even third-rate.

Lord Berners

I owed my friendship with Lord Berners to David Cecil. I was unaware of him and his work, chiefly known for his music, until the second German war drove him back to England from his residence in Rome. The name Lord Berners naturally meant to me the famous Tudor translator. The title was an ancient one, created for that man's grandfather, John Bourchier, in 1455. The barony was a peculiar one, for it had been dormant during two periods, and had the distinction of passing through the female line. It came to my friend via his grandmother, the Baroness Bourchier, in her own right. Her grandson did not set much store by all this, for he was uninterested in history, quite unsnobbish, and utterly wrapped up in the arts. Three of these he practised, music, painting and literature, and left evidences of his creative gift in all three.

Because of his distribution of his talents in this way he was regarded as a dilettante, in the pejorative sense; and because of his addiction to jokes and japes, people thought of him as a playboy, a light-weight. It was some disadvantage to him that he was a peer. He contributed to this under-estimation; he was determined not to be bored, as he had been by the county-family upbringing of his youth. His epitaph for himself was:

> Here lies Lord Berners,
> One of the learners,
> His great love of learning

May earn him a burning,
But, praise to the Lord,
He was seldom bored.

Anyone who was at all close to him knew that his devotion to the arts and things of beauty was total. His work as a composer of music came first, and his centenary has been celebrated with the revival of some of his works, with appreciation and respect from the critics. In this realm I am not qualified to judge, nor have I had the opportunity of hearing his music performed. But as a writer he was a conscious artist, a stylist – something like Max Beerbohm, though less mannered. He read the manuscript of *A Cornish Childhood* for me; so I know, and profited from his corrections and emendations. His own style, easy and urbane, with its quiet irony and puckish humour, I cannot fault at a single point (except for his addiction to 'different to' instead of 'different from').

He was born into a country family which took hunting, shooting and horsemanship seriously, while denying him the exercise of his real interests and talents: neither at home nor at school was he taught music or drawing, for which he had inborn aptitudes. When my book came out, with its depiction of my own struggle away from an impoverished working-class background, he said agreeably: 'Talk of Mr Rowse's struggle: it was nothing to the struggle I had'. We laughed, but there was something in it. We were both faced with utter incomprehension, but he had had consistent, conventional opposition to put up with. No wonder he emerged so determinedly unconventional, independent-minded, something of a rebel. He was a joker in his pack, as I was.

Genius is a sport, and unaccountable. No one could account for Gerald Berners, with his odd appearance and unexpected array of gifts. He certainly did not look English, more Continental, with his dark, sallow complexion, large, luminous black eyes and thick lips; his fluttering, moth-like eye-brows, and big expressive nose apt to twitch with amusement. Bald, he described his sculpturesque head as 'an angry egg'. He spoke in what I used to describe as 'peers' falsetto' (Lord Ilchester spoke like that too).

Some people thought of Gerald as Jewish – no detraction in that, it would account for his exoticism and intelligence. In fact, there was supposed to be a gipsy strain in the family, and he may have been a throw-back: he looked it rather. But there was enough in his immediate background to account for oddity. His maternal grandfather, a very rich old man sunk in melancholia (Gerald was subject to fits of melancholia), would rouse himself to howl the house down with his cries. Gerald's father, a Naval officer almost always away from home, was a clever, sophisticated man with a cynical turn of wit. *His* mother, the Baroness Bourchier, was an appalling Victorian dowager, of repressive Low Church piety, a Sabbatarian who created a desert around her, turning secular pictures to the wall on Sundays: a strong personality, but a perfect horror. No wonder Gerald rebelled against all that. When very young, told that God would punish him for some naughtiness or other, he answered back: 'Nonsense! God doesn't care WHAT we do'. Clever little urchin: he adhered to that principle throughout an amusing, well-considered, thoroughly creative life.

Better perhaps give some idea of the family background and of the external concerns of his career before coming to my own contacts with him. In his delightful *First Childhood* he plays round with names of places and people, so that one needs to set them down in sober fashion. He was born Gerald Hugh Tyrwhitt, 18 September 1883, the only son of Commodore the Honourable Hugh Tyrwhitt and Julia Mary, daughter of W. Orme Foster, MP, at Apley Park, near Bridgnorth, Shropshire. In the book Foster appears as Farmer, Apley as Arley, Bridgnorth as Southbridge: other names are similarly treated – it gave him more liberty in writing about them. Apley was a vast early-19th-century mansion with a tower and turrets, Gothic and castellated, and an atmosphere that was 'highly romantic' – otherwise he does not seem to have cared much for it; he never spoke highly of it to me, and I do not know whether it survives.

For the rest, 'The only conclusive fact that I have learnt
about heredity is that, in the later Victorian era, there were
certain disadvantages in being a sport (in the biological sense)
in an exclusively sporting environment.'

He was evidently, like David Cecil, a mother's boy. But
what a contrast! Gerald's mother was hidebound in conven-
tionality, hardly read a book, appeared at her best on
horseback and – not to put a fine point on it – was obviously
stupid. Not much love lost between the parents: the clever,
wayward naval officer had married her for her money, with
a father immensely rich. She must have thought her only
child a changeling, as he grew away from her. The sense of
humour came from the father; she had none, was so innocent
as not to understand his rather naughty jokes. 'It was some
time before I came to understand the lack of affection that
existed between my two parents. I thought at first that it
was the normal relationship between husbands and wives.'
It evidently had an enduring effect upon his own emotional
make-up, reserved, undeveloped, not really adult. In many
ways he remained a boy – a certain childishness often goes
along with genius.

In music his mother's taste was represented by 'The Lost
Chord', and when the son looked at the picture he felt that it
was just as well that it was lost. Significantly, his first
musical excitement came visually, when he looked at a page
of arpeggios and cadenzas, Chopin's *Fantaisie Impromptue*,
for example. Ultimately he learned to play it. Oddly, I had a
similar experience. In my great-aunt's house was a good
piano, with a volume of Beethoven's Sonatas, which I used
to open at the 'Moonlight', with its rhythmical waves of
notes. I was impassioned by it, and implored my cousin to
play it to me. In working-class homes girls were sometimes
taught to play the piano, not boys; she had been taught, up
to a point, but could not play the 'Moonlight Sonata', of
course. She had no talent. Gerald says for himself, 'both in
the earliest developments of my individual taste, as also in
later life, the visual sense has always predominated.'

We do not need to pursue him into the recesses of
Shropshire county life and its odd denizens – we have a

gallery of portraits of them in his delightful, and funny, autobiography. One neighbour might not have been so welcomed if he had not been distantly related to a duke, for he had an undulating gait, effeminate ways and took particular notice of the men servants. 'When he declared one day, "I often think that the best things in life are behind us", my mother was inclined to agree with the sentiment and was a little puzzled when my father broke into a malignant guffaw of laughter, which seemed hardly justified by the innocent nature of the remark.' Similarly with egregious old Lady Bourchier describing herself in *Who's Who* as 'distinctly low', 'an epithet which must have caused some surprise to those who were unaware of its sectarian significance'. As he observed, 'a sense of humour, to be of any real value to its possessor, must be untrammelled by any kind of conventional bias'.

It is odd that such a brilliant butterfly should have emerged from the sleeping chrysalis of Salopian county life, and he confesses that in its waste spaces he became something of a bird-bore. The child is father to the man. All that most people know of the later Lord Berners is that, when they approached his house at Faringdon, a cloud of exotic birds flew up arrayed in all the colours of the rainbow: the pigeons had been dyed.

Nor need one follow him in the details of his schooling, comic as they often are. There was his inability to cope with arithmetic: 'I had an active distaste for figures and the mere sight of the simplest addition sum filled my soul with nausea.' Like some other rich men, when depressed he had an odd conviction that he was on his way to the work-house. In one of these moods at Faringdon I had to go through the year's account with him and, so far as I could see, he was over £100,000 on the safe side. He was in this rather like the 18th-century aristocrat who happened to be Chancellor of the Exchequer, to whom 'any sum of five figures was an impenetrable secret'.

His days at prep school were, as might be expected of such a boy, pretty glum, overshadowed by games. When he went back some years later 'with a view to refreshing ancient memories, I noticed a definite alteration in the atmosphere; there was a feeling of gaiety, of irresponsibility in the air': it had been converted into a lunatic asylum. For all his being odd-boy-out, he was not without common sense and worldly wisdom; he learned thus early that bluff was 'important in our dealings with our fellow human beings'. Conventional people are apt to regard as 'eccentric' those who have the courage to follow their own tastes regardless of others' opinions. In this sense Gerald was never wanting in courage; he was not a talker, except to make a joke, and kept his own counsels, so he went his own way without ever getting into trouble or controversy. And eventually he discovered that 'places could be more important than people'.

His Eton days he wrote of in a second volume, no less fascinating, *A Distant Prospect* (1945). He inscribed a copy for me with his usual mocking mixture, 'with feelings of reverence and esteem'. It had a nostalgic frontispiece, Eton Chapel beyond the wide expanse of river, meadow and trees. Painted by himself, it has a Regency flavour of the plates to Gilpin's volumes of Picturesque Scenes. Sad to say, Eton was a disappointment; he happened to be placed in one of the least good houses, where the masters were a dull lot. Just ordinary humans, they made their subject as uninteresting as themselves. One must allow that ordinary teachers, dons, professors have no living interest in what they profess: they are just there to get a living. He speaks out quite severely about this, says that it was no wonder that boys left with an incurable dislike for the Classics to which they were then yoked. He resented 'an institution that was to render me incapable of working seriously for years to come'.

This was a pity, and I feel sure it has been put right at Eton in our time, with such outstanding Headmasters as Alington, Robert Birley, Eric Anderson. It is not always the fault of the masters. One trait I find so silly comes from the boys themselves – the way they can make it the thing *not* to work, discourage a 'sap' or a 'swot'. Average humans – I never took any notice of them at school, unpopular as it was to be intelligent and interested. It was an advantage that I went to a co-educational school; it is an improvement to take girls into the public schools today: they have more sense.

Gerald writes, 'boys who worked hard were not admired. "Saps" were despised, and sometimes even persecuted. And most of the masters seemed to think more highly of success in games than in work'. The one exception to this stricture was of course a distinguished man himself, A.C. Benson, who became a prolific and successful writer. For the brief period that Gerald sat under him the Classics came alive. 'If it had been impressed on me that the study of Latin and Greek grammar was going to enable me to read Latin and Greek authors in the original, and that some of them were really worth reading, I might have been more willing to put up with it.' Not only was his interest never engaged, but his real enthusiasms were not provided for. 'There were drawing classes at Eton, but I was not allowed to attend them any more than I was allowed to have music lessons.'

However, his passion for music was not quenched, and he advanced his knowledge in his own inimitable way. 'My interest in music had been aroused in the first instance by the sight of musical notation on paper. I was attracted to it pictorially.' In an Eton bookshop he spied the complete score of Wagner's *Rhinegold*, and used to visit it surreptitiously to study it, until one day a tip from his father enabled him to buy it. 'The possession of the *Rhinegold* score acted like a magic gift that had the power to transform my surroundings.' He advanced from Chopin to Wagner – if that was an advance; anyway, this was a complete orchestral score. The future was foreshadowed.

For the rest, there seem to have been no Early Intimations of Immorality to reveal. He did once tell me that the naughtiest boy in the school, 'a byword for scandal', became a bishop, 'a revered dignitary of the Church', but would not reveal to me his name. Intellectually frustrated, he settled for a sensible hedonism. 'Space is often a more rapid healer than Time, and local grievances are luggage that one readily leaves behind.' I never learned that lesson; nor that which the gregariousness of public school life enforces, 'to let bygones be bygones and, above all, to avoid recrimination'.

Gerald and David together characteristically tried to rescue
me from recrimination against my local bishop, one Hunkin,
a former Nonconformist, who had unforgivably attacked *A
Cornish Childhood*. I had gone out of my way to be friendly
to him, when he was not at all my cup of tea. In vain: I
never spoke to the man again: his loss – I did not want to
know him.

This was, I knew quite well, lower-class behaviour, disapproved of by my friends; but nothing would have stopped
me from giving the man what he asked for. Unsnobbish
again, Gerald made friends with a rather rebarbative type at
Eton, who professed atheism and challenged social conven-
tions. He invited him home during the holidays, where he
did not go down at all well: Gerald's mother, who was easily
shockable, was shocked, though the boy made the concession of going to church. Gerald found the Rectory rather
more congenial than home – though it contained a good
many objects such as Henry James described, in a favourite
passage David Cecil was given to quoting: 'gimcracks that
might have been keepsakes for maidservants and nondescript
conveniences that might have been prizes for the blind'.

There then ensued a bad bout of rheumatic fever, and he
was withdrawn from school, which had not been a success.
'Eton was for me an Alma Mater beloved for her beauty
more than for any other quality, and the memory of it was
the most valuable of her gifts.' But what was he to do in life?
What was to be his career? Army or Navy was unthinkable
for him, and the Church no less; so the family rather casually,
but ingeniously, hit upon the diplomatic service.

From boyhood Gerald had been passionately anxious to
travel abroad; but Abroad was disapproved of by his reces-
sively country family. An uncle had got sunstroke in Florence, his mother had lost a bracelet at the opera in Milan,
and grandmother found a bug in her bed in Bologna. 'These
mishaps were often referred to when anyone spoke too
enthusiastically of foreign travel.' Now was his chance. He
went off to Germany to learn the language. It always

surprised me that his feelings towards Germany were friendly. This was only partly because he was apolitical, and had no historical understanding of the German record – for that matter, he had no understanding of, or interest in, politics either. Secondly, his was the old-fashioned provincial Germany before its manic anxiety to get on top, which has ruined our century, was quite in evidence – though under Bismarck the tokens were clear enough to be read by reflective minds, the great historian Burckhardt and Nietzsche, for example. Oddly enough, Gerald was partial to Nietzsche. Myself, I have never been able to take him: genius and madman, a typical German combination.

In the diplomatic service Gerald made only one or two friends; he had not yet found his *milieu*. One of them was another Gerald, a Cornish friend of mine of the Robartes family, who became Lord Clifden and succeeded to Jacobean Lanhydrock, now the headquarters of the National Trust in Cornwall. For a time the two shared a house in London. Gerald Clifden was a man of taste, a connoisseur, too; but he had political understanding, knew the European situation and was a convinced anti-Appeaser.

In this way I was a link between the two old friends, who saw little of each other in later life. Gerald Clifden was naturally 18th-century in his tastes; he did not care for Gothic Lanhydrock, heavily Victorianised after a fire, and much preferred Georgian Wimpole, which had come into the family recently. To meet heavy death duties he sold it to Elsie Bambridge, Kipling's daughter (a formidable dowager, like her American mother, Carrie Balestier).

Gerald Clifden envied Berners's beautiful Faringdon, built by John Wood of Bath, he told me – which he bought, on succeeding to his inheritance, Ashwellthorpe, an uncongenial place in Norfolk. This had come into the family through the Tudor translator's grandson marrying a Knyvett heiress. Gerald sold it; but on the springy two-branched staircase at Faringdon hung attractive Elizabethan portraits of Knyvetts, just as Gerald Clifden had transferred fine gilt Kent furniture from Wimpole to Lanhydrock. When Gerald Clifden acquired two splendid bronze urns from the Comte d'Artois's 'Bagatelle', it was Gerald Berners's turn to be envious, when I told him. That was where their hearts were (mine too).

A less congenial companion in the diplomatic service was the young Harold Nicolson. He was clumsy physically, accident-prone, not very good at clambering on the bandwagon politically, though later on he tried hard enough. When the two were serving together in Constantinople a typical game was played on Harold Nickers (as I sometimes called him, though more usually Uncle Harold). A rather compromising visitor was expected, no less than Ronald Firbank, exotic personality, outrageous appearance. Young Harold was persuaded that it was his duty to take Firbank on a conducted tour of the harbour, etc. Harold was flustered, but gave in. When the boat duly arrived at the quay, no Firbank of course, but a consignment of roses.

Gerald knew Firbank as few did, he was such a recluse and lived an unhealthy life, mostly by night; he hardly ate, but drank and smoked. I once saw him for a moment on the pavement outside All Souls, a tall, tottering, etiolated figure, wide panama hat, ring in his ear. He looked, or rather – as Lady Ottoline said of a man in the theatre – 'leered', at me and went on his stilt-like way down to his rooms in Longwall, where my friend Sanders the bookseller used to visit him. Gerald was on his wavelength and appreciated his oddities. Firbank had told Augustus John as a deadly secret that his father 'was a Member of Parliament'! In spite of appalling health he would embark on – in those days – arduous journeys. Once he wrote on one of the square blue cards he used for his communications: 'Am off to Haiti. I hear the President is a perfect dear.' I once shocked Geoffrey Faber by quoting Firbank on the youth who fell for a much older woman: 'he adored to distraction her little schoolboy moustache'. (Geoffrey was less conventional than the rubicund Rugby face he put on the world would give one to suppose.)

Gerald went on teasing Harold Nicolson and 'Rye Vita' as he called Vita Sackville-West, and lured me into the game. In Harold's book on Byron he made a scathing attack on

Edward John Trelawny, condemned him as a liar, etc., when he was only a *fantaisiste*. This called up the Cornishman in me and led to a passage of arms, which Gerald encouraged me to conclude with 'Come off it, Mr Nicolson!' It did not improve relations with Uncle Harold.

With Gerald it was almost anything for a joke. As John Betjeman noticed he hardly ever spoke at length – usually a snappy sentence, sometimes a naughty schoolboy pun. He was much amused by Raymond Mortimer's dismissal by an eminent French writer he was making up to. Mortimer was artistically arrayed in a long flowing cloak and big floppy panama hat. 'Allez-vous-en, affreuse bergère!' said the Frenchman. (Note the gender imputed.)

Mortimer thought of himself as an intermediary between French and English culture. Practically the only book he produced, amid his hundreds of reviews, was a small volume collected from them, *Channel Packet*. Gerald referred to it as Chanel Packet.

An odd thing happened to Raymond when quite elderly: he fell violently in love with Uncle Harold Nicolson, even more elderly. The ways of the human heart pass understanding. By middle age sex had extinguished itself for Gerald – to his relief. I find that sad. I suspect that his addiction to jokes was partly to fend off the hereditary demon of depression.

Gerald's long periods of residence abroad much increased the impression of exoticism, of foreignness he gave. At one time he shared a house in Paris with Diaghilev and Stravinsky – he told me the large Russian's saying, 'Il m'est absolument nécessaire de faire l'amour trois fois par jour.' With the little Russian Gerald applied himself to improve his technique in musical composition. He also took lessons with the *avant-garde* composer, Casella, in Italy. For all his jokes and antics he was fundamentally serious about art; ordinary numbskulls took the one for the other, whereas he was really a dedicated artist, especially in the realm of music where his chief contribution lay.

I am unable to speak about this, as there was not much opportunity of hearing it, as John Betjeman complains in his notice of Berners in the *Dictionary of National Biography*. Most of it was composed and performed abroad, in France and Italy. Here I can only record the findings and opinions of others. Stravinsky judged that Berners's talent was for the smaller musical forms, 'the miniature, the burlesque, the musical pun and the parody'. Stravinsky was never generous about the work of his contemporaries, and this omits Berners's opera, and his ballets. It is interesting that now, on his centenary, his music is being performed and more widely appreciated.

An early work consisted of funeral marches, characteristically for a statesman, a canary, and a rich aunt. The *Fantaisie Espagnole* of 1920, a parody of Spanish mannerisms, has been described as 'a small masterpiece of Firbankian *tristesse*'. He was usually seen as an English Satie, with a comparable combination of eccentricity, shyness and sadness.

Le Carrosse du Saint Sacrement was successfully performed at the Théatre des Champs Elysées in 1923. Gerald merely told me that it ended with the overthrowing of the coach, the conjunction of that with the Holy Sacrament probably attracted him to Mérimée's subject: a streak of naughtiness was characteristic of him in everything. The ballet, *The Triumph of Neptune* was produced by Diaghilev in London, Paris and Monte Carlo in 1926. Richard Buckle, our authority on ballet, describes it as a mixture of Victorian pantomime, really a satire on it, and Jules Verne. At school Jules Verne was Gerald's favourite as against Henty (who was mine). Sacheverell Sitwell did the scenario; in the Schottische, typically we have imitation bagpipes and yelping Highlanders. The polka of the Sailor's Wife and her Dandy was broken into by a drunk singing the sentimental 'Last Rose of Summer' – typical Gerald joke. 'The musical numbers for four Harlequins, the Hornpipe and the Apotheosis were smash hits.' I should much like the chance to hear it.

The ballet *Luna Park* – Christopher Wood did the *décor* for that – was produced in Cochran's 1930 Review. The ballet *A Wedding Bouquet*, for which Berners did the sets himself, produced at Sadler's Wells in 1937, had a chorus with words by the then fashionable Gertrude Stein. A critic speaks of the

camp elegance of the score and the bizarre text; *Music and
Letters* describes *A Wedding Bouquet* as one of the best of
British ballet scores, and Berners as 'England's first *avant-
garde* composer'. He must have known everybody in *avant-
garde* Paris. He was a friend of the Princess de Polignac, who
used her American Singer fortune as a generous patron of
music and musicians. Two more ballets followed: *Cupid and
Psyche* in 1939, and *Les Sirènes* produced at Covent Garden
in 1946.

Smaller works were his clever *Fragments Psychologiques,*
'Hatred', 'Laughter', 'A Sigh', which Harold Acton describes
as far more than parodies of other composers: 'they are
stylistic reflexions of his moods'. Parody much appealed to
him, apparent in his *Valses Bourgeoises*, in various orchestral
pieces, and songs taking off national idioms and manners,
English, French, German. *Hoi polloi* were more impressed
by the fact that he had a piano keyboard built into the back
of his big motor-car: it never occurred to them that it served
a useful purpose. He was always at work; he worked hard at
his music, his total output not inconsiderable. When he filled
in his *Who's Who* notice, 'Recreations: None', it was not a
joke: he was always at work, if not composing, then painting
or writing.

For his music I have to rely on others – I have heard only
such pieces as he played to me on the piano. I do not much
care for musical wit, unless it has a tune to it, as in Walton's
Façade; I prefer music in general that has recognisable tunes.
Berners clearly belonged to the Paris School of Les Six –
Chabrier, still more Eric Satie, odder even than Gerald, with
his mania for collecting umbrellas. I prefer Debussy and
Ravel, and in England Elgar. Constant Lambert was an
admirer of Berners's music, and after his death arranged a
Third Programme performance, with a few days later a
concert, for which he arranged his friend's *Caprice Péruvien*.
A photograph exists of Lambert pushing Gerald's antique-
looking car on the gravel outside Faringdon House.

In those inter-war years it was the fashion to depreciate
Elgar, as it was Kipling. Berners, as one of the *avant-garde*,
did not care for Elgar, but he knew what a mastery of

technique he had. He told me that somewhere in his work there is a grand *tutti* with just four notes for the oboe; everybody said that one would not hear them, but one *can*. Elgar would always know better than his critics. He had had so much to put up with, coming from the bottom of society, that it made him a touchy and difficult man. Gerald was philosophic, and rather consoling to me about that: much better, he thought, than to have a good time when young and to be disappointed later. He may have been right – but it leaves scars; Elgar, for all his success and fame, was a resentful, reserved man, who would not allow people to know him.

Though Walton was then one of the *avant-garde*, having genius himself he was above such meanness about Elgar. When he came to write his own Violin Concerto, it was recognisably influenced by Elgar's, with its leaping octaves. Gerald and I went along together to hear the work; Gerald's brief 'Well played' to him after made me wonder whether there wasn't a slight touch of envy at the far greater success the former Christ Church choirboy had achieved.

Berners's devotion to music was deeper than mere avant-gardism. We went again together to the Sheldonian to hear Beethoven's 'Eroica'. In the interval I went outside, to encounter a woman-don, who was a friend; she had deliberately stayed outside all through it, chain-smoking (she eventually died of cancer of the throat). 'One simply can't put up with middle-Beethoven: only the last quartets.' I was angered by such silly superciliousness: it revealed that she had no real sense of values, no *real* feeling for music – all a cultural pose. When I got back I told Gerald. All he said was, 'But the 'Eroica' has *everything*.' There was the difference between real values and bogus, between a man of genius and a culture-vulture.

In the intervals of other activities Gerald painted. From schooldays he had been keen on drawing; now he was free, and rich enough, to do what he liked. It came third in the list of his accomplishments, second in point of time. For in the Thirties he had two successful exhibitions of his oils, agreeable landscapes, at the Lefèvre Galleries in 1931 and 1936. I did not see much of his work; there were too many fine paintings he had collected at Faringdon, and usually too many people about to study them.

Here again his taste was quite independent and, for all his jokes, sincere. Though he was a friend of Dali and the moderns of the school of Paris, he liked Corot, and his own landscapes were in that manner. He had other manners too: as in the frontispiece to *A Distant Prospect* which is after the style of a Regency engraving. I never saw any of the satirical pictures à la Douanier Rousseau which Betjeman mentions. Gerald was the last person to thrust any of his productions under one's nose. I recall now a charming interior of his house in Rome, 3 Foro Romano, with Gerald himself at work and Robert Heber-Percy, his companion, hovering beside.

One could not but see at Faringdon the unsleeping sense of beauty, not only in the pictures and furniture he collected but in everything around him. Again, what was characteristic was that pictures were on the small scale, nothing large and pretentious. He had a number of early Corots and Constables; among the moderns Dérain, Sisley, Dufy, Matisse. I remember particularly a beautiful early Matisse, a cliff scene on the Channel Coast: I prefer it to later Matisse, that endless series of women's curvaceous bottoms.

He went on collecting during the week at Oxford, when Robert would load up the car with acquisitions for Faringdon at the weekend. Gerald and I would stroll into Mr John's shop next to All Souls – always lovely things there, especially oriental rugs and carpets – I remember still a splendid Bessarabian carpet, spoils of a ruined Europe. And there would be pieces of tapestry, silk hangings: some of these spoils repose now at Trenarren, more at Faringdon. There Gerald's bedroom was just inside the front door; he slept in a remarkable gilt Empire bed curved like a ship, prow and stern.

A continual stream of schoolboy jokes kept us amused. Knowing my devotion to Neville Chamberlain, Gerald sent me a propaganda postcard from Conservative Central Office of the great man, and provided with gnashing fangs in red ink by Gerald. When he was himself drawn by Gregorio Prieto, a good likeness, the artist depicted him cherishing a lobster – appropriately, for there was always lobster for lunch at Faringdon.

When one got upstairs to one's bedroom a poster on the door announced, MANGLING DONE HERE; within, one was bidden not to let off fire-arms or make other unsuitable noises in the night. Beside the bed was a musty old Victorian Bible, such as might have belonged to the Baroness Bourchier. One opened it to find that it was the cover for an improper French novel by Paul de Kock, or some such. Nancy Mitford appropriated several of Gerald's jokes for her *Love in a Cold Climate*, where he appears as Lord Merlin. He was friendly with the Mitfords, but knew better than to introduce me to the Mosleys, with their humiliating sucking-up to Hitler and Mussolini. Nancy Mitford, the most intelligent and sensible of them, disapproved of their pro-Nazi antics as much as I did. Gerald was so unpolitical that he saw no objection: anything for a quiet life, so long as he was not interfered with in the more important matter of pursuit of the arts. An engaging innocence – today much to be said for it.

In 1934 he produced *First Childhood*, the delicious volume of autobiography which is the best of his books; it is such an evocative portrait of an idiosyncratic childhood in a vanished Victorian world. Two years later came a novel, *The Camel*, which I have not read, most of his books being out of print and unobtainable. Sir Harold Acton describes it as 'a rococo pastiche of a Victorian moral tale with macabre undertones'. For it is based on one of the incongruous juxtapositions Gerald delighted in: 'the humped quadruped appears at an English country vicarage in mid-winter and takes a furious fancy to the vicar's wife'. From his own exotic background he looked on English life, and not only country life, with an odd eye.

Then came *The Girls of Radcliffe Hall*, a naughty skit which he published privately. Miss Radcliffe Hall was a Lesbian of an old-fashioned sort, who was much in the news at the time for the childish prosecution of her novel, *The Well of Loneliness*. Gerald takes the amusing goings-on at a boys' public school, some of the characters recognisable, and transposes them more amusingly to a girls' school. A piece of literary transvestism, it gave one a good laugh, with its 'Keep off the grass!' at awkward proximities.

That sort of thing much amused him. He celebrated George V's Jubilee in 1935 in a memorable way. Across the main road into Faringdon, on a hill opposite his park, he built a folly: a tall Gothic tower which could be seen from his front door, until the pines and conifers grew up around it. It was an imaginative 18th-century thing to do; but it roused the ire of a tweedy, mannish lady in the town, who wrote to the papers that something more useful would have been in order – perhaps a boring children's crèche. Usefulness was the last thing he considered. He replied in a brief letter under the pretended assumption that the protest came from a man, perhaps a colonel.

He had a painting made of it, by John or Paul Nash. In fact the tower is an addition to the landscape, which only he would have thought of, and it has given its name to the eminence on which it stands, Folly Hill. One can just see its pinnacles above the encroaching trees. Every time I go by on the road this appreciative passer-by at least directs a shaft of thought to dear Gerald's memory.

Count Omega is a rather nightmarish fantasy, for there was a sombre side to his manic-depressive make-up. The only novel in which a composer is the hero – if that is ever the word for it in a Berners book – he becomes infatuated with a young giantess, 'whose virtuosity on a trombone seems to offer the perfect climax to a symphony he is composing'. Then, by the way, there is a comment that betrays what the author seriously thought. 'He thought that the actual state of music was far from satisfactory. The atmosphere of the concert room, he considered, had become like that of a museum and the works of even the greatest composers only called forth the same kind of emotions as those aroused by museum pieces. Serious music had ceased to be vital.'

This reveals to us something of his motives. He not only wanted to liven things up, but to shock people to attention. In *Far From the Madding War* there are some more clues. 'Lord FitzCricket [i.e. himself] had always been interested in the pleasurable aspects of art, and he thought that a work of art should never be tedious. . . . If you're setting up to be a national composer, the English have a tendency to judge art by size and weight.' Still more the Germans: some leave-takings were 'as protracted as the finale of a Bruckner symphony'. I have myself walked out before the end of a Bruckner finale going on and on, while the (largely German) audience in the Carnegie Hall in New York were worked up to delirious enthusiasm. There *is* a nimiety, a too-muchness about the Germans: they never know when to stop. Look at Hitler!

The commonsense side to Gerald knew well enough the ways of a successful promotion in the arts.

> A 'white hope' (thus a critic had described him) of English music – his compositions, though slightly lacking in originality and inclined to be long-winded, were very much appreciated by the more serious-minded of the English musical critics. . . . He set out to get to know all the most influential musical authorities in the country. He professed great humility, sought their advice, listened to their opinions . . .

This was far from Gerald's mind: he *was* original, and he was not long-winded. Thus his work was overlooked by the Trade Union of conventional critics. Yet, when one hears the works of the second rank of English composers of whom they approved, how boring!

He had written a song, which I have not heard, 'Red Roses and Red Noses'. *The Romance of a Nose* is a fantasy about Cleopatra, whose nose was too long ('more like a limb than a feature', said Margot Asquith of hers). Plastic surgery enabled Cleopatra to subjugate Caesar. A characteristic detail reveals Gerald. Cleopatra released a papyrus box of large flies that had tiny streamers of coloured silks. 'Like miniature birds of paradise they filled the air with swirling colour as they flew out into the courtyard.' Like the fantail pigeons at Faringdon.

Percy Wallingford and Mr Pidger, a slight affair, I have quite forgotten. But I could not forget *Far From the Madding War* (1941), for it is a portrait of Oxford in wartime and I was much with Gerald when it was written. Scenes, names, characters, slightly altered, are recognisable to one who lived among and alongside them, and have now become nostalgic. The best of his novels, it has a touch of *Zuleika Dobson* about it; dedicated to David and Rachel Cecil.

With the war he came back from Italy, but needed to vary country life at Faringdon with an urban scene. Bombed London was out of the question. One must remember an important clue to him: all his life he had two admirations, the world of scholarship and the world of fashion. (I could hardly lay claim to the latter: our friendship came under the first heading.) Oxford was obviously indicated. At first he lodged in the Warden's Lodgings at Wadham with Maurice Bowra. That did not work out; I expect Maurice's boisterous ebullience was too much for Gerald's nerves. At any rate, he got one of his attacks of depression, which used to take the odd form, for a rich man, of thinking he was reduced to poverty.

He moved out into lodgings of his own in an old house that looked out on St Giles's. Here I used to see him often, would sometimes get him to play the piano, a tricky piece by the difficult Granados, or one of his own compositions. I once asked him *how* one composed. With few words, as usual, he explained that one took a first theme and developed it; then one took a second, crossed the two and developed that. In the season he lunched every day off the morels Robert brought in from the woods at Faringdon. Gerald's landlady, Miss Alden, from a good old Oxford town-family, was quite a character: her hair 'simply wouldn't grow grey', and in her knowing way she thought Robert Lord Berners's illegitimate son. Actually Robert was indispensable. Inclined to be wild earlier, especially on horseback, he not only ran the estate, the gardens and grounds, but the house and the

housekeeping. Like the ducal Bertie Russell, Gerald couldn't
make himself a cup of tea – though at least he did not write
telling the world how it should be run (and getting a Nobel
Prize for it).

Moreover, there were always guests in that hospitable
house. As I see it now it seems always to be summer, a light
breeze blowing in through the white silk curtains of the
dining room, across the immense space of mown lawn, the
tower of Faringdon church in the background, the spire
having been shot off in the Civil War. Gavin Faringdon
would descend, with guests, from the eminence of his Buscot
Park. A devout Labour peer, he would usually have Cabinet
Minister Susan Lawrence in tow. (A civil servant, who went
in for his first interview with the rigid Minister, came out
with: 'perfect specimen of the *virago intacta*'.) More con-
genially, there would be the Betjemans, Penelope bringing
in her horse to afternoon tea. There is an enchanting photograph of the group around the table, the well-bred white
horse with muzzle hovering hopefully over the sugar basin.

Gerald was much amused by the spectacle of Oxford life and
its folklore, which he had missed when young. Wartime:
'The sky, above the old university town, seemed to have
become a rendezvous for aviators, a kind of non-stop meet;
they were for ever circling, wheeling, and diving overhead
and the ancient walls never ceased to vibrate to their dron-
ing. . . . The sound was a reminder of the precarious age we
live in.' According to my usual wont I shall attempt to sleuth
him through his book. 'The war had come as a very
unpleasant surprise . . . Being neither a keen nor a very
conscientious student of politics, [the heroine] had put her
trust a little too implicitly in the words that fell from the lips
of some of the eminent statesmen who occasionally came to
the house.' That spoke for Gerald: he just had not noticed.

It was a markedly different kind of life that predominated
from pre-war days when the university was in the ascendant.
'There had been lately so great an influx of refugees . . .
Czechs, Austrians, and Germans crowded the pavements.'
We used to say that on the buses to North Oxford one

needed to speak German. Various institutions had been evacuated from London: Chatham House, for example, which appears as Cheatham House, whose principal war-work was reading foreign newspapers. For some reason Gerald was taken by a well-known figure in this *galère*, a Cambridge diplomatic historian, who was a decent sort of man but a somewhat gallumphing personality; when he lunched at All Souls I noticed how clumsy his table manners were. Gerald found this good man comic, and gave him a typical Berners scene, espied fondling his inamorata among the dinosaurs and brontosauruses – the vast skeletons of the University Museum – 'the most incongruous, the most uninspiring spot for a lovers' rendez-vous'.

The traits of the Provost of Unity are recognisable Bowra – with his habit of enjoying telephoning round bad news: '"I've got a very funny piece of news for you. Prepare yourself for a good laugh. Mrs Trumper [the inamorata in question] has hanged herself." No intrigue, no drama, no love affair, however recondite, could occur within the precincts of the university without his immediately becoming possessed of its every detail.'

The university is visited with some condescension by a former alumnus, Mr 'Lollipop' Jenkins. ('Lollipop' was a nickname he was known by in the House of Commons.)

> He had been invited by Jimmy Guggenheim Junior; an American undergraduate who, though continually exhorted by his parents to return to America, was staying on 'to see the old country through'. He was very much impressed by Mr Jenkins, and indeed Mr Jenkins had all the qualifications for impressing an American undergraduate. In the course of an unchequered career he had been in turn author, journalist, and Member of Parliament and now he was all three at once. His political novels, his biographies of statesmen ran into countless editions; high prices were paid for his articles. In the eyes of the world he was a success. Yet as he approached middle age his more thoughtful friends began to suspect that something was going a little

wrong. Although outwardly the rose retained its rubicund exterior intact, they scented the presence of the
invisible worm . . . People began to feel that there was
something really rather terrible about an *enfant terrible*
who was growing middle-aged and slightly pompous.

Who could this condescending MP be? Clues are the
rubicund appearance and the pomposity. The American is,
of course, the notorious 'American Sergeant' who ran
through wartime society over here like a knife through
butter, and was a particular friend of Harold Nicolson. 'The
Sergeant has taught me so many things about America,' said
Harold to Lady Colefax, who said to me, 'Silly old thing,
when I have known Harold for twenty-five years and to
think that he could get away with that!' Sybil was no fool,
and I have seen her at Faringdon getting away with a load of
flowers for her famous shop in London, Colefax and Fowler.
    Gerald appears, with singular objectivity, as Lord
FitzCricket:

> a stocky little man, who had now become completely
> bald, and when he was annoyed he looked like a
> diabolical egg. He was always referred to by the gossip-
> column writers as 'the versatile peer', and indeed there
> was hardly a branch of art in which he had not at one
> time or other dabbled. He composed music, he wrote
> books, he painted. He was astute enough to realise that,
> in Anglo-Saxon countries, art is more highly appreci-
> ated if accompanied by a certain measure of eccentric
> publicity. This fitted in well with his natural
> inclinations.
>   He had a collection of strange masks that he used to
> wear when motoring. He dyed his fantail pigeons all
> colours of the rainbow, so that they flew over the
> countryside causing bewilderment to neighbouring
> farmers.

We are given his reactions to the war.

For a time the war knocked me out. I felt as if I had
been pole-axed. I was unable to do anything at all. I
offered my services, but I was advised to go on doing
what I was doing, and God only knows what that was.
I couldn't compose music, I couldn't write or paint. I
believed it was the end of everything, and certainly of
people like me. You see, I'm all the things that are no
use in war. My character is essentially pacific and
hedonistic. I like everything to be nice and jolly, and I
hate to think of people hating one another.

So Gerald muses in the character of Lord FitzCricket,
going on further to depreciate himself characteristically. He
need not have done so: after all he was essentially construc-
tive, in a world given up to destruction. It was enough to
depress anyone, if it had not been a question of survival. He
did not care about that for himself. In the book his character
considers a bout of psycho-analysis, and Gerald did undergo
that deleterious exercise. Oxford did better for him: it took
him out of himself, gave him something new to study, a
new subject, new friends – and he had a gift for friendship,
quite unsentimental but steadfast and loyal.

We need hardly explore further, though I recognise more
denizens in the menagerie. A.J.P. Taylor's first wife, Margaret, figured in it and entertained us (in both senses) – 'he is
working so hard, he has little time for poor little me'. 'I am
always the one who is left out', and Holywell Ford, where
Alan grew vegetables and we all dined well, was 'just a little
country cottage'.

We can trace Gerald's earlier avatar, continuous from *First
Childhood*, in his irreverent jokes – irreverence was very
much part of him. 'When I was a child', someone says, 'I
used to think that the Day of Judgment meant that we were
all going to judge God, and I still don't see why not.' 'Like
the people who looked for the Holy Grail, I felt I wouldn't
know what to do with Him when I found Him.' On a more
serious note the heroine wonders 'whether the God or
Demiurge who was responsible for the design was beginning
to find that it was not coming out quite as He had hoped,

and whether He were not at present engaged in destroying it
bit by bit – just as she was destroying the embroidery.' Her
warwork was unpicking a large piece of tapestry – about as
useful as that of the busybodies of Cheatham House.

And I like the underlying common sense of 'There's not
much to be gained by formulating questions about the
unknowable.' Also, 'It's a mistake to be priggish about
platitudes. I'd rather be guided by a few honest platitudes
than by any amount of metaphysics.'

Thus Oxford drew Gerald out of a nervous breakdown
and gave him something to observe and write about. His
unqualified admiration for scholarship meant that he was on
friendly terms with the greatest scholar there, J.D. Beazley;
he knew him well enough to know the hidden side to that
life immured in scholarship, they shared a taste for improper
French novels. For a time Gerald was on terms with Marie:
he fell for her exotic cooking, one of her many talents, and
in from Faringdon would come the fresh vegetables. But one
couldn't be friends for long with Marie without a tiff, and
they broke off. I expect Gerald was bored with her nonsense.
How Jackie put up with it I can't think; of course, she was
indispensable to him, but he grew a protective wall of
deafness against her philosophisings.

A no less exotic creature represented Gerald's other great
admiration, the world of fashion – no one more so than the
notorious Daisy Fellowes. She was the descendant of Louis
XVIII's boyfriend, the Duc Decazes, her mother a Singer –
American money enabled her to throw her weight about.
(Princess Bibesco to me: 'Tous les Singers sont fous.') Was
there a streak of that in Daisy? A famous beauty, she was of
an incomparable selfishness. Her first husband, Prince Jean
de Broglie, had been killed in the 1914–18 war. On the
strength of that she had herself presented at the English
Court arrayed all in black, train, plumes and all, a striking
figure in the mist of *débutantes* in virginal white. Gerald,
glamourised by her, was much impressed by that. (*Ich nicht*:
mere exhibitionism.)

A war-widow, she then married Reggie Fellowes, of the
Blenheim family, a cousin of Winston Churchill. As a Singer

she providently transferred herself across the Channel, and took a house near Faringdon, Compton Beauchamp. Gerald took me there – a house that enchanted me, on the edge of an escarpment of the Berkshire Downs. The entrance front was Queen Anne, but looked a little like a French château, with an internal courtyard; the other front was Elizabethan, with a moat, the garden border running away laterally, little church below. Perfect place – would it were mine! But not with Daisy at any price.

The moat reminds me of a story about her. A moonstruck Italian count, or some such, was protesting his passion for her – in that case, he would prove his devotion by jumping into the moat beside which they were. Dusk: he did; the moat was dry – and he smashed his nose. There were several stories of this sort, mostly showing that what she chiefly wanted was to exert her power over men. From some grand affair in the City she was given a lift by the other guests who happened to have, in wartime, a chauffeur. She insisted on sitting in front beside him. She needed a chauffeur; by the end of the drive she had got him away from his employers – bribed, I suppose.

She is the only person who got me to break a rule of the Codrington Library at All Souls. We had the two volumes of Memoirs of her ancestor, Decazes. She got me to lend them to her out of the Library. I doubt if she meant to return them, until in the end I made a fuss through Gerald and got them back. This little experience alerted me as to the lady – a worse one I will not relate.

However, I was bidden to stay at lovely Compton Beauchamp – I can see it now, at nightfall, a footman hurrying across the courtyard with a lighted candelabrum, the candles flickering. Next morning I got up early to walk to Ashdown – no car and no petrol at that time – a Caroline house built by the Lord Craven who entertained a romantic devotion to the 'Winter Queen', Elizabeth of Bohemia. Ashdown was further than I thought, and I was away all morning till lunch, when the footman informed me that Madame was much disappointed – she had specially come down early to take me for a walk herself alone.

A little bird must have told her that I was immune to her glamour, as Gerald was not. I see her now presiding at the large round tea-table in the hall, and spilling hot tea over his trousers. He behaved beautifully, as always, merely giggling nervously and said it was nice and warm. Daisy Fellowes next settled for an exquisite 18th-century Gothic house not far away, Donnington Grove, and filled it with the choicest furniture, especially her bedroom *en princesse*. I never penetrated it. She had an extreme sense of beauty, but one can pay too high a price for that.

Gerald adhered to a regular routine, Faringdon at the weekends, where he entertained guests constantly: he liked company, partly to keep away the blues; Oxford for the week, when he worked. He was always working at something. At one time he wrote a play, in which we all lent a hand, Robert bringing in furniture for the stage from Faringdon – did Daisy produce the curtains? I co-operated by writing it up and, not unwillingly, lending the hero my uncongenial first name. For a complete Celt it should have been Arthur, not Anglo-Saxon Alfred, so popular with the Victorians, whence it went right down among the people, where I picked it up.

At Faringdon the handsome, black-haired Robert embarked on an unexpected adventure: he married Jennifer Fry. The advent of a baby called out an improbable feature in Gerald's character: the lifelong bachelor became fond of the baby, positively avuncular, pushing her about in her pram. (The marriage didn't last: with her luscious chocolate background there were other arms awaiting her.) Everything showed that Gerald was really a great dear. I do not suppose that there had been much sex in his life: he told me, when approaching sixty, that it was all over, and 'a good thing, nothing but a nuisance'. I found this too rather odd; I fancy that the products of loveless marriages may be expected to have cool temperaments.

He was singularly without illusions – about people, politics, religion – and without any form of self-deception. John Betjeman says that he was extremely self-critical and destroyed much that he did. We may regard his lifelong pursuit of beauty in every form as his religion. One saw that in all that he created and surrounded himself with: Faringdon in point, that distinguished house upon which the father of the Poet Laureate Pye overspent himself. With the infallible taste of the 18th century he had chosen a perfect situation for it, the terrace at the back overlooking the valley of the upper Thames. One saw that it belonged to that procession of historic houses, along the gentle ridge, of which the noblest was Coleshill – destroyed by a malevolent workman leaving a charcoal-burner alight in the roof. (There should be punishment to fit the crime: such people are all too easily replaceable, Coleshill for ever irreplaceable.) The entrance front of Faringdon had curved wings with niches; a photograph shows Gerald posed in one of them in his peer's robes.

Eventually the melancholia inherited from his grandfather got him down. He was sixty-six when he died in 1950. I did not see him in that last sad phase. But it meant that he never went on with his autobiography, his best book – and what a story he had to tell! Germany, Constantinople, Paris, Rome; Diaghilev, Stravinsky, the Sitwells, Walton; music and theatre, painting and writing. He told me, perhaps in fun, that he would call it 'Second Childhood'. I do not know if any of it exists in manuscript, but he is alive to us in the work that remains, and enlivens my memories as in life.

I append a last sad little note, from a pocket notebook of 1950.

> May 15th, Faringdon: back for the first time to the house without Gerald. Robert is in the garden, working as usual. I find tea waiting for me – the familiar things around which I remember Gerald buying, from Mr John's seductive shop next door to All Souls. We used to go there together. Here are those superb Dresden vases with parrots and flowers; the odd little silver-gilt owl; the bronze-gilt cockerel on the table with attendant fish.
>
> Sleepy from my afternoon Maytime journey through Berkshire, massed lilac and may, banks of tulips and

variegated wallflowers, heavy green foliage brushing the bus-windows as we pass through Longworth and Buckland, nearing Faringdon – I am dying for tea, *my* drug addiction.

I stand up walking round the room drinking in with every gulp the associations of this place – Gerald's whims and oddities, the extraordinary figure at the head of the table, moth-like eyes blinking or twinkling with amusement or mischief, trim moustache twitching with pleasure at a joke, the gesture of touching his bow-tie, the alto voice (peer's falsetto). In these last two years the pathetic figure drooping and plaintive, unable to work, in dressing gown and slippers. Still shining through illlness and despair, that instinctive courtesy and kindness.

I have never known him angry, at most betraying nervous irritation. His presence, his taste – impeccable but original – is everywhere. Robert keeps the bedroom where he died locked up and sacred to his memory – on the right hand as you come in at the front door, with his gilt bed curved like a ship, characteristic of him. I suppose he brought it away from his house in the Foro Romano.

Everything here speaks of him – except oddly the ancestral Elizabethan portraits on the double staircase of the Norfolk Knyvetts, through whom Ashwellthorpe came, which Gerald found uncongenial and sold for lovely Faringdon. All the same, they showed his descent from the original Lord Berners, the Tudor translator, though one didn't think of Gerald as an historic figure like David Cecil: Gerald was altogether contemporary, modern, *avant-garde*.

Though Robert keeps faithful watch over everything, and nothing has changed, the spirit has fled.

Sir Maurice Bowra

Maurice Bowra has been much written about, and described as 'the most discussed personality at Oxford since Jowett'. He certainly was an outstanding personality, the brightest begonia in the parterre there in my time. Strangely enough, though I knew him intimately, I was not one of his circle. Though he was the most hospitable entertainer in Oxford, I rarely had a meal with him, and I do not remember asking him back to All Souls – he usually appeared there as John Sparrow's guest.

There were reasons for this. Though we knew and were friendly with the same people, our circles were different, intersecting, but with a different centricity; overlapping, but with a contrast. Maurice's were essentially social: for him social life was an end in itself, and how it buzzed and whirled! Mine was intellectual: I was not interested in social life, or even company, for its own sake. I had a number of intimate friends and, for company, one never needed to go outside All Souls in those days. Maurice's Wadham was a small college, and not well off; he was jealous of All Souls, as a good many others were. It might be said briefly that he was extrovert, I introvert, rather solitary amid all the normal life going on around me.

Our relations fell into two distinct phases over the years.

When I was first elected at All Souls Maurice, five or six years my senior, used to turn up after lunch to take me for a walk. I suppose he was thinking of taking me up; I was not thinking of being taken up. And I much preferred going for a walk by myself, with a pocket notebook in which I jotted down the way things looked, the Meadows, Mesopotamia, the river, people observed, flowers and phrases, lines for poems that came into my head as I looked. Even a friend who became nearer and dearer to me, Charles Henderson, I once told in my rude way that there was no one I wished to walk with every afternoon. Some idea of this self-sufficiency must have transpired to Maurice and he gave up. Anyway, I was surprised by the gregariousness of these public school boys, who never seemed to be sufficient to themselves and were not happy unless in company. I was content with my own, All Souls for background.

Then something awkward happened. I observed that one of Maurice's closest *protégés* was rather taken with a golden-haired youth among the College servants; I was alarmed for him – that was all – and warned him off. 'Keep off the grass!', in the words of a character in Gerald Berners's *The Girls of Radcliffe Hall*. No business of mine, but I was behaving like a prefect at school with a junior, with perfectly friendly intentions. They were not well received, and were misinterpreted. Both Maurice and his friend regarded me as a 'persecutor', quite wrongly; they did not know that my sympathies were really with them – I kept them to myself.

Then too I did not like the tone of Maurice's circle: all that eating and drinking, wining and dining, loud and boisterous and, I thought, vulgar. I couldn't have put up with it, even if I had been able; and I was increasingly ill all through the Thirties, endless duodenal trouble, then operations, over-strained and miserable. Maurice and his friends were enjoying life, both at Oxford and abroad together every vacation, France and Germany, the Riviera, Italy, Greece, the Aegean Islands – Cyril Connolly, John Sparrow, John Betjeman, Evelyn Waugh, Adrian Bishop and the rest of them. When I went abroad, nothing like as much as I should have done – I gave up my vacations foolishly to my Cornish constituency – I went abroad on my own.

One day Maurice said, in his staccato way, not unkindly, but rather dismissively: 'Social life – not your thing.' Para-doxically, after the war, when I got better and Maurice was immersed in the College and university business, I moved on the margins of a grander, if quieter, social life than his. Again, it did not mean all that much to me, but as an historian I wished to see something of the way of life of the society of the past, before it collapsed into the dreary monochrome of today. I was only just in time; I observed and noted, in Journals and Notebooks, its last sputters. Even so, I was more interested in the architecture, the places and houses, than in their denizens. Privately, I could not see Maurice's loud and ebullient manners fitting into it.

By that time our relations had entered upon a new and more satisfactory phase. Older, I had come to realise that Maurice's aggressive manners were a cover-up for an inner lack of confidence. I think he was genuinely grateful for this understanding, though nothing was said of it between us. Our *rapport* was an inner one. We still didn't entertain each other, there was no need to. I was not interested in academic society; we were both busy, he with his very efficient administrative work, and writing as a second string, I with research and writing, which to me was all in all.

Maurice was a public figure, a devoted public servant; I, deliberately, was no longer, after I gave up the chore of being a political candidate. Our relations were private, but we gave each other moral support, and Maurice showed himself a loyal friend and supporter at various junctures. His need for reassurance was rather touching – I don't know how many of his public friends could see that. Two Celts perceived it: Anthony Powell, with his novelist's feeling for people, but also Hugh Lloyd-Jones, who wrote: 'Sir Isaiah Berlin thinks that his self-confidence was undermined by the destructive criticism of H.W.B. Joseph, but the roots of his diffidence must lie further back.' In the end I came to feel an affection for him, which not all of his more public circle displayed.

A turning point came with his first venture into modern literary criticism, *The Heritage of Symbolism*. He was apprehensive about this book. What was he afraid of? (There was a nucleus of fear behind his offensives.) He was afraid of being laughed at – he was a short, stocky little man – and he

had been put off by the clever boys around him, Cyril
Connolly, Goronwy Rees, John Sparrow and such. Fancy
allowing oneself to be put off by anything they might think!

I wrote a welcoming review of the book in the *Oxford
Magazine*, making the point that so obscure a poem as Paul
Valéry's 'La Jeune Parque' needed a classical scholar, inured
to textual exegesis, to work out its meaning. Maurice did
not work much of it out, it was so obscure, and perhaps
most of it does not have meaning. Valéry was following in
the footsteps of his master, Mallarmé. Maurice was markedly
grateful – and relieved; after that our relations never looked
back.

But the long period of suspense had an unfortunate effect.
I had looked on Maurice a bit disapprovingly as a playboy,
when I was worn down with anxiety through the Thirties
by the helpless way things were going. Of course there was
the playboy side to him, and I am glad now that he enjoyed
himself, as I could not. But I did not know then how
seriously concerned he was about Germany, nor about the
contacts he had there, which told him exactly how things
were, so that we were in entire agreement as to the outcome.

Maurice was not so overcome, as I was, by the historian's
sense of the folly of mankind; he was more of an optimist,
where I became (and have remained) a defeatist. After all, I
had been defeated all along the line, which did not improve
my opinion of them, only corroborated Swiftian contempt.
Maurice was more human; the point here is that we were
not in touch about politics; I did not know how deeply he
too felt about it, and tended to disconsider him in consequence. This was a pity, when I learn now from Hugh
Lloyd-Jones that 'Bowra loathed everything that was associ-
ated with the predominance of men like Baldwin and Neville
Chamberlain'. That was exactly as I felt and expressed it in
Politics and the Younger Generation.

Maurice had fought, when no more than a boy of nineteen
and twenty, on the Western Front in 1917–18. He found the
experience so unspeakably horrible that he would never talk
about it; at the time he accepted it fatalistically, did his duty
and bore no resentment against the Germans. But when he

went to Germany after the war he learned what they were
really like.

> Their thesis was that the Germans had never been
> defeated, but had been betrayed at home by the 'stab in
> the back', which led to the Armistice, and that the Allies
> had taken advantage of this to impose the 'Diktat' of
> Versailles. It was useless for me to talk about the battle
> of 8 August 1918, which I had myself witnessed and
> which Ludendorff had called 'the black day of the
> German Army'. They claimed that this had been a
> strategic withdrawal; as for the Armistice, it had never
> been accepted by the German generals, whom they
> regarded as faultless. The arguments were interminable,
> and an alarming indication of how even quite civilised
> Germans falsified the past in their desire to prop their
> neurotic honour.

The fact is that neither Germans nor Russians have proper
respect for truth. This was the material Hitler so successfully
worked upon, and he had their support to the very end.
Maurice attended one of the Nazi demonstrations thus early:
the audience were 'so carried away that they could not
restrain themselves, and then they burst into maniacal demonstrations, shouts and yells, umbrellas opened by women,
daggers slashed from sheaths by young Nazis. Everyone was
in a state of wild exaltation, convinced that his sorrows were
over and that he was master of the world.' The *Herrenvolk*! –
of all European peoples the least qualified to rule.

'I had little doubt that Hitler would soon gain power, and
equally that a majority of Germans wished him to do so. I
had read the unexpurgated text of *Mein Kampf* and was
convinced that he meant what he said.' *Ich auch*! I had no
doubts of his ruthlessness or of what a government directed
by him and his party would mean, not only for Jews, but for
anyone who opposed them. In England no one would take
notice, and dismissed what they were told by those who
knew.

> In 1934 I was convinced not only that the Nazis were a
> fearful menace to all civilised ways of life but that they
> wished to rule Europe and were preparing to do so by
> war. The concentration camps were already in existence,
> and it was easy to find out about them. Bernstorff was
> well informed on their hideous character, and denied
> that the Germans did not know about them. . . . What
> particularly embittered me was the cold-blooded indif-
> ference which the Appeasers showed towards the bar-
> barities of the Nazis. Themselves gentle and humane
> men they refused to look facts in the face, and invented
> disreputable sophistries to avoid them.

Maurice was perfectly right, the humane fools!

In July of that year came the blood-bath when Hitler killed
some 1,250 of his opponents within and without his party,
and received the thanks of senile President Hindenburg for
the riddance he had made. Just before, Hitler's predecessor
as Chancellor, the respectable Brüning, managed to escape
or he would have been murdered. He came to Oxford,
where Bowra met him and saw that such a type, ineffectively
reasonable, was no match for a Hitler. Anyone who thinks
the masses are reasonable is blind to the facts. When Brüning
was brought to All Souls I asked him if he had not known
that the armaments manufacturers, Krupps and Thyssen,
had backed Hitler massively. No, he had not known. It was
his duty to know. Such a high-minded type was no match
for a Hitler.

'On the night of 9–10 November 1938 there was a
"spontaneous" outburst against the Jews in Berlin. It was
highly organised by Heydrich, Jewish shops were set on fire
and many Jews were murdered.' Maurice's friend, Ernst
Kantorowicz, a distinguished scholar, was sheltered by
Bernstorff and got away to Oxford, where I met him: a
survivor of the poet Stefan George's circle, author of a
celebrated biography of the Emperor Frederick II. Maurice
had known the Impressionist painter, Max Liebermann. 'Old
Frau Liebermann, left alone in Berlin, killed herself in 1939.
Bernstorff, who had saved Ernst's life, survived the first

years of the war; but in July 1943 he was arrested and sent to
prison in Berlin. Two days before the Russians arrived, he
was let out and at once shot.'

Albrecht von Bernstorff was in the German Foreign Office
with Adam von Trott. Here Maurice's contacts and mine
came together, for Adam earlier had been my close friend. I
had ceased to see him, for private reasons (he had a gift for
creating unhappiness) as well as for public – one could not
be sure. When he came to see Maurice, he too

> felt uneasy: I could not believe the Gestapo would allow
> so obvious an adversary to go about the world express-
> ing his views in this fine manner. I became suspicious.
> My suspicions became worse when he went on to argue
> that we should let Hitler keep all his conquests, and so
> remain at peace with Germany. I then decided that von
> Trott was really on the side of the Nazis and asked him
> to leave the house.

Maurice went further and wrote to influential friends in
USA, warning them against Adam. When he was hanged –
on a butcher's hook, in Plötzensee prison – we learned at last
that Adam had been a genuine anti-Nazi; 'and my rejection
of him remains one of my bitterest regrets', Maurice wrote.

We were all unsure, such were the dilemmas in which we
were caught in that evil time. The last time I saw Adam he
made the same point to me – that Germany was constricted.
What did this come to but Hitler's demand for *Lebensraum*,
for expansion in Eastern Europe? What about the people
whose land it was, the Poles and others? Maurice had already
noted in the Twenties the Germans' 'total contempt for the
Poles, regarded as sub-men'; and of course during the war
they treated them as such (so did the Russians: Katyn!).
Adam was a 'good German', but a German patriot – regarded
today as a Resistance hero. But leaving Germany in possession of Hitler's conquests would mean letting Germany rule
Europe.

There was a fundamental ambivalence not only in von
Trott's position, but in his personality. In the German
Foreign Office he was working on the 'Free India' campaign.

Of course, the war hurried forward the independence of India from British rule, and the scuttle from Africa – the Sudan, Uganda, Nigeria, Rhodesia. (Are any of them the better for it? – massacring each other in hundreds of thousands.)

And, inside Germany, could anything be more pitiable than the endless talking, the ineffectiveness of the Resistance to Hitler? Adam and his friends went round and round in circles discussing what should take place when Hitler had been got rid of – instead of one brave man, among thousands of his victims, killing him. (It would have saved the lives of millions.) What transpired when the 'Generals' Plot' was eventually blown was the revelation that it had no support among the idiot German people: they fought for Hitler to the very end, and brought their own fate, so richly deserved, down upon themselves.

Bowra's own family exemplified the widespread contributions the English have made around the world. His father spent his life propping up a disintegrating China in the Chinese Customs – profitably for China and also for himself. He had caught a glimpse of the enamelled face of the able (and evil) last Empress hurrying by in the streets of Peking, when it was still its beautiful Imperial self, not wrecked by the ignorant Philistinism of Communist rule. Maurice himself was lost in wonderment at its beauty, its brilliant colouring, for he was born in China, 8 April 1898. He several times went to and fro via the Trans-Siberian Railway (he would have known Gerald Berners's joke, 'When in Russia, mind the Steppes!'). Then, on his mother's side, he was descended from a natural son of Lord Cornwallis, of the American War of Independence and later Governor General of India. So that, when Maurice was asked on his first visit to the United States if he had any connexion with America, he could answer, 'Not since my great-great-grandfather surrendered at Yorktown.'

The name Bowra always struck me as odd – Maurice merely told me that it was a good old Kentish name, and that there had been a well-known cricketer of that ilk. It is in fact a medieval name, occurring in various forms, more commonly Bowrer, meaning a dweller at the bower. Nor did he talk about his early Chinese experiences, or his schooldays. He had not been particularly happy at Chelten-ham, nor was he popular with his schoolfellows: no good at games, too clever, and talked too much. He made up for this, as Connolly did at Eton, by making up amusing stories about people; this set a (rather scandalous) pattern for later life. I got the impression that he was not proud to be a Cheltonian, would rather have been an Etonian, or even a Wykehamist, though the imagination boggles at the thought of the latter.

New College was very Wykehamical, and turned out to be important in his make-up. He had won a scholarship there, and took it up when he came out of the Forces in 1919. His scholarship gave him £80 a year, his father contributed £350: Maurice could afford to entertain and have a good time, and did.

There was one great snag. He encountered the formidable H.W.B. Joseph, the notorious philosophy tutor for Greats. This man was an inhuman logic-chopping machine, who put his pupils through third-degree; hardly a sentence of their essays could pass muster without 'What do you mean?', 'What does the word, or phrase, mean?', 'What is it that we really see when the train goes by?', 'But what does the word "real" mean?'. Fellows who had come back from the war could not bear it. My friend, Deane-Jones, who had had a bad crash in the air force, was driven crazy by it, and sensibly went over to Modern History. Maurice gave up on Joseph, and confessed to Warden Spooner that he could not under-stand what Joseph meant. Wise old Spooner replied, 'Neither can I; but it doesn't matter.'

It did matter to Maurice. Some people thought, as he did, that it undermined his confidence. The explanation for that lies farther back, and goes deeper. What it did was to undermine his intellectual confidence: he was not much good at theorising or generalising, his mind was essentially practi-cal. And a good thing too; an historian thinks most theoris-ing – well enough for mathematicians – a waste of time.

Some of Joseph's pupils who were abstract-minded took to it, and made a cult of the old boy: Roy Harrod, Douglas Jay, Herbert Hart, John Sparrow. But Maurice thought that the sausage-machine did no good to this last ewe-lamb of his, and I agreed with him. He thought that 'Joseph's influence on John was deleterious. He seemed likely to crush the poet by turning him into a logician, and that of a not very sympathetic kind. . . . The gap between the lover of poetry and the young logician widened, and it became more difficult for John to bring the two together.'

It was certainly contrary to my gospel, and I disapproved of Joseph on other grounds too. My view was that one should accept one's nature, develop and fulfil it to the best of one's ability – that way lay fulfilment; not impose something alien and constricting upon it – that way lay frustration and ultimate negation. Maurice would have agreed with that. All the people who have paid tribute to Bowra's influence – Connolly, Powell, Betjeman, Noel Annan – all agree that it was a '*liberating*' influence. What were they liberated from? – their middle-class conventional upbringing.

Post-war New College was a much more distinguished place than it had been earlier. Dear old Spooner was succeeded as Warden by an eminent historian, H.A.L. Fisher. A Liberal Rationalist, he made the concession of attending Chapel on Sunday evenings, 'with a fine aloofness as if he had no interest in what was happening'. Dick Crossman said that he appeared there like 'an up-ended sarcophagus'. Then there was Jack Haldane, brilliant but rude; he once offered to exhibit his small penis to a surprised Julian Huxley. They made the poor chaplain, Lightfoot's, life miserable with their militant atheism, when he was already sufficiently uncertain of the grounds of his Christian faith. When David Cecil gave an address, expressing belief in the Resurrection or something, Lightfoot said, 'But you were *exceedingly* bold.' David was tougher where religion was concerned: 'To think that Chapel services which have been going on for centuries should be suspended on account of a Haldane or a Huxley!'

It happened that some of Maurice's undergraduate friends at New College became friends of mine later, notably Cyril

Radcliffe and Roy Harrod. Cyril became a Fellow of All Souls and one of the ablest lawyers of the day. Tiring of the law, he turned to public service, and presided over numerous commissions. He entered into history with that which partitioned India from Pakistan. A certain coolness developed between these two, Cyril and Maurice, who was not without envy for those who made a public career in London. I detect the note in Maurice's reference to Cyril, 'who had been a subaltern in the Labour Corps and published a volume of poems called *Spring's Highway*, which reflected with much dexterity the influence of A.E. Housman and Austin Dobson'. I never knew that: the eminent lawyer kept that quiet.

Maurice did not commit that kind of indiscretion, and had been a (superior) gunnery officer. Noyon Cathedral was a German outpost in the war, and Maurice hesitated to shell it – until he remembered that the odious Calvin, that 'enemy of the human race', came from there, and levelled his gun at it. I should have remembered Robert Louis Stevenson rather, and his stipulation that, if ever he joined the Catholic Church he might have the charming *évêché* of Noyon-sur-l'Oise.

Roy Harrod became a closer friend. It so happens that over him I witnessed Maurice in action as the expeditious committee man he was. When he was Vice-Chancellor an election to the chair of Economics came up, which I attended when Sub-Warden of All Souls. Maurice loyally said his piece on behalf of his old friend. We were then all steam-rollered by Lionel Robbins, in his overbearing way, to elect his candidate (whom, as it happened, I had defeated years before in the examination for the All Souls Fellowship). There was little to choose between them; both distinguished economists, both excruciatingly theoretical, but one was presumed to have the better judgment. To what effect all the theorising about a subject essentially one of practice? I have had a sceptical view of theoretical economists ever since 1931 – today no less at sixes and sevens with their conflicting views. Academic economics has become an industry; a little of it is enough.

The economist who was preferred for the Chair declared

in his inaugural lecture that the dollar shortage 'was in the nature of things and would continue for as long as could be foreseen'. Within a very short time the shortage of dollars had turned into a glut! Yet 'the economists who promoted the idea of a permanent shortage appeared to suffer no loss of esteem or revision of their reputation' (*Times Literary Supplement*, 30 January 1987). They had little to lose with me, sceptical of their judgment ever since 1931, when they were all at sea in the same boat and all wrong with the exception of Keynes, who was disregarded when right.

In 1922 Maurice became the classics don and dean of Wadham College, where he lived for the rest of his life. It is not too much to say that he turned the beautiful little college, then a back-water, from a third-rate into a first-rate institution, one of the best colleges in Oxford. And he was always popular there, especially with the undergraduates, exceptionally with such a job as being dean, responsible for discipline. I have witnessed how popular he was, from dining in Hall there, boisterous and jolly, one of the boys, standing them drinks. He was genuinely generous, and spared no expense. He may not have realised how much he owed his flair and his popularity to the camaraderie he had learned in the Army.

When he went to Wadham it was poor and undistinguished. An appalling Victorian Warden had wasted its resources and made a large fortune for himself. (Maurice spent his on it.) Gone were the golden days of Warden Wilkins and young Christopher Wren, from which the Royal Society arose. The clue to Maurice's success came quite early, when with his abounding energy he drove through the sale of a neglected part of the Warden's garden to the Rhodes Trustees for £30,000 (worth twenty times that amount today), on which to build Rhodes House.

I have always been opposed to any further building in the historic centre of Oxford, though it has gone on all my life, to the detriment of its beauty. Yet in this instance I was wrong, Maurice right, though Rhodes House is no beauty, with the Zimbabwe bird on the roof of its dome (and the tomb of the Unknown Rhodes Scholar beneath?). That transfusion of cash paid for another Fellowship and more scholars, and one may see Maurice's enlightened sense of quality in the people he recruited to the College. As dons, David Cecil and Humphrey House – a promising authority on the poet Hopkins, who created a problem as Chaplain by losing his faith. (No problem for Maurice, who had none, but sturdily went, surpliced and hooded, to Chapel.) His recruitment of scholars was equally perceptive – such promising young writers as Rex Warner and Day Lewis who, though not a memorable poet, became Poet Laureate and wrote good detective stories. Maurice had his blind spots – he always depreciated Wystan Auden, 'the Martin Tupper of our time'.

He made a centre not only of social but of literary life of those sunny rooms of his, high up in the south-east corner of the front quadrangle. The staircase was supposed to be haunted, but then all Oxford staircases are (especially my earlier one at All Souls). To these there came those promising young writers and also Henry Yorke, who made a name as novelist as Henry Green, who went down rather than face the bullying C.S. Lewis as tutor at Magdalen, any more than John Betjeman could. (I had to take on the historian John Cooper for the same reason – the ablest pupil I ever had, and the most troublesome.)

Down from her eyrie in Old Headington came the young Elizabeth Bowen. One does not have to read far in her novel *To the North* before one recognises Maurice's figure and lineaments. The *dénouement* of the car-crash at the end is rather forced, and improbable. Maurice could never learn to drive a car – and was self-conscious about it – any more than he could throw a ball: feminine characteristics. David Cecil told me that at a charade they had Maurice dressed up as Queen Victoria: it was *too* convincing, for he had just the figure. At this time a scandal gave us much amusement: a Wadham undergraduate had been discovered on the canal bank in flagrant delight with a mechanic. Maurice, as dean, had to appear in court to give evidence as to character. The magistrate addressed him, 'Stand up, Mr Bowra.' Maurice was supposed to have said, 'I *am* standing up.' (John Foster of All Souls, when Recorder of Oxford, used to dismiss all such childish cases, wasting people's time.)

Here was a source of Maurice's inner lack of self-confidence. Another was his private life, none too private. He was in fact bisexual, and did not neglect the women (better equipped for them than Jack Haldane, who got into trouble over them with the anachronistic Sex Viri at Cambridge, instigated by the no less anachronistic Proctor, the Nonconformist Hunkin, later Bishop of Truro.) Of one well-known Oxford woman Maurice gave me his staccato summing-up: 'Fucked her for years; much enjoyed it.' But she would not marry him. When he became Warden he had to do all the entertaining himself as a bachelor and it was all the better for it.

I used to shore up his confidence by saying that he could never achieve all he did if he were married, with the joys of family life to contend with. He worked all day at college and university work, tutoring, lecturing, examining, committees; then far into the night he did his reading and research, and wrote his books, both on the classics and on modern poetry, for which he had a passion and a most retentive memory in several languages. He could never have got through all he did if he had not had driving energy, robust health and was free of entanglements.

This burden he carried with ease, and even enjoyment, when I should have been immeasurably bored and have broken down under the strain. Actually two successive Vice-Chancellors did break down, and Maurice easily stepped into the breach. He served his own term of three years and then two or three years of others' sentences. It gave the impression that he was permanent Vice-Chancellor; and he was probably the best of the century. Though we saw little of these humdrum chores, a successor, Kenneth Wheare, reminds us that

> he did an enormous amount of work as a member of committees of Council and of the General Board of the Faculties, the Curators of the University Chest, and as chairman of many committees of these bodies, as well

as faculty boards. The amount of detail involved in this work made it repugnant to many people, but Maurice tackled it as part of the job, devoting hours to preparing his agenda. You knew that, if such business could be transacted painlessly, Maurice could do it and hardly anybody else could.

One does not want to write about the drudgery of committees; one caught sight of him frequently enough when he surfaced – the sturdy little figure on his way from Wadham across the Broad to the Clarendon Building, cap on the balding head, gown flapping in the wind against the short legs. Hundreds of hours were consumed in ceremonies alone. I was pleased when I took my doctorate that it was Maurice before whom I knelt to be capped, brief Latin formula, a kindly smile, then on with the next. It was his speed, sheer quickness of mind, not a moment wasted – unlike so many wordy academic committee men – that got him through. Wheare says that he was sometimes too quick, and members would ask for a little more time.

It was the same with the work he took on as President of the British Academy. He told me that that took him two days a week in London. As President, he, with another man of action, Sir Mortimer Wheeler as Secretary, carried through something historic in the history of that hitherto somnolent body. They drove through an entirely new inquiry into research in the humanities and social sciences, and the possibilities of development. This bore fruit in a large government grant to meet the needs explored – 'the first definitive grant of the kind in the history of Treasury benefaction'.

Nor was this all. 'The second outstanding episode of Bowra's Presidency was the establishment of a flourishing British Institute of Persian Studies at Teheran – a major operation.' This fell in with his lively interest in the Near East, the abiding passion of his life, the love for Greece and all things Greek. Not for me to sing his praises as the most memorable, the most popular and resounding lecturer on Hellenic cruises – I never was on one. But I am touched by an episode when the British ship was passing through the Dardanelles: with a brief ceremony a wreath was committed to the waters, in memory of the poor fellows who had lost their lives there. Witnesses were moved, but Maurice was knocked out: 'Had to go below. Lie down for *half-an-hour* afterwards in my cabin', before he recovered. It showed the depth of feeling beneath the busy, brash exterior, dear Maurice; and also how much the War had meant to him.

When one thinks of all the external work he accomplished – for his college, the university, the Academy – one wonders whether Gerald Berners wasn't right afer all in his suggestion, in *Far from the Madding War*, that Maurice was a man of action rather than a scholar. Of course, he was a scholar, but not a pure scholar in the sense of A.E. Housman or Jackie Beazley or even Gilbert Murray.

I am not qualified to follow his work in the classics, though I can his aims and intentions. He was not a textual scholar; he belonged not to Housman's school but to Gilbert Murray's. He was after the life expressed in Greek literature, and to make it intelligible to us in modern terms. 'I thought that I might remove some of the obstacles which stand between us and the Greek poets and, by placing them in their historical context, show more clearly what they were trying to do and how they did it. This was more history than criticism, but I could not keep criticism out of it.' The work was all the better for bringing the two together in his early *Ancient Greek Literature* in the Home University Library (1933).

With my regrettable ignorance of Greek, this was a useful introduction for me. I remember asking him on a later walk how great a loss of Greek literature we had suffered. He thought that much of the best had survived. Even more interesting was his open-ended view of Greek literature; he did not think of it as ending with the classical age but continuing in the Byzantine world. We did not speak of Cavafy, but he was sympathetic to Maurice on not only literary grounds: he translated some of the poems and would read them to friends. Cavafy's poetry is immersed in history;

and Maurice would have made a good historian. This comes out in a later book, *The Greek Experience* (1957), which all account one of the best books ever written on the subject – the *life* in 'the glory that was Greece'.

He was not thought highly of as a writer, or stylist: Powell describes his prose as 'unhandy'. I think it was unduly depreciated by his fastidious friends. He was no aesthete; his prose is plain and practical, even business-like, like his committee work. It is true that in his writing, at any rate his published writing, he was withholding something of himself, afraid of giving himself away. That is not like a real writer, who gives himself away in all he writes, and is not afraid to do so. But when Maurice writes about Greece something lights up in him, and he is at his best; the psychological reason for that is not far to seek.

In seeking to bring the experience behind Greek literature alive for us moderns, especially for those without Greek, Bowra was following in Murray's footsteps. And he has an effective rebuttal of Eliot's notorious denigration of Murray's translations into 19th-century verse. Murray and Bowra knew immeasurably more Greek than Eliot. Bowra's answer is clear and convincing: 'If we stick too closely to the Greek and translate literally word for word, we get only the bare, dry bones and extinguish the living breath.' What is wanted is something equivalent. 'The problem may be insoluble, but at least there is a problem, and Murray solved it to the satisfaction of his own generation. His translations were often acted with success on the commercial stage.' Though not produced now, I can testify to their impact on our generation: Sybil Thorndike in the *Medea* for example, produced on the steps of the Library at Christ Church, that noble proscenium, held us breathlessly enthralled.

Murray had the recognisable stigmata of genius. Bowra, who knew, says that Murray's translations into English were remarkably close, for all the difficulty he gave himself in sticking to rhyme. On the other hand, his translations from English into Greek were of a matchless simplicity and limpidity.

The source of Murray's strength in scholarship was that
he knew the Greek language and Greek literature
extremely well. He knew large tracts of Greek poetry
by heart and had so absorbed them that he was entirely
at home with them and understood them from the
inside. This was why he did not need and did not much
respect the German method of learning Greek from the
outside, of approaching a text with an enormous appa-
ratus of commentary and explanation. He thought that
this was far less effective than a mind so well trained to
the language that it grasped almost instinctively not
only its plain meaning but its nuances and associations.

Mutatis mutandis this is precisely what I stand for in the study
of Shakespeare.

All the same it was a bad blow to Maurice when he did
not succeed Murray as Regius Professor, when he had laid
himself out to do so and everybody expected it; perhaps still
more when he found that Murray did not want him but had
opted for a purer scholar, E.R. Dodds, an Oxford man but
brought in, rather unwillingly, from Birmingham. At the
time it was a bitter blow, and Maurice's supporters behaved
badly, particularly at Christ Church, where they made it
clear that Dodds was not welcome. Fur and feathers flew far
and wide in Oxford about this affair – just as a boy at school,
Maurice himself had talked too much about it. Fancy letting
people know what he hoped and felt! – ingenuous of him.

He did not realise until later that the rebuff was a blessing
in disguise – as Shakespeare points out, such a set-back often
turns out the best thing possible. Maurice was to find this in
becoming Warden of Wadham, for which he was much
more suited. At the end of his life he wrote, 'I knew at heart
that I was not a good enough scholar for so central a post. I
might have certain talents, but they were not of a professional kind.' In the educational inflation of today, professors are ten a penny; Maurice's combination of talents was
much rarer, and he need not have repined. His account of
the episode reads curiously modestly, if that is a virtue:

modesty is apt to be a middle-class convention, and easily becomes sheer humbug.

We must return to the personal. In spite of his (somewhat muted) passion for literature, especially poetry, he was no aesthete. He had not much taste, for pictures or music or furniture. David Cecil would have made that distinguished house, the 17th-century Warden's lodgings at Wadham, quite beautiful. Maurice furnished them briskly: David went to inspect the result, and was overheard to say, behind a doorway, 'Just like a Trust-house.' And so it was – Maurice should have taken advice. I gave him as a house-warming present a 17th-century style, high-backed oak chair for the hall. But I could not approve the new buildings he put up in the back quadrangle: a third-rate effort by an old Wadham man, who happened to be an architect, and Maurice got him cheap. On the other hand the appointments of the lodgings were of the utmost comfort; Maurice was a sybarite – his figure and complexion showed that – and did himself and his guests extremely well.

It seems to me odd that such a man should be possessed with a *passion* for poetry. Cyril Connolly thought that he was a poet *manqué* – wrong judgment in my view: it was Cyril who was the poet *manqué*, and wrote the most poetic prose. (Then he was an Irishman, though he could not bear to recognise it.) Maurice enjoyed himself writing a lot of pornographic verse, for the delectation of his friends, and mostly at their expense. Their names recur in the verses, or one can recognise the references. Those to Dr Parr refer to John Sparrow's long obsession with that celebrated pedagogue. John's mother used to ask me, 'Mr Rowse, can you do *nothing* about it?' What indeed could I? Gerald Berners would surreptitiously print on the title page of a volume of the *Works by Dr Parr*, 'and CELEBRATED BORE'.

But I do not know to whom the following refers:

> When the dusk has descended,
>   He wanders afar,
> And enjoys a gay tussle
>   With Jolly Jack Tar.

> Or expounds to stout guardsmen
> The claims of Cézanne:
> He knows all the ways
> Of a man with a man.

Then there is a parody of *The Waste Land* – *The Old Croaker*. (Eliot's family had come originally from East Coker.)

> Little Jack Horner
> Sat in Cosy Corner
> Pretending to be pi.
>   Asked me to take him for a honeymoon in Venice
> To the Vierjahreszeiten with Wystan Auden
> Kennen Sie Sir Christopher Isherwood?
> Of course I just live for Art and Music . . .
> Lead blindly tight amid the revolving room:
> I'm tight and stark, and fed up, far from home.
> Das ist die Liebe der Matrosen.
>   O maisons! O gâteaux!

One sees that a select knowledge of contemporary poetry went into these pieces. John Sparrow may be said to have got some of his own back when he questioned what would be left of Maurice in literature since 'his verse is unprintable, and his prose unreadable'.

A remarkable memory for verse is no evidence that a man is a poet. Yeats, whom Maurice greatly admired, and got him an honorary degree at Oxford (I watched the ceremony and the expressions moving like clouds across his face), could hardly remember any of his own lines; A.E. (George Russell) could remember yards of his – and was not much of a poet. However, Maurice's enthusiasm led him to dig further and further into early poetry. He knew some Russian and to this added Jugo-Slav epics and ballads, then dug into the rebarbative chants, the oral verse, of primitive peoples, and emerged with a book, *Primitive Song* (1962). I dare say it threw some light on the composition of, and the oral element in, the Homeric poems, such a happy hunting-ground for academic dispute. It seemed to me that he over-praised the poetry of Edith Sitwell – though this did him no harm with her.

The 'Greek experience' indeed! – it was said at one time that the visit of two famous Oxford figures doubled the prices of the boys on the beaches in the islands. For all his unconventional private life, Maurice's outer standards were conventional: public duty and service, and public recognition in return. His attitude was not that of a finer and more rigorous scholar, A.E. Housman, who had more pride and a contempt for such things. Maurice would say to me, 'The OM – then gaga.' In the event he achieved something rarer, the Prussian *Ordre pour le Mérite*, which, he pointed out to me, Carlyle had received. (He refused honours from his own country, the tasteless old Teuton – though, from his name, provenance, and temperament, Carlyle should rightly be a Celt.) I recall a pleasant occasion in the garden of the *Maison française* at Oxford, when a luncheon celebrated the award of the Legion of Honour to Maurice. The big *gâteau* was inscribed *Preux Chevalier. (O saisons! O châteaux! Quelle vie est sans repos?)*

He was a natural and spontaneous wit – David Cecil said that he should have been made an earl for his jokes alone. I don't know whether he thought them up beforehand, as he certainly did the stories he invented about people, the more scandalous the better. About the satyr-like Professor Dawkins, for example – Baron Corvo's 'blubber-lipped professor of Greek' – or the equivocal character of Dundas at Christ Church, with his moonlight bathing with the boys in the Meadows. When younger I was ingenuous enough to be taken in by some of these stories. But there was no doubt about the jokes, even if he disclaimed the one about Enid Starkie, who prowled the streets of Oxford in the red-white-and-blue of the French *mâtelot* – 'dressed in all the colours of the *Rimbaud*' (she had written a book on Rimbaud).

I had a couple of Roman clerics as friends, David and Gervase Mathew. Their mother on her death-bed said, 'Now neither of my sons will ever wash again.' This appeared true enough for Gervase, a Blackfriar (confidant, if not confessor, to Graham Greene). David, the elder brother, was arch-bishop and enjoyed the more than usual fatness of a Roman prelate: when he sat in a chair his person overflowed on all sides. Maurice to me on this phenomenon: 'a prime example of the Word made Flesh'.

Towards the end of his time as Warden he told me that he had spent some £26,000 on entertaining, and 'the College will have to do something about it'. Wadham behaved well to him, as it should have done (not all colleges do to their most distinguished, and memorable Fellows), and set him up, albeit in an ugly building, for which he had been responsible, in the back quad.

There I went to see him for the last time. He looked *dépaysé* in that bleak environment, hemmed in by heavy furniture, out of place. And rather sad – like those who have been used to a court around them. Deafness was an affliction to someone who had lived so much for conversation and the rattle of repartee. He could no longer hear what the under-graduates said – not that that was much loss; he felt out of touch – fancy minding that! and, what was odder, that he 'no longer understood them'.

What matter? He had done his best for them, and for many others too. It was he who got John Betjeman, after he had been sent down, a job on the architectural journal, which set him on the right road; and he was only one of many.

Sir Arthur Bryant

My long friendship with Arthur Bryant began in the happiest way. After a couple of desperate duodenal operations in University College Hospital in 1938, my spirits were low indeed. I picked up his *Samuel Pepys: The Man in the Making*, the first volume of his biography, with its vivacious portrait of the gaieties of the Restoration – and was taken out of myself and my troubles. I was indeed grateful, and for the first time wrote a fan-letter to an author. He responded with enthusiasm, an endearing and enduring characteristic, and asked me over to his charming Elizabethan house on the Verney estate at East Claydon.

I had not known much about him, though he had begun with a resounding popular success with his *Charles II*. That had not been much to my taste, for, where the Merry Monarch was concerned, I held the Whig view that he sold the interests of the country to Louis XIV and contributed to France's domination of Europe. So perhaps I should begin with a brief sketch of Bryant's career for background, before coming to our long friendship and (very full) correspondence – we each kept the other's letters, as conscientious historians should, though not all do.

Arthur Wynne Morgan Bryant was born on 18 February 1899. His names already give us a clue: he must have been of Welsh descent, though he made nothing of it and never mentioned it. He was all for England, and made a most successful career out of his patriotism and singing her praises. This was quite genuine, an abiding inspiration in all his work

– histories, essays, lectures – but had it not something of the
engouement that England markedly arouses with outsiders, or
those who can see it partly from the outside?

Both Stanley Baldwin and Winston Churchill, each strong
on this theme, were partly outside: Churchill as half-American, Baldwin as a Macdonald on his mother's side. Lloyd
George on him: 'Understand Baldwin? Of course you can't:
he's one of us.' Patriotism was an immense inspiration in the
heroic years 1940–5, when Britain was fighting for civilisation against a bestial Germany. I wrote *The Spirit of English
History* against the background of continual defeats and the
sickness of hope deferred, finding consolation in the unique
record of the island's past.

It reached its term in those years, and went out in those
flames. Britain became a second-rate power in the world,
demotic society naturally a third-rate affair, every wrong
turning taken. I watched with disgust how things were
going, with the scuttle out of Africa and the dismemberment
of the Empire, and I considered Arthur's sounding-off in
praise of England into the Silly Sixties and the Squalid
Seventies just a worn-out gramophone record.

I wondered whether some characteristics at least were
those of a Celt, unconscious of them as he was. His thinking,
for instance, was largely emotional – the reverse of a very
English Attlee. Everything he wrote and said had a personal
inflexion, no impersonality whatever; and he had the intui-
tive sympathy, the warm-heartedness of a Welshman.

He was born in the purple, his father, Sir Francis Bryant,
a courtier for half-a-century; I think he became Comptroller
of the Royal Household – all Arthur said was 'in the service
of Edward VII and George V for fifty-one years'. The only
thing Arthur told me of his father was his useful (?) instruc-
tion: 'Never trust a man who uses scent, my boy.' I suspect
that this was a shaft against his fellow courtier, Lord Esher,
whose tastes – or at least preferences (for he did his duty by
his family) – were actually for his own sex. He was a great
servant of the State, to whom we chiefly owe the formation
of a General Staff, etc., only just in time for the first German
war. Poor old King George V, who had not had much

education, was vastly impressed by his servant having a son who could write a book – in contrast to his own sons. Sir Francis retired to a grace-and-favour residence at Hampton Court, and Arthur had noteworthy advantages in knowing any number of important personages, political and social. Again, he never mentioned that – he was entirely unsnob-bish, his bent was too democratic, one might almost say populist, for that.

His tastes were those of an artist. He had a passion for beautiful historic houses, an equal sense of the beauty of nature, landscape, hills, trees, coast and sea. He loved fine old furniture, *objets d'art*, painting and portraiture, but par-ticularly if historical. I learned a lot from him in those ways, and he was a good teacher. He also had a keen eye for the beauty, and not only the beauty, of women: I used to tease him as an old 'Edwardian *roué*'. He had no eye for the looks of his own sex; and used to tease me back about my unresponsiveness to his lovely ladies, my 'bachelor impreg-nability' he affected to deplore. I, like Arthur Balfour, 'fancied a career for myself'. Actually, Anne, Arthur's second wife, used to say that I was his only man friend, it would seem the only fairly intimate, personal friend; the others were apt to be Army comrades, men in the Services, club-mates. (He was a member of half-a-dozen of the best clubs.)

After Harrow, where he made no impression, he served in France in the 1914–18 war; and, on coming out of the Army, was at Queen's College, Oxford for a couple of years, where again he left no impress. He was anxious to get on with life and, with abounding energy and marked natural gifts, embarked on an extraordinarily variegated career. For a couple of years he was Principal of a Cambridge School of Arts, Crafts and Technology; then for ten years a lecturer in history for the Oxford Extra-Mural Delegacy, 1925–36. This was a hard-working job in popular education, travelling around the countryside to small towns and villages; but this laid the foundation for his immense success as a lecturer. Except for Kenneth Clark, a more finished performer, Arthur was the best lecturer I have known – he made up for lack of finish by enthusiasm and extreme charm. The word is impossible to avoid in speaking of him: in every respect, public and private, he could charm a bird off a tree, as they say. Plenty of aristocratic tact – he was never one for making enemies and could in fact deflect an opponent into useful channels. Also he had persistence, a good deal of obstinacy.

His gifts were first-rate. In the 1920s he wrote and directed three pageants, one at Cambridge, another for Oxfordshire, and a third for Fenland. This activity culminated in a splendid Naval Night Pageant at Greenwich, lighting effects upon the Thames, I think in Coronation year. It must have been spectacular – a pity it was never filmed for the record and so it was lost.

In 1924 he married a daughter of a Cheshire baronet, Sir Walter Shakerley of Somerford Park, and thereby hangs a tale, in fact two. In that house he first happened on the delights of historical research, which he has described in an enchanting essay, 'On Discovering the Past was Real'. It had never occurred to him before, at school or at Oxford, but now he penetrated into a muniment room loaded with letters and papers, 'almost all that remained of the life record of countless Cheshire men and women'. Here was 'the stuff of which history was made. . . . All this, which others learn from books or teachers, I came to discover for myself. What began as a relaxation from the monotony of a winter holiday in a lonely country house soon became a regular hobby.'

In the best sense of the word he was an amateur; but, taking to original research among the documents, he became more of a professional than most academic historians. Moreover, the pursuit of the past became a passion: what he was looking for and was riveted by, was the life revealed in the letters 'still folded as their long-dead recipients had left them, the very sand from the sand-dishes of their first writers glittering in their folds'. From this there came about his gift of transcribing the vanished life, with its excitements and its pathos, into his books.

There was a further consequence.

It was not till the last hour struck in the history of Somerford and the great house, dismantled, opened its doors to a barbaric invasion of antique dealers and auctioneers before its final agony at the hands of the estate breaker – product characteristic of our petulant, uncreating age – that I was able to survey the full scope of the work before me

in sorting and transcribing. Thus 'the education of an historian had begun'.

The destruction of Somerford – all too characteristic of our levelling age – was unforgivable; Arthur did not forgive it, but he learned from it. He rescued what he could of the papers, and the portrait of old Peter Shakerley,

> dearest of all the dead men and women I grew to care for. Though the house he built is now perished and the tall trees he planted all felled, his careful, far-seeing spirit still broods over the wasted parklands of Somerford and in the little panelled chapel which alone survives of the ordered paradise he created in what was formerly a wilderness and has now, by man's greed and folly, been made a wilderness again.

Arthur once described the folly to me – the thoughtless way everything was auctioned off, exquisite Regency sofa-tables going for a guinea, a grand set of Chippendale dining-room chairs for a few score pounds, which today would be worth thousands. Thus he learned to appreciate fine furniture and to become a collector; something of this, how and where to collect, he handed on to me. The houses he came to inhabit were filled with beautiful things; I learned from him.

In the 1930s he got rapidly into his writing stride, in 1932 producing a little book on Macaulay; this too rested on some original research among Macaulay's papers at Trinity College, Cambridge. For all Arthur's instinctive Toryism his historical models were those Whig historians, Macaulay and G.M. Trevelyan, who had the art of recalling the past to life. Throughout the decade he carried on his research work on Samuel Pepys, until the biography was almost complete in three substantial volumes.

He had other strings to his bow. Along with serious history he brought out little books of popular appeal – one might call them *livres de circonstance*: on *The National Character*, *The American Ideal*, *George V* in the year of his death, *Stanley Baldwin*, to cash in on his retirement, and anyway a fellow Harrovian. More attractively, he made use of his 17th-century research to fill out with a little book, *The England of Charles II*, *The Letters and Speeches of Charles II*, and a delightful volume of selected letters, *Postman's Horn*, some of them from unpublished Shakerley manuscripts.

By the summer of 1937 he was writing that it was a pity that we should be opponents politically, when we agreed about many things. Next year I stayed with him at the White House at East Claydon, and he took the opportunity to introduce me to the historic house of the Verneys – familiar to me only from their famous Letters and Papers – who subsequently became friends. Then it was, in his view, 'only foreign affairs divide us'. It is true that in home affairs, domestic policy, he was no reactionary and ready, in a muddled, kindly way, for social 'progress'. To use a cliché: he wanted working people to have a better deal.

To me foreign policy, with Hitler's Germany rearming night and day to reverse the defeat of 1918, was crucial; the muddle and confusion and concession, in the vain attempt to appease her, disastrous. It is true that the Labour Party's opposition to rearming was senseless in the circumstances; but they could not trust a government on a course of collusion with our enemies. An Anglo-German Naval Agreement, which Hitler never kept, and only chagrined the French, our allies; the supine acceptance of the German remilitarisation of the Rhineland; the fiasco over Abyssinia, throwing Italy (our ally in 1915–18) into Hitler's arms; Non-Intervention in Spain, which helped to ruin the Spanish Republic; the passive acceptance of Hitler's annexation of Austria, paving the way for the destruction of Czecho-Slovakia.

1938 was the year of Neville Chamberlain's Munich, which Churchill described as Britain's gravest diplomatic defeat, as it was – and was shouted down for saying so by the House of Commons, which had supported Baldwin and Chamberlain through thick and thin, all along. One could expect nothing from these old men. Knowing Germany as I did, I was beside myself with anguish and foreboding. Neither Baldwin nor Chamberlain knew Germany or German history, the German character, or its potentialities for evil. No one would believe what they proved capable of.

Arthur Bryant was a foremost proponent of Appeasement, wholly committed to Baldwin and Chamberlain, whom he regularly referred to as 'S.B.' and 'Neville'. One might regard his tribute to Baldwin as sycophantic, except that he genuinely liked the man, was always telling me what a good committee man he was, etc. As a private person Baldwin was a nice man, a kindly man, public-spirited in his way. But that was not enough: his indolence, his refusal to face what the long-term interests of the country demanded, helped to ruin it. When Churchill came down to All Souls, he called him 'a whited sepulchre'; and privately again, he described Chamberlain as 'the most narrow-minded, the most ignorant and ungenerous of men'.

For some years Arthur was educational adviser, and eventually a governor, of the Bonar Law College at Ashridge, and was anxious to persuade me to give a lecture there – an historical one. In the event it turned out most exciting politically. In March 1939 Hitler went back on the Munich understanding, broke his word to Chamberlain and marched on Prague – ending Czech independence and, incidentally, gathering in giant Skoda to reinforce German armaments.

What would Chamberlain do? Give way once more? Such were the signs. But at length the Foreign Office revolted. Chamberlain was to speak at Birmingham that night. Halifax went up in the train with him, and prevailed on him to change the message to warning and resistance – at last! At Ashridge we listened to the news of the reversal of policy with excitement – I with approval, though it showed the utter bankruptcy of the course followed ever since Hitler got power in 1933. There should have been *no* concessions to him, the ring held firm around Germany, so that when the abscess burst, it should burst inside – that would have swept Hitler away.

Arthur had no idea of this. That June 1939 he wrote to me that he was writing a book which no doubt I should regard as 'pernicious rubbish'. It was. The book, *Unfinished Victory*, which came out when the war was upon us, actually advocated giving Hitler all that he asked for, not only colonies but everything. It was crazy, and the publishers knew it. Harold Macmillan, who was no Appeaser and knew what nonsense the book was, took the liberal-minded view that they were publishers, not policemen, and it was not for them to suppress it. However, it was the last time that Macmillan's published a book for Arthur – and, in the event, he did repent of it. But fancy being so muddle-headed about Germany as ever to have written it! I do not want to excuse him, but I think he was carried away by sentiment: he knew the horror of war, and he was taken in by all the propaganda against the Peace settlement at Versailles.

It was on the issue of policy that we had our one and only upstanding row – or rather, a seated one, for it raged in a car across the county of Dorset while Anne (his second wife) was driving. She thought that we should never speak to each other again, tempers were so high. Not a bit of it: it was not a personal quarrel, but a man's debate on an intellectual issue. It had no ill effect on our friendship – Arthur saw to that; all the same we never had another argument.

He placed all the blame for the perilous state of the country on Churchill, of all people! I was thunderstruck. In 1924, as Chancellor of the Exchequer, he had initiated the Ten Year Rule, by which the state of our armaments need not be reviewed during that period.

Very well: that brought us to 1934, when Hitler had been in power only a year, there was as yet no danger – and Churchill was out of power all that dreadful decade, not responsible for the confused course pursued by Baldwin and Chamberlain.

I argued that policy came first, the prime consideration; armaments came second, and were to be considered in relation to the policy decided on. Arthur could not see that.

He kept repeating that lack of armaments was responsible for the mess we were in. I urged that policy was the end, and primary; armaments the means, and secondary, to be related to the policy pursued – and the right one. It was the hopeless policy pursued ever since Hitler came in that had built him up (in fact, it was practically collusion: they were mesmerised by anti-Communism and thought that he would pull the chestnuts out of the fire for them. Actually, in the 1930s weak and distracted Russia, purges and all, was no danger: Nazi Germany was the almighty danger.).

Churchill – as anti-Communist as anybody – saw that simple, overwhelming fact. Arthur could not. He kept obstinately repeating that lack of armaments was responsible, and that was Churchill's fault. Way back in 1924! Actually Churchill, as we know, pushed for armaments throughout the Thirties. It was the policy that was at fault – at first confused and muddled with Baldwin (who took no interest in Europe or foreign affairs), and then positively collusive with Chamberlain's attempted appeasement of both dictators, Hitler and Mussolini. Utterly mistaken, in practice humiliating and totally without effect.

There is an interesting psychological point here, which nobody has gone into. Why did all the Chamberlainites get so hot in their defence, actually furious with those who disagreed, and so set on finding a scapegoat? *They must have had some inner doubt and felt that they were wrong.* I came across that curious phenomenon several times over during that period. Fancy their blaming Churchill! whom they all detested (he returned the compliment).

Arthur, a convinced Chamberlainite, was furious. (Actually Chamberlain as Chancellor of the Exchequer kept down the level of armaments, in the interest of lower taxes – and what a good time the upper classes had in the Thirties.) I was no less angry, and was reduced in the end to saying that not to see that policy came first, armaments second, to be regulated in accordance with it, was second-rate thinking. And, of course, purely intellectually Arthur was second-rate; it was his gifts that were first-rate. He never dared to venture on an argument with me again – nor would I have wasted time on it: he could not see the logic of it.

Unfinished Victory made a bad impression, and his popularity temporarily slumped. *Unfinished Defeat* should have been the proper theme, and the proper objective: the Treaty of Versailles only half-did the job. As a German-Swiss professor succinctly summed up to me, 'Europe cannot live with a united Germany'. 1945 finished the job.

I do not know what happened about that book, one never sees a copy about. The bad smell did not last long, people had other things to think about in 1940. And shortly Arthur rehabilitated himself (he was very good at climbing on the bandwagon) with a very patriotic book, *Social England*, which caught the mood of the time – for he was a genuine patriot – and reinstated him in public favour. Defensively or no, he told me that he had done the research for it some years before, and later admitted, rather reluctantly, that he had been wrong about Appeasement.

At Ashridge there ensued a tremendous tug-of-war between Arthur and the Chairman, Bernard Paget, which broke into public controversy, long letters in Arthur's fashion on his side and his characteristic persistence and obstinacy. He may have been right for all I knew – I never did know the rights and wrongs of it, not involved anyway; but it must have taken a lot of time and energy.

In 1942 came out my own bestseller, *A Cornish Childhood*, about which he wrote me the first of a whole series of consistently flattering letters. I fear dear Arthur was a flatterer – no doubt they were genuinely felt but, I felt, rather undiscriminating. Like John Betjeman, he had made up his mind never to criticise – a good technique for success, humans being what they are. He did tease me a bit for 'slogging old S.B. and Neville' – their day was over, but we were now faced with the appalling consequences of their careers, the country in the gravest danger, after all the nation's effort of 1914–18.

He was now working on the first volume of his trilogy on the war against the French Revolution and Napoleon, those comparable years of trial and failure, *Years of Endurance*, and asked if he might dedicate it to me. (He was always courteous and spared no trouble about that sort of thing.) In return I fixed up a Cornish holiday for him on the spectacular cliffs of Crackington Haven near Bude. He wrote me a descriptive letter in the train, passing evocative historic spots like Wardour of the Arundells. (My friend, the last peer of that ancient Cornish stock, had been taken prisoner at Dunkirk, spent the whole war in the horrible prison-camp at Colditz, and did not survive.) Arthur put his views on education, in which by now he had a wide experience, and questioned what I had written about the public schools, where I now think he was right and I wrong.

It was on the cliffs of Bude that he was picked up by a pathetic stray terrier, who became quite a celebrated character in his own right in the Arthurian saga. He wrote a little book about him, *Jimmy*, and an account of the annexation in an irresistible essay, 'A Dog that Chose' – for it was Arthur and Anne who were annexed and subjugated by this tyrant. My relations with him were ambivalent: we were supposed to have an attachment on grounds of Cornishry, but in fact I thought him outrageously spoiled. Arthur could never go abroad 'because Jimmy wouldn't like it', etc. On the other hand, every now and then he would drop a hint in his *Illustrated London News* articles that his dog liked chocolate more than anything, and boxes of scarce wartime chocolate would arrive and pile up for that spoiled, temperamental dog.

Arthur had taken on the job of writing a weekly article for that admirable old periodical, in succession to G. K. Chesterton, in 1936 and continued it to the end of his life, nearly half-a-century, though latterly it became a monthly chore. How he managed it beats me. I used to think that, if it fell to my lot, I might be able to keep it up for a month or so. He said peaceably that at school he had had to write a weekly essay, now he was condemned to it for the rest of his life.

How on earth did he do it on top of everything else? It was a remarkable feat to keep such a good standard. There were of course regular themes, the recurring seasons, celebrations, festivals of the Church – he was an old-fashioned,

believing Christian. He had his Armed Services contacts and
experience to bring into play; the dramatic sense of occasion
which had made him an outstanding director of pageants. A
constant sense of good-hearted humour, wide human sympathies, and an astonishing memory – he could always call
up an apt quotation, any amount of verse ran in his head. It
is said that that incessantly scribbling woman, Queen
Victoria, accomplished some two or three million words in
her long life. Arthur must have beaten her. It was always
'scribble, scribble, scribble' wherever he was: not only at
home at 18 Rutland Gate or in the country, but while
weekending away, in trains, cars, taxis, or afternoons in the
Park, while Jimmy picked quarrels with any dog larger than
himself.

Next year Arthur cashed in on Dunkirk, with one of his
topical books I have not read. He was keen on another
holiday in Cornwall, and I fixed up for him to stay nearby
me at Pentewan. He wrote lyrically of his memories of
Mevagissey Bay, but found himself swamped by his war
commentaries for the Ministry of Information. Meanwhile
he was finishing the second volume of his Napoleonic book,
Years of Victory. Since it came out appropriately in 1944, D-
Day and all that, I suggested that he dedicate it to Churchill
– I think he did not feel on strong enough ground for that
yet.

Still, it was an admirable book, full of his characteristic
zest. With his Army experience and contacts he was well
equipped to write about Wellington and the Peninsular War.
I remember still his unerring eye for landscape, not only the
set pieces of the battles but the cross-country hunts in the
intervals of the fighting. Some officers took over their
hounds to the Peninsula with them. Those were the days for
the fighting aristocracy that held back the French Revolution
from swamping Europe, and gave Britain a grand century of
security.

In September 1946, 'after seven years of war and near-
war', he was taking a holiday in Wales: a fine drive through
Central Wales, 'that dog' (my words for him) barking all the
way with excitement, then turning north to the coast. There
it rained every day except one, while the Army practised

bombing on the beach below: 'such is human progress'.
However, next year he returned: he had fallen in love with
Wales, from an eyrie in the hills above Portmeirion, and
with Welsh folk. 'Why have your people allowed English to
oust their lovely language?' Welsh warm-heartedness: in
those days of appalling scarcity – food shortages lasted right
on to 1952 – he and Anne had been sent off with a basket of
peaches and a dozen eggs. Returning to London, he was well
into writing the third, a Regency, volume: *The Age of
Elegance*. Here again, I thought how well equipped for it: not
only the gaiety and glitter of Regency society, the architecture, Carlton House, Wyatville's Windsor, Brighton, but
popular life, the riots, pugilism, fisticuffs, sport of every
kind. At the end of his long haul, he was to have his tonsils
out, but 'I adore anaesthetics'.

From this time on there enters a new theme: his passion for
country houses – they had to be old and historic – and his
restlessness in suiting himself. I was involved in every move,
right up to the last phase. He would not, or could not, make
up his mind until he had my opinion; it was not so much
advice, as my impression of the house he wanted, my
reaction to its atmosphere. I shared his feeling, though in
fact he was more exquisitely sensitive to atmosphere, a
perfectionist, for ever not satisfied. Willing to be of use, I
could not quite understand it; but would be carried across
country from Oxford, Anne driving, in the car with that
dog always clambering up in front to obscure the view. And
I was as constantly pressed to come and stay to test the
house, while one or the other of his old girl-friends would
be laid on as a lure – in vain. The houses were fascinating.
   The White House at Claydon – endearing, as it was, and
full of memories (earlier he had kept an untameable mon-
goose there, like Cyril Connolly's lemur) – had become too
small for his possessions, collections, and a wife. In 1945 he
had settled for an adorable 17th-century manor in the Cotswolds, Rapsgate, up in the hills looking towards the Severn,
not far from Cirencester. I had been to stay there with him,
and thought it perfect: panelled rooms, candle-lit, harpsi-

chord to play 17th-century music on, immersed in fantasy.
Arthur described it as 'my future home'; actually it was not
his countryside.

At last he had the chance of a personal chat with Winston.
This was after his shattering, and so undeserved, defeat in
1945. The immense Labour victory really represented
people's reaction to twenty years of Tory rule that had
brought war down upon us in the worst possible circumstances. The brunt of it fell unfairly upon Churchill, as even
my Labour following in Cornwall felt. Fatally advised by
Beaverbrook, he had fought the Election on the wrong foot;
realising it afterwards, he summed up to Arthur that the
people wanted 'pap, not pep'. That was about it. Arthur met
the grand old man again at Gray's Inn, and this time 'fell
completely for his magic'. He had been editing 'poor
Neville's speeches', but would not send this work to me lest
I should 'burst with apoplexy'. It would certainly not have
been welcome.

With the war I had ceased to be a Party man or to be
interested in Party-politics: it was then a question of survival.
After the war, in the appalling dangers of a nuclear world,
Party divisions lose real significance: I see not much difference, for the human race, between Labour and Tory, Dem-
ocrat and Republican, between Britain and the United States:
we are all in it together, in so dangerous a world. In any
case, Britain no longer exerts influence on world events – as
could have been done in the Thirties: all now depends upon
the relations between the United States and Soviet Russia.

Arthur did not really feel settled at Rapsgate, the wild
Cotswolds were not *home*. He had written an *ILN* article
about the house, 'belonging to the wild woods and the
clouds and the noble rigours of that stern countryside'. He
preferred gentle, elmy North Buckinghamshire. He did not
deny the beauty of Rapsgate, which 'in clear frosty weather
acquires, especially at night, a curious elfin quality; one
almost expects to see True Thomas ascend in the moonlight
from the woods, or hear de la Mare's horseman clatter up to
the door'. He thought of writing a fairy story about it, 'The
Frost Princess'. But it never could be *home* like Claydon.

So off we went careering around the country looking for

other possible houses. From Oxford we visited historic Canons Ashby of the Drydens; he thought it the most beautiful of houses: 'It spells the heart of England to me and fires the imagination. Being an artist, one wants a base that gives a constant inner glow.' Canons Ashby was all that Arthur felt about it, drenched in history, dreaming of the past, full of memories, nostalgic painted rooms, atmospheric to a degree. But it was a large proposition, far gone in disrepair after wartime occupation, and his housekeeper couple put their foot down against the antiquated kitchen arrangements.

Meanwhile, in summer Rapsgate smiled: 'sun bathing the tree-tops beyond the lawn with a light so translucent, green and unearthly'. And to heighten the effect the Third Programme had ceased broadcasting *Beowulf* in the original, and was playing Elgar's 'Introduction and Allegro' with the wind from his Severn Valley beyond the trees.

London, meanwhile, was spoiled. 'But I know it will become again the gay busy shining London of my youth, and the proud invincible London that used to bring tears to my eyes whenever I saw it in the Blitz winter and the summer of 1944.' Yes, indeed, one wept to see it; but would it ever become its old self again? Not on your life. He was an inveterate optimist. That again is a helpful technique for success. People don't like being told harsh truths – the duty of the uncompromising historian. And, of course, London will never be again what it once was. As for Jimmy, he was in perpetual trouble in the Park, his only sexual interest being in his own sex; and now he had nearly met his death trying to attack a swan, 'scuffling and clucking like a Dame of the British Empire disturbed at a committee meeting'.

Arthur could not decide between Rapsgate and Claydon; Anne not liking the country, he wanted me to have the casting vote. There was Rapsgate,

> perched over space and hanging woods in that wild austere country – so lovely at times it makes one's heart ache, I can't think why. Walking out last thing at night onto the lawn and seeing the pure cold Gloucestershire

stars and the chestnuts on the terrace towering in glorious silhouette over the house . . . Enchanting in sunny weather, it has its drawbacks.

Now Canons Ashby has 'a hall and courtyard like a miniature Oxford or, rather, Cambridge college – indeed to live there would be the next best thing to living in one.' What about a place near Oxford? He was thinking of taking Jacobean Water Eaton, asleep in its meadows by the Cherwell. It would be convenient for the Bodleian Library, and he could go in for market gardening and farming. Would I find an architect for him to put it into repair? Everything was in disrepair everywhere after six years of the mad Germans' war. I duly put our All Souls architect on to him. Nothing came of this; eventually Carr-Saunders of the London School of Economics rehabilitated Water Eaton.

Now he had fallen in love with exquisite Chettle House in Dorset and wanted me to go and see it with him. It was not far from his father's grave and his second home at Wincombe. His restless thoughts were turning towards Dorset. At length he settled for Smedmore on the astonishing shale coast at Kimmeridge Bay (I expect today it is improved by oil installations). I remember the house, cream stucco and grey stone with lavender mottlings. David Cecil describes it as

a record written in stone of the life and character of the persons who lived there. . . . The hall, the main sitting rooms, the parlour, the drawing room and the dining room are in the highest degree welcoming and reassuring, but they also stir the imagination. For me, the sense of a past period evoked by Smedmore is that of the Napoleonic wars. It was this coast that was in most danger from Napoleon. Indeed, the instructions about evacuating people and goods in Dorset in the event of a French invasion were issued over the name of William Clavell of Smedmore, Sheriff of Dorset in 1797 [the year of the Mutiny at the Nore].

Once more the Channel Coast had undergone the threat of invasion. Smedmore had been occupied by the Army with the usual consequences; Arthur had a tremendous job in putting it to rights. In the winter of 1948–9 he was moving in, 'capturing room after room, knee-deep in dust, dirt and mess'. He described it all in detail to me,

> the Queen Anne oak-panelled room in which we mainly live, opening onto a sheltered walled garden, a suite of 1762 rooms compact and elegant, early Georgian stair-case, pretty bedrooms, Georgian front, a Wren-like façade on the garden, an early 17th-century stone range – compact yet spacious. Haunted by the sadness of all it has been through, from Army vandalism and dirt.

(One knows too well what ordinary humans are, and what they will do.)

Now, it was 'slowly convalescing', the garden beginning to look beautiful. Scenery magnificent, cliff after cliff: 'in a wild storm I could see the whole coast line from Portland to the Isle of Wight'. Sea-mists and gales, 'but when the sun shines and the gardens are full of blossoms and birds, its magic and loveliness are beyond my describing'. On top of all this he was going to go in for farming, with a dairy herd of Jerseys. I simply could not understand a full-time writer taking on such burdens. Anyway, I never knew about Arthur's financial operations; I just assumed that he had good business sense – where I had none, and knew it.

At that time, with the appalling weight of taxation – both American and British tax doubled on one's earnings – astute writers, like J.B. Priestley, took up farming, where they could offset losses against their royalties. Penal taxation was not only a disincentive but a loss to the country. I remember Charles Morgan receiving an offer from America, of some 50,000 or 60,000 dollars for a couple of stories. When he totted up both double British and American income-tax, plus surtax ditto, he would receive some 3,000 dollars. He reported this to Hugh Dalton, then Chancellor of the Exchequer, who replied that as a private person he sympa-

thised, but such was the law. So Charles Morgan turned
down the offer, and the country went without the dollars of
which at that time it was in dire need. I know that, in regard
to my own small affairs, I could have doubled my dollar-
earnings if I had not been hampered, discouraged, obstructed
at every turn. Very well, a country unappreciative of one's
efforts can go without them.

Arthur's affairs baffled me. Like Balzac, he seemed to need
to work in a whirl of complications which would have
driven me to distraction. He was involved in getting the
Cambridge University Press to transfer publishing his Pepys
volumes to Collins, and had worked out comparable sales-
schedules (beyond me). At the same time he was involved in
getting his earlier family-house at Wincombe in North
Dorset into order, planting up the woods. He took me to see
that attractive Regency house. What was wrong with that?
Why not settle for that? I think his farming operations
combined the two in some way I did not fathom.

He regarded himself as a 'poor farmer', but in a couple of
years he had a hundred pigs and twenty Jerseys. The pigs
gave off a strong smell; as for cows, did I know that they
were so stupid that in the lush time of the year they would
go on eating grass until they blew up, and had to be lanced
to let out the wind or they would explode? Also, they would
eat barbed wire if not prevented. No; though a countryman
born, I was not aware of these proclivities. Still, 'I like to
feel a house resting on the earth out of which it grew', and
Smedmore was now 'a dream of beauty'. I cannot remember
how many cows he ended up with; but he had a first-class
farm-manager, and by 1953 his Jersey herd was top in Dorset
and won a prize.

I was bidden down to stay, though farm operations were
beyond me. I remember a rainy weekend, when I was put to
work on an early volume of the History of England he was
writing. I had forgotten how much work I put in on the
typescripts of all the successive volumes of this work –
though privately I did not see the necessity for yet another
History of England. His letters are full of discussions of these
matters, jokes about William Rufus, etc.; he was very

amenable to criticism and suggestions, not only mine, willing to change titles of chapters and take endless trouble. In fact, writing his books proceeded in the same Balzacian whirl of discussion and continual rewriting. Other books were on the stocks at the same time: his editing of Alanbrooke's wartime Diaries, for example, and turning them into a continuous narrative. This took shape as two big volumes: *The Turn of the Tide*, 1957, and *Triumph in the West*, 1959, and practically amounted to a history of the second German war, as seen from the perspective of the British Chief of Staff. There was a complicated fuss about this book too, Arthur doing the work for 50–50 returns. And about the same time the affairs of Ashridge College, of which he had become Chairman, blew up into a crisis.

There now enters another theme – people, especially if they were the bearers of historic names. The grandest of these, indeed a prime grandee, was the duke of Alba, to Arthur another Jimmy. He had the double interest of being the descendant of Philip II's repressive agent in the Netherlands, and of James II and Arabella Churchill; also a great-nephew of the Empress Eugénie. I owed my introduction to him to Arthur. To me he meant simply history, of which indeed he was a connoisseur, and financed the publication of historic documents, including three fat volumes of the correspondence of his famous ancestor, which he gave me.

When I was travelling round Spain – for the benefit of my book, *The Expansion of Elizabethan England* – I lunched with him in Madrid, where he showed me some of his treasures. Among the 16th-century collections was the only known scrap of New World coastline by Christopher Columbus himself. In the room devoted to the Stuarts was a portrait of Arabella Churchill's fine soldier son, the duke of Berwick, victor of Almanza, to whom Churchill pays tribute in his *Marlborough*. Then a room full of mementoes of the Second Empire. I remember two eloquent interiors: the Empress's boudoir in the Tuileries, dominated by the bust of Marie Antoinette, whose fate she was afraid she might share; and Napoleon III's study at Saint-Cloud at night, littered with papers, candles guttering. Both palaces of course burned down by the idiot people in the Commune of 1871.

Alba was more than kind, he was interested, and pressed me to come and stay at his palace in Salamanca. This, however, was not in my plans, and I never did. When his daughter and heiress came to London, I was bidden to dinner to meet her and her husband. A ducally-connected English guest made rather a nuisance of herself pressing her attentions on me, determined to conduct me home from the party. I was equally determined to catch the midnight train for Oxford, in readiness for my departure for America on the morrow. I was in a cold fury at anybody thinking they could overbear me. 'I'll spend your money for you' – she would too, if she could have got her hands on it. Arthur, with masculine imperceptiveness, could not make out what this unspoken clash of wills was about, but never forgot the mounting atmosphere when the lady left, on her own, in high dudgeon. 'I hope you haven't been unsettling the lovely Duquesa, *homme fatal* that you are, and uncaring at that. How awful it would be if I had your chances.' The poor little Duquesa had had her features bitchily criticised the moment she had left: 'No bone-structure' – the big Flanders mare herself all bone-structure, of course. That had not recommended her either to the Henry James type, watching the scene and giving nothing away.

Since the laurelled Betjeman has admitted that he liked architecture better than people, perhaps I can hardly be blamed for wanting to see historic houses – a duty for an historian – rather than their occupants. I owed my acquaintance with the Spencers to Arthur; the reigning Earl bade me over to see the treasures of Althorp – Lelys by the score, a second set of the 'Windsor Beauties', a magnificent library, for all that the original one constitutes the nucleus of the John Rylands at Manchester, the muniment room he had constructed for the family archives. He added to his kindness by taking me to see Queen Mary's Marlborough House – very useful, too, since it had been built by Duchess Sarah, and I was writing the family history of the Churchills. Little did he know that I was aware of *his* story: that Queen Mary planned to marry him to Princess Mary, and his Cynthia to the Prince of Wales, the later Duke of Windsor. On getting wind of that, Jack Spencer and Cynthia at once hastened into each other's arms.

Arthur was well in with the Kemsleys, owners of the *Sunday Times*, which had awarded him their Gold Medal for his *Age of Elegance*. Here there was an unattached daughter I was supposed to find 'ravishing', and made to conduct back from another dinner party to Chandos House. I was not ravished. I had expressed admiration for Jacquetta Hawkes's admirable book, *The Land*. Arthur regarded her as 'the Helen of Oxford', and 'I am nervous for you; bachelor gents with country houses to get in order, like Trenarren, are in peril.' But it was Mrs Hawkes's prose that I admired; she was to find comfort in the arms of J.B. Priestley, and a country mansion appropriately called Kissing Tree House. Arthur had not forgotten the Potiphar's wife episode at the dinner for the Duquesa de Osorio: 'Your long Bir Hacheim stand of bachelor impregnability is a challenge and an affront to the entire sex.'

He had almost missed Lady Spencer's fascination the first time he met her – 'I wish it wasn't so far away and inconvenient.' Next the Spencers laid on a private party for a few writers to be presented to the then Queen. At the end I was graciously bidden to present my new book. This presented rather a problem, like Queen Victoria requesting the new book by Lewis Carroll, which happened to be on the Differential Calculus, or something equally unsuitable. Mine was hardly less so, for it was a volume of wartime poems of love and loss. Arthur hoped that 'the Queen would not read *all* the poems aloud in the family circle – a few were scarcely *suitable*. Had it been Queen Mary it would have been different.' He concluded that he liked writing me *long* letters – I can't think how he found time for it; obviously he liked teasing me, and signed himself, 'Yours affectionately, Arthur, Bishop of Smedmore, Rural Dean of Wincombe, Archdeacon of Rutland Gate, Pluralist and Simoniac.'

He was as much of an enthusiast for female beauty as for houses – no eye for male good looks. This was very un-

Renaissance of him, but appropriately 17th-century, his favourite period in which one saw him best. (I had no liking for his 'jovial' Edward VII: to me, as to Max Beerbohm, a vulgar Philistine.)

I certainly owed my acquaintance with the Buccleuchs to him. He was already a friend of the beautiful Duchess, on one occasion 'ravishing in a tartan'. Henceforth I was included in the summer house-parties when they came south to their Northamptonshire house at Boughton. This was no less than a palace, a French *château* of the 1680s added on to the already large Elizabethan house of the Montagues.

One cannot begin to recount its historic treasures – but now that it is open to the public they may be appreciated by those few who can appreciate such things. There was the splendid silver box, in the form of a great shell, which had been presented by the Goldsmiths' Company to Queen Elizabeth I upon the defeat of the Armada. (Princess Margaret: 'Then, what's it doing here?' Answer: 'Probably parted with by Charles II to his bastard Monmouth, from whom the family descend.') The earliest woven English carpet, with the Montague cipher 1586, had been sent up to Westminster Abbey for George V's coronation. The library wing at one end of the façade had never had its interior completed. But all the boards and panelling were ready waiting: it would have been completed, had it not been for the recent war: another of its casualties. In the attics were the rich stuffs, brocades, gold tassels as fresh, such was their quality, as when they had come from their makers in the reign of Queen Anne. Signed French furniture of Louis Quatorze, which even the Louvre envied. All this, and more, to appeal to the eye of an historian with any visual sense. Few have, but Arthur was carried away by such things: a collector himself, he communicated the taste to me. It was significant that our admired Trevelyan, the complete Victorian, had little, except for landscape and countryside.

These visits formed a useful introduction to Northamptonshire, richest of all counties in grand houses, and I came to know the roads well. But for the Duchess, I should never have penetrated inaccessible Drayton, of the Stopford-

Sackvilles, a wonderful sleeping princess; still filled with relics, mementoes, all Lady Betty Germaine's blue-and-white china, Swift's friend. There on the threshold was Lowick Church, with its Greene monuments – of Richard II's 'Bushy, Greene and Bagot'. I already knew Deene Park of the Brudenells, going back to Henry VII, but with Cardigan's Balaclava Hall.

And what of the vanished, and ruined, palaces? Holdenby, grandest of Elizabethan houses: we owe its destruction to the odious Civil War. Lovely Kirby – Sacheverell Sitwell described its bays like the hull of a galleon anchored in those green meadows – had had most of its roofs gambled off by an idiot Winchelsea heir in the gambling days of the Regency, feckless Charles James Fox setting the pace. O to be a Rockefeller or a Mellon, put the roofs on and call the life back within those Elizabethan and Caroline walls, with their echoes!

It was then too that I met a fellow-historian, Kisty Hesketh, *châtelaine* of Hawksmoor's monumental Easton Neston – to become a friend, who accompanied me around all the places I needed to see when writing my *Ralegh and the Throckmortons*. I had learned from Macaulay to *see* the places I was writing about and to describe them as they lay under my eye – Paulerspury of the Throckmortons, Whittlebury Forest of the Wakes. Joan Wake, admirable historian, of that ancient family – did they go back to Hereward the Wake? – was a good friend too. (Lord Spencer thought that she considered him 'insufficiently feudal': true, the Spencers were a more recent family.)

When my book came out, it was attacked by a Leftist Liverpool professor (to whom I had been helpful) for venturing to thank these Northamptonshire folk who had been generous and hospitable. Arthur had a more successful technique for dealing with such types: his publishers said that he had the habit of feeding the hand that bit him. In short, he made up to them. Myself, I wouldn't dream of it: I give them some of their own back, after an interval.

Several times Arthur expressed himself indignant at an 'outrageous' review of a book of mine by Harold Nicolson –

to whose son and nephew I had been kind as a don at
Oxford. When young, I had clumsily rejected a pass he made
at me. Cecil Roberts: 'And did you ever get a good review
from Uncle Harold again?' In fact, I never did. When his
wife, Vita, wrote enthusiastically about *The Expansion of
Elizabethan England*, inviting me to Sissinghurst, I never
went; merely commented that it should be pronounced, in
the old English way, Sissiehurst, and never spoke to Harold
Nicolson again. He had the decency to express regret after-
ward, but to his close friend, John Sparrow, not to me, an
old friend of his sister's family. Such are reviewers, but *he*
should have known better.

There was little enough that I could give Arthur for all his
continued kindness. True, I put in a good deal of work on
the successive volumes of his History of England – though I
did not see the necessity of writing it: plenty existed already.
Our correspondence is full of suggestions and criticisms, and
Arthur was very long-winded in his letters, all written by
hand. However did he find time? Nevertheless, it is always
the busiest who do.

Rarely enough he would come away for a weekend at All
Souls, when I would have a large lunch-party in hall; then
he would usually leave before Sunday was over, ready for
the week's work on Monday morning. Naturally he met my
friends. John Betjeman, who had names for everybody, used
to call Anne 'the Rajah's niece', for she was one of the
famous Brookes of Sarawak (vanished world!). Arthur came
to know Wyndham Ketton-Cremer through me, and stayed
with him, as I regularly did, at historic Felbrigg: now, thanks
to Wyndham, safe – with all its belongings, portraits,
furnishings, decorative plaster-work – in the hands of the
National Trust.

In the 1950s, foreseeing how things were going to go with
this country, I decided to see how things were in America. I
did not emigrate for tax reasons, as one or two writers and
artists were rewarded with CHs and OMs for so doing –
anyhow, the country did not profit from their presence.
Ambivalent as always, I divided my interests henceforward.
Several of my friends had made the acquaintance of the

United States when young; I had been unable to through illness and would make up for it now. In the event I more than made up for it, at last seeing practically every State in the Union over the years. The bulk of the Cornish were in America anyway – one day I would write a book about my people over there.

This meant that henceforth I saw less of Arthur, though we kept regularly in touch, and met when I came back for the summers. He didn't know America; most English people who write about it do not. Their view is a superficial one, of a country that is really a vast continent: how it holds together in freedom, with free institutions (no Siberia), is the political miracle of our time. Those people who are mean about the United States – usually, though not wholly, on the Left – do not know what they are talking about. For long baffled and uncomprehending, it has taken me years to get the hang of it.

Nor did his books appeal in America – too much centred on England, too insular. When my forebodings were only too clearly borne out in the Sixties when everything went wrong – irresponsibly importing a racial problem we did not have before, bringing more people into an over-populated island – Arthur wrote, 'What you say is true, but somehow I cannot despair of England whatever my brain tells me.' He was right that the English past recorded a wonderful achievement, the impress the small island had made on the world – but all that was past; as I wrote at the time, 'The past of this country is a great deal more interesting than its future is likely to be.'

In 1954 he got a knighthood, for what that was worth in a demotic society – some point in it in the Elizabethan age, when such things were few and far between. Arthur did not attach importance to such things; much to his credit, he regarded only the work. And he was as hard at work as ever on the gramophone record: a succession of volumes, *Makers of the Realm, The Age of Chivalry, The Fire and the Rose, The Medieval Foundation, Protestant Island, The Lion and the Unicorn*, etc. What was the point of them now?

That is not to say that he was not conscientious about the

work he put into them: he told me that he had written the
Anglo-Saxon volume, with *The Coming of Christianity*, five
or six times. He got no credit for this from the academics,
though far more readable than they; in the breakup of an
integrated society, they constitute a sub-culture, writing for
each other rather than for society at large. And, though he
got various 'honours', he got little recognition from them.
When Oliver Franks left the Provostship of Queen's at
Oxford, to become ambassador in Washington, I wondered
whether Arthur might not become Provost of his old college.
No one thought of it: they elected a non-entity, one Jones.
They never even made him an 'honorary' Fellow, nor did
the University recognise his life's work with an 'honorary'
degree – any more than it did Margaret Thatcher, an historic
figure of our time. I remember A.J.P. Taylor reviewing one
of Arthur's histories as 'a piece of scissors and paste' – he
was conscientious in quoting from original sources. When
there was a banquet at Vintners' Hall for Arthur's eightieth
birthday, Taylor was there, I noticed; another instance of
Arthur's talent for feeding the hand that bit him.

In July 1955 it was – could I get Sir Bernard Paget
honoured by the University or city, as a son of a bishop of
Oxford? I think that this was the man with whom Arthur
had had such a prolonged tug-of-war over Ashridge; but
there followed a long account of Paget's career, culminating
with 'what he did for training D-Day armies is comparable
to what John Moore did for Wellington's Army.' Of course
I couldn't: I never had any success with suggestions I made.
I thought Jules Supervielle, a writer of rare distinction, a
suitable choice; and what about Montherlant? I twice suggested J.B. Priestley; though I was not in sympathy with his
populist Leftism, it would be a proper gesture to a Cambridge writer. No response.

I had luck only once, in suggesting the American historian,
Professor Allan Nevins – but he was a recognisable academic.
When C.S. Lewis, the most eminent member of the English
Faculty, became a bestseller, Helen Gardner, a second-rate
figure who *was* a professor, said that he ought to resign. The
usual envy of the uncreative for the creative, of the second-

rate for the first-rate. The Faculty would never have him as professor: he took off for Cambridge, where he was not really at home. Arthur was well out of the academic snake pit.

In 1956 there was a crisis about Smedmore. He had spent £14,000 on it, and now all the roof timbers had to be renewed. What was he to do? Move herd and farm and employees up to Wincombe which he owned? I never understood these tangles he got into, and so did not involve myself in them. He held Smedmore on a lease, so there ensued complicated negotiations about compensation.

At the same time there was a crisis about Jimmy, who dominated their personal lives (Arthur would never encumber himself with children). Anne faithfully gave up months to nursing that dog round: he survived, 'and now bites anyone at sight like an irascible retired Edwardian colonel'. I remember Arthur turning up at a publisher's party with his nose bitten. 'What have you been doing with that dog?' I inquired. I assumed he had been exciting him with gross attentions: 'He is my friend.'

In June 1958 he was moving from lovely Smedmore, into which he had put so much work, to Wincombe, where he was farming several hundred acres and woods. Now he was on his way to stop at Holyrood, as a guest, to attend the Assembly of the Church of Scotland – as I did somewhat later. As historians we were much impressed, attending the banquet in the Long Gallery in which Bonny Prince Charlie led off the dance in '45. (Actually he was a swarthy, Italian-looking foreigner.) I was fortunate enough to attend the Assembly in which one saw the Scottish nation representatively gathered – when relations with the Church of Rome were debated. An unreconstructed Calvinist struck up the old cry of the 'Whore of Babylon'; I saw the sinister figure of John Knox planing over the Assembly, as he used to 'ding the pulpit in blads' in St Giles's. I was less impressed by my bedroom at Holyrood, hung with portraits of Queen Victoria's German relations.

In the early 1960s Arthur sold Wincombe; he decided that he could not 'both farm and write the history of England'.

Still, he had revivified the place and replanted the woodlands. He had known it for nearly sixty years, and had sold it to someone who would appreciate and cherish it. Himself had now fallen for a wonderful place in his best-beloved North Buckinghamshire: the splendid group of Queen Anne buildings at the Grenvilleses' Wotton Underwood, the centre-piece a handsome mansion, something of a palace, with two detached pavilions symmetrically placed before. The Merchant Adventurers of Bristol had bought this lovely house for demolition. Elaine Brunner, with courage and gallantry and not much money, had only just managed to save it from these brute Philistines. Heart-breaking how we go round England today trying to pick up the bits and pieces, the relics of an élite society that had taste and distinction, and made the country great – while today . . .

Arthur had fallen in love again: 'that baroque fantasy of Wren's three red-brick buildings suddenly rising out of the Buckinghamshire meadows and elms [alas, vanishing too] is one of the most beautiful architectural effects I have ever seen'. He had bought the South Pavilion, which had been the original coach-house, one enormous room. He would have to reconstruct the interior entirely, and open out the basement on to the lawn. He did not want to give up his Jersey herd, and hoped still to farm. He wanted me to come over and see Wotton 'with its great Hampton Court windows lit up'. I stayed with him in the Pavilion, beautiful, but it made an odd house with its one vast room, in which he had disposed his pictures and elegant furniture. By this time he had had his special collection of Battersea enamels burgled from Rutland Gate. Of course.

Together we attended one of the Claydon Concerts, by which that devoted couple, Ralph and Mary Verney, have brought back to life their historic Buckinghamshire house, and saved at least that from the ruin of our time – by musical talent and sheer hard work.

In May 1960 I was called upon to suggest illustrations for an edition of his Charles II book, with which he had first achieved popular success (I will not use the *cliché* 'acclaim', so worn out by the media). In May 1962 he had been writing his regular article for the *Illustrated London News* for twenty-six years, though he had never once been to the office; nor had 'my illustrious predecessor', G.K. Chesterton in thirty-one years. Arthur had a happy relationship with a congenial editor, Sir Bruce Ingram. I feel sure that quite a number of Arthur's articles would bear reprinting better than G.K.C.'s repetitive pieces. Still, Arthur had his popular record. In 1967 he 'comforts' himself with Pitt in 1797, 'I am not at all afraid for England; we shall stand till the day of judgment.' But then England was on the way to Trafalgar and Waterloo, which gave us a certain primacy in the world, and a century of security. And today? . . .

In the 1970s he turned out a number of his patriotic little books, not all of which I have read, for the day for those was really over: *Nelson, The Great Duke* (Wellington), *A Thousand Years of British Monarchy. Jackets of Green* was, I think, his tribute to the Green Howards: he was well qualified to write military history. In May 1961 he had been in the Highlands 'with two soldier friends', Dick O'Connor and Harry Houldsworth, seeking out Bruce's hiding places; thence on to the MacEwens' Marchmont, to be shown over Flodden Field by scholarly Kisty Hesketh. In May 1968 he found it 'fun to be living in the same century' with me: in the Silly Sixties we were both amused at the 'dockers hooting at Leftist intellectuals'.

I suppose we both found work an anodyne – I at any rate from grief at the way things were going with the country. Arthur's moods went up and down; in November 1969 he wrote me a rather autobiographical letter – would I come and dine 'in this decaying city'? In September 1971 he was slogging away at his biography of Wellington, writing an eighteen-hour day, a seven-day week. Devout Trade Unionists, regulation strikers, please note. He was borne up by enthusiasm for a splendid past, against 'the shoddy and supine present'; his public stance was, however, an optimistic one – I used to think 'whistling to keep his spirits up'. I had no use for such an exercise, and no need to sustain myself with illusions. Politicians perhaps have to have some opti-

mism – otherwise how could they keep going? 'Pour agir il
faut espérer' (De Gaulle) – but I do not hope: I gave that up
in 1945.

Even when away on supposed holiday Arthur worked as
hard as ever. One autumn someone lent him a villa on Cap
Martin at Menton, where he wrote at the current book till
2 a.m., and all day in the open 'sitting among olives,
cypresses and umbrella pines, looking across to Monte
Carlo, which looks very pleasant as long as one doesn't go
within four miles of it'. In August 1970 he was in South
Africa being entertained by H.V. Morton, the bestselling
author who had retired there for tax reasons. So many
authors have thus been driven abroad. Even as late as the
Twenties literary life centred on London, with such writers
as Shaw, H.G. Wells, Arnold Bennett, Barrie, Belloc, Chesterton, Somerset Maugham, with Kipling, Hardy, Henry
James still coming up to town; and with a whole younger
generation in the Bloomsberries, Lytton Strachey, Virginia
Woolf, Keynes, Eliot, and so on. Today literary life consists
mainly of literary journalists and media men. Mary Renault,
excellent writer, had also absconded to South Africa from
wartime nursing in bombed London, but she was not on
Arthur's wavelength (more on mine). The bachelor Morton
– *In the Steps of Our Lord*, *In the Steps of St Paul*, and other
sacrosanct persons – had 'a magnificent Zulu butler, whose
attitude towards the Cape Bantus was rather like that of a
Guards' Regimental Serjeant-Major to the hippies in the
Park, and whose own father had been one of those tremendous warriors who broke a British army at Isandhlwana.'
(Not an army, only an isolated section of one.) One sees that
the situation in South Africa is by no means the simple one
of Black v. White as liberal intellectuals would make it.

In the 1970s we did a Christie Minstrels turn together with
John Betjeman at the St Albans Arts Festival. I was surprised
at the amount of correspondence it took Arthur to fix an
engagement, where I wasted no time, Yes or No. Letters went
to and fro; it was characteristic of him to tangle himself up:
letters to me would begin with a whole page of apology for
not having written, long explanations why not, etc. When we
arrived on the platform we were ensconced in enormous,

black-leather dentists' chairs, trussed and tied up with every kind of microphone and TV gadget, a blinding flood of lights, and a vast blackness where was a large audience. For once in my life I was rather daunted, until dear John took up blandly with a topographical account of St Albans, which he had providently prepared. Then Arthur followed, smoothly, suavely, long-windedly. Some crank objected afterwards to my forthright, candid opinions; it was not the reaction of the audience at large, for I was asked to the Festival on my own next year, and yet again the year after. It is amusing that it is always the third-rate who are so difficult to please. Why? I venture to suggest that it is their only way of getting their own back. But one should *never* set oneself to satisfy them, with their standards, and after all one must amuse oneself.

A large proportion of our correspondence dealt with Arthur's work, not mine. After all, I did not need his opinion on the Elizabethan age, or on my continuing Shakespeare work, or anybody else's for that matter. Who was there who could combine an intimate knowledge of the historical circumstances surrounding Shakespeare's life and work, with the practical qualification of writing poetry? For all that one had to put up with academic obscurantism, giving no enlightenment to the poor mutts of the media, I knew quite well that there was no answer to the discoveries I had made about Shakespeare. It was no matter for surprise that they should have been made by the leading authority on the age. Neither Agatha Christie nor Arthur had gone into Simon Forman's papers in the Bodleian – no 'Shakespeare expert' had done, except Halliwell-Phillips more than a century ago; but both Agatha and Arthur saw separately that in creating Cleopatra Shakespeare was remembering someone, an intense experience of his own, as Arthur wrote, 'when it was over and recollected in tranquillity'.

Meanwhile he assured me that he had kept all my letters, 'love ones and Baldwinian denunciations too'. He knew, as few did, how much I had been scarred by the intensity of the struggle I had been through – to get to Oxford in my youth, then years of illness, the hopeless struggle as a political candidate all through the Thirties against the Old Men and

Appeasement. I often think of my campaign for common sense about Shakespeare in terms of that, which at any rate inoculated me against ordinary humans' obtuseness.

Arthur made one last move, a final one, and this time quite improbably. I don't know why he made it: I suppose he fell in love with a house again. And I do not pretend to understand his relations with the female sex, to which he was an express devotee. What was what in that quarter? I never inquired; I know only that he could be very jealous over his women folk, like an old Pasha with his harem. (Perhaps I was his 'only man-friend', as Anne said, because I was not a competitor. That was a race for which I did not enter: it left me even more free for work.) His first marriage was not a success, and was dissolved. Eventually, he and Anne had a separation, but remained good friends. She preferred living in London. I cannot but think that Arthur must have been difficult to live with, for all his well-practised charm; most writers are (better not to take the risk).

In 1975 he sold the Pavilion at Wotton Underwood to John Gielgud, who has made a thing of theatrical beauty of it. Arthur moved to a perfect Queen Anne house in the Close at Salisbury, somewhat improbably in the bosom of the Church. Here, away from London, which he had at last given up, he felt very much out of place for a time, surrounded by arch-deacons and canons, constant bells calling to cathedral services – much more in my line than his: Arthur was not a bit clerical. I am sorry that I did not go to see him there. It was off my route between Cornwall and Oxford, from which I retired in 1974. In one of his letters he describes it all to me, the meadows running down to the Avon, the scene so often depicted by Constable. In 1978 he had a cancer operation, 'with a gash from breast to crotch', but recovered and was still working. He had a cat problem. He had a resident cat, and a resident nurse; but two of the Close cats were always attempting to live in the house. Meanwhile his own cat was sitting on him, trying to prevent him from finishing the Elizabethan volume of his History, which he wanted me to read for him.

This had grown from a chapter into a book, *The Eliza-bethan Deliverance*. I was surprised: he was in his eightieth year – and it was one of the best things he had ever written. In spite of his illness, it had such vitality and sparkle, all his old enthusiasm and exuberance; and, in my view, his grasp of the essence of the age was quite right. He, Sir John Neale, and I agreed: there was no denying the marvellous achievement of that small people, only five million of them, in only half an island. No point in mean-minded academics denigrating it, who cannot bear to pay tribute where it is due, in contrast to the squalor of today's unlovely society. And now – one more change – he could not but feel 'optimistic about the future of society'. This, in spite of a collapsed back from stooping so many years; after treatment in London he was returning to his 'ecclesiastical compound'.

The last times we met were on public occasions. His eightieth birthday was celebrated with a banquet at Vintners' Hall, a grand turn-out in his honour: an archbishop of Canterbury, two former Prime Ministers, politicians, historians, writers, journalists – the best speech made by Harold Macmillan, coming up for ninety. And even Arthur's eighty-fifth was celebrated with another such gathering, when Michael Foot and I made the speeches in his honour.

The last occasion of all was, happily, back at Oxford at a dinner in Merton hall in honour of Thomas Joy, the Oxford town boy who rose to be head-boy of bookselling, at Hatchards in London. Arthur and I were the speakers. A curious experience befell me: I fell in love with the beauty of Merton, the high midsummer pomps, honeyed light on stone, the garden within the city wall, the limes and roses, the outlook on Christ Church Meadows of my undergraduate days. I could have been a teaching don at Merton, which gave me my first job, had I chosen. How would life have been if I had opted to spend it within those walls? For twenty-four hours I lived in a dream, as if I had.

Strangely enough, that night in an Oxford college had a similar effect on Arthur: he too fell in love with lovely Merton. Or, perhaps it was not so strange, for we had so much in common. Next morning at the gate we were photographed together – I felt for the last time – before we went our separate ways home.

Hensley Henson:
Controversial Bishop

I am old enough to remember the days when bishops were prime public figures, and the public in consequence attended to their pronouncements. Of these the one who commanded most news-value was Hensley Henson, Bishop of Durham, a 'stormy petrel' in the Church. He had always been a controversial figure from early Oxford days. An *enfant terrible*, he looked like one: a shrimp of a man, compact of energy, positively vibrant; with ill-fitting, clattering false teeth which emphasised the effect of his speech, with hissing s's; striking querulous eyebrows, of which he was proud – a gift to the caricaturist. As a young preacher he could fill any church in London; when he preached his farewell sermon at St Margaret's, Westminster, hundreds were turned away. When he retired from the bench, ten publishers competed for his autobiography. Those were the days for bishops!

He was one of the four All Souls bishops, and the most notable – except for Lang, by right of his primacy; the others being Headlam, Bishop of Gloucester, and A.T.P. Williams, Bishop of Winchester. Not one today!

In colleges seniority is a matter of some significance. Herbert Hensley Henson, elected a Fellow in 1884, was a couple of years senior to Cosmo Gordon Lang, elected in 1886. In the private Common Room proceedings testifying to a candidate's personal qualities before election, Henson made a speech which ended 'In short, Mr Lang is a person of second-rate intellect, and first-rate gifts.'

I do not know if, in the course of their long, comparable, and almost competitive, lives Henson changed his view of his junior. But it certainly vexed him that the junior got a long way ahead of him up the ecclesiastical ladder. Even at the end, when Lang became Archbishop of Canterbury, Henson could not help fancying himself as Archbishop of York – though there was no likelihood of it. The relations of these two College prelates were always ambivalent; Lang thought that Henson married for money; Henson thought Lang a snob.

I one day said to Lang when, after his retirement, he was prepared to let his hair down (by that time he had not got any, except a little downy white fluff): 'One can't expect to have prime responsibility, and continue to say whatever one likes.' 'Well, exactly', said the sage archbishop. Henson could never just shut up. It seems an art that bishops of Durham find difficult to acquire.

There is a good Life of Henson (by Owen Chadwick); and he wrote a long, fully documented autobiography, *Retrospect of an Unimportant Life*. I'll bet he did not think it unimportant: the title suggests a lingering reproach at his not becoming an archbishop. This book was a favourite with my friend, the historian K.B. McFarlane; and I know why. McFarlane had a marked vein of malice in him: he found the book very amusing – in a sense not intended by the author.

As usual in these sketches of people, I must keep as far as possible to personal contacts with them. My first meeting with Henson was shortly after my own election to All Souls. There was this diminutive figure, in episcopal gear, gaiters and all, lying full length along the hard, uncomfortable red-baized bench, from which the politically-minded Fellows liked to think the Empire (when there was one) was governed.

Henson had evidently heard that the new Fellow was a young Leftist from the working-class. So his opening salvo was 'Isn't it time for a little blood-letting for the working-class?' I caught the twinkle in his eye, and from that moment understood something about him. (Too much of a cliché to say 'we became friends', though we became friendly: I liked him.) He had, exceptionally for a bishop, a sense of humour – and that got him into trouble. He *was* a trouble-maker. Could one imagine Cosmo Láng saying anything of the sort? Henson was all too human.

I gradually learned that he had always been popular in College, Lang not – rather unfairly, I thought. But to Henson All Souls was home, the first really happy home he had had.

His first home had been miserable – so much so that, though talkative about everything else, he was extremely reticent on the subject, and we knew nothing about it. His mother died when he was six. His father was a fanatic of a Plymouth Brother, who would hardly allow his clever boy to go to school for fear of his being morally contaminated. For a time he attended some inferior little school at Broadstairs; the boy made up for it by gorging himself with serious reading, history and theology. Then the old fool would not allow the adolescent youth to go up to the University, until finally over-persuaded by the sensible German step-mother. Even then he would not allow his son to go to a college, for fear of 'impurity', and young Henson came up to Oxford as a non-collegiate student – known contemptuously in those days as a 'tosher' – living solitarily in impecunious digs.

Henson resented all his life that he had not had a good classical education, like his public school competitors. He always felt odd-man-out, and that he had been put at a disadvantage in this regard. His queer education had some advantages he did not consider – independence of mind, for one, fulfilment of his own very individual personality, for another. But the rough-and-tumble of a public school would have smoothed away some of the edges, softened his asperities, damped down the arrogance and egoism, taught him to be a better colleague. He was always a difficult colleague – what his friend at All Souls, Grant Robertson, would call a *mauvais coucheur*. On the other hand, he was brilliant and gifted, and could not be ignored – had no intention of being so. When hardly more than an undergraduate he flatly contradicted the great Jowett at his own dinner-table.

Still, no wonder that, in his first phase, he loathed Dissent and described the Plymouth Brethren, with undue serious-ness, as 'poisonous schismatics'. 'Fatuous asses' would have been more to the point.

It was not until, quite unexpectedly, he was elected to All Souls that he found happiness.

> I was welcomed with a generous kindness which made me feel immediately at home. I formed friendships which have enriched my life. I loved everybody from the Warden to the scout's boy, and even now, after more than half a century, I never enter the College without emotion. It would be difficult to overstate the importance of All Souls in my life.

Indeed, life opened out for him. The poor young fellow had been starved of emotion, when actually he had an emotional nature and was rather lovable. He had a special relationship with Warden Anson, himself a bachelor – married to the College, which regarded him as almost a second Founder: to young Henson a foster-father.

In this family environment the impish personality bloomed; everybody seems to have taken to him and, above all, he enjoyed himself. His pranks became part of College tradition – how, in energetic argument, he mounted the marble mantelpiece in the Common Room, Arthur Hardinge at the other end, to orate more effectively over the heads of the assembled Fellows. There were constant arguments – one memorable one with Belloc, then a candidate for a Fellowship, over the Dreyfus affair. Henson was one for ferreting out the truth; Belloc came out with some 'fact' which no one knew whether true or not – Belloc never minded whether what he said was true. I do not suppose that he had Henson's vote on that occasion.

Henson had a formidable power of advocacy – he consid-ered going to the Bar – and also of persuasion, another matter. The famous constitutional lawyer, Dicey, did not attend Chapel: after an hour's talk with Henson he became a regular attendant. He had an immature gift for leadership: quite young, he founded the Stubbs Society, still going as the chief historical discussion club in the University. He started a Laymen's League in support of the Church. Sir Charles Oman told me that they would all follow Henson's lead – until he began to change his mind as to where he would lead them.

Oman was apt to be late for Chapel. So he received this reproof from his junior: 'You arrive not only late for the General Confession, but late for the Absolution you most stand in need of.' A good deal of an actor, he had a self-conscious stylish way of speaking which betrayed itself in antitheses. Rejecting a plate of cold mutton at lunch in the buttery: 'I accepted it without enthusiasm, I part with it with alacrity.' What a vanished Victorian world it bespeaks. A fortnight of vacation at Sidmouth was ruined by an organ-grinder playing daily outside his lodgings: 'it combined the *ennui* of eternity, with the torments of the damned'. Later, his notorious phrase, 'the Protestant underworld', helped to lose the cause of the Revised Prayer Book in Parliament.

All Souls was like a family in those days: a small body of the choicest spirits in the University, two chosen each year by a strenuous examination when those were the only Prize Fellowships going. And most of the elect were on their way to distinguished public careers in Church and State or at the Bar. One derives some sense of the fun they had when they came together – especially at All Souls-tide, 2 November, when they religiously returned to the bosom of the family – from the Betting Book, an historic feature of Common Room life.

When in residence Henson has the most frequent entries; in fact other Fellows wagered on the number – something like a half of the total during the period – and lost more often than won, and gaily paid up, sometimes years after. At All Souls-tide 1885 Pember, who was Henson's 'mate', i.e. elected at the same time, wagered that he, Pember, would not weigh fifteen stone by the time he was fifty. Henson paid up at the All Souls weekend in 1913, twenty-eight years after.

Doyle, College librarian, bet Henson one shilling that the person who distinguished himself as a shot with Mr Wardle was Mr Snodgrass, as against Mr Tupman. Henson, unquestioning, paid up. But why? It was Mr Winkle who, aiming at a rook, shot Mr Tupman in the shoulder at Dingley Dell. Once more Henson lost to Duff who wagered that Roger Wildrake was of Squattlesea Mere, in Scott's *Woodstock* – Henson was thinking of the real Whittlesea Mere Scott had in mind. The assured Curzon, who would have known, bet Henson two shillings that his racket weighed less than fifteen ounces. Again Henson paid. In those days the Fellows played tennis on the lawn in the big inner quadrangle – today only bowls. Another bet with Curzon was to the effect that Henson weighed four stone less than the immense Oman.

Most of the bets are political – about the prospects and results of Elections, Home Rule, ins and outs of parties and cabinets. I suppose that they have a certain historical interest in registering expectations. Twice Henson bet ten to one that Germany would beat France in the next war – this was 1887 when Bismarck was bullying France again.

Personal bets are more relevant. The most frequent are on the subject of Fellows marrying – for, when they did, they forfeited their Fellowship (unless they were professors, regarded as helots by the real, i.e. Prize, Fellows). Henson was clear that he would not be caught in the toils for some considerable time; in fact he did not marry until 1902, at thirty-nine or so.

In 1886 he was betting Headlam five shillings that Headlam would be married before Henson took his DD. This he won, for Headlam married in 1900, and Henson did not get a Doctorate of Divinity until Glasgow conferred it upon him in 1913. Already the question was mooted whether he would go into the Church. Duff bet him half-a-crown, in 1886, that he would not be a clergyman of the Established Church in two years' time. Henson was ordained on 5 June 1887, and Duff paid up the same day. Before this Henson had promised Duff five pounds against his ever becoming a bishop. He did not become a bishop until 1918, and by then Duff was long dead.

We may note here that Lang made only one bet in the whole book, and this he won: that F. W. Bain (author of *The Digit of the Moon* and other such Indian stories) would marry within five years. Bain married in less than one; but then Lang, half a Highland Celt, was rather psychic.

Henson went through much heart-searching, in the Victorian manner, before he eventually became ordained. All his life he kept a diary, in which there is self-accusation – and also constant self-dramatisation. 'Sincerity is an enigma to me.' Was it? He tried hard enough to achieve it. 'I am constitutionally hypocritical.' If we take the word in its harmless, literal meaning of being an actor, that was true enough: he was always acting up. 'All this comes of an arbitrary character and an unfortunate history.'

All the same I find his dedication of himself to the Church rather moving. 'There in Iffley church, and standing before the altar, with my hand upon it, I dedicated myself to God and the Church. Registered in the Archives of Heaven is my vow.' (Was it?) He added 'and here also, in the time to come, a reminder to me not to forget'. A diary may as well serve that purpose also.

He was ordained deacon on Trinity Sunday, 5 June 1887, in Cuddesdon church. Three of the Fellows walked those miles out to witness it – Headlam, Hardinge and Tom Raleigh. No member of his family came. In those days it was a custom of the College to take long Sunday walks, by paths and fields and meadows. This continued to my time in the Thirties – until the suburbanisation of the country round Oxford ended it.

He left Oxford, to become Head of Oxford House in Bethnal Green, and devote himself, looking hardly more than a boy, to the well-being of boys in the East End. Then followed the big substantial College living of Barking. Legend had it that his first sermon began, 'Ye Barking Christians'. In no time he became a noted preacher. Warden Pember told me that Henson took to writing all his sermons, otherwise he became too prolix – and too excited. He always had too much to say. Shortly his tergiversations began, which, as Oman said, made it impossible to follow him or for him to lead.

He regarded himself as also dedicated to telling the truth, and speaking out. (Here we may see him as a chip off the old block.) What then did he believe? He began as a High Churchman – very High in the sense of clerical claims and pretensions; when he looked into them, he began to have doubts. The doubts went further – did he, could anybody truthfully believe in the Virgin Birth? He switched round, and became distinctly Low: a Protestant, an Erastian, with Modernist sympathies.

Thus he became, and always remained, a controversial figure. Like Bertrand Russell – he would have hated the comparison – he was wholly convinced when he changed and took up the opposite view which he had held hitherto with equal conviction. Both were egoists, both were conceited and intellectually arrogant. Being concerned with themselves was not the same thing as self-knowledge. Why did it not occur to them that a little scepticism in regard to their views might be in place? Why such vehement conviction, and then change, equally convinced of the opposite?

Of course it made Henson an interesting personality – people went to hear him; it made for publicity, but one could not trust him. Though All Souls remained always friendly, the University would not have him. His junior, the wary Lang, was made vicar of St Mary's, the University church, not Henson.

However, as canon of Westminster and rector of St Margaret's, the church of the House of Commons, he had much more réclame. He had admiring politicians in his audience. Having started as a protégé of Lord Salisbury, and a familiar at Hatfield, he now had Asquith and Lloyd George to listen to him. He had a knack of tuning in on the topical, and getting into the newspapers. He took up Roger Casement's campaign against the horrors of the rubber plantations of Putumayo. (He can have had no idea of what was what about Casement. Henson was a straight, unreconstructed hetero.)

Meanwhile, Lang, born in the moderate purple of the Church of Scotland – his father indeed a Moderator –

advanced up the episcopal ladder. Bishop of Stepney in his thirties, Archbishop of York in 1909, 'the youngest Archbishop of York since Paulinus'.

It took a Lloyd George to make Henson a bishop – no one else would have done so. A Nonconformist, he had no truck with ecclesiastical proprieties (or others either): he could appreciate pulpit oratory and by now Henson had come completely round to chumming up with Nonconformists. In 1918 Lloyd George made him, at last, Bishop of Hereford.

There broke out an almighty row. Bishop Gore, leader of the Anglo-Catholics, and by nature an Inquisitor, led the opposition to Henson's consecration. Gore had already inhibited, i.e. prohibited, Henson from preaching in his diocese (Birmingham). Henson kept the inhibition framed on his study walls to his dying day. Did he, or did he not, believe that Jesus was born of a virgin? It was pretty obvious that he did not. Who could? And what did it matter?

Gore sent round a printed protest, for all his fellow bishops to sign, appealing to the Archbishop of Canterbury to refuse to consecrate Henson. Several lined up with him. Gore had been an early friend, and sent it to Henson with an affectionate letter. An ordinary layman would regard this as humbug. The Archbishop was put in a tight spot. The newspapers raged and built it up into 'The Hereford Scandal' – the diocese which was to receive the 'heretic' as a mixed blessing.

Not for nothing had Randall Davidson been brought up in the nursery of statesmanlike Archbishop Tait at Lambeth, married to his daughter. (Tait had had similar trouble in his time.) Only a few years before there had been the 'Kikuyu Controversy' over Anglicans and Nonconformists communicating together in the wilds of East Africa. Over that the Bishop of Zanzibar had taken a strong line, and young Ronnie Knox (on his way to Rome) had perpetrated a limerick:

> There once was a Zanzibarbarian
> Who dreamed that the whole world was Arian,
>   So he cabled to Randall
>   With bell, book and candle –
> Who lay low, for our Randall's a *wary-un*.

Archbishop Davidson was a good man, a simple believer, but with immense, far from simple, diplomatic skill, a practised tight-rope walker. The protests rolled in, various bishops indicated that they would not attend the ceremony, if there was one – among them the Archbishop of York, Lang, and an old Hatfield friend, 'Fish', Lord William Cecil, Bishop of Exeter. At the Athenaeum 'divers bishops looked away, or cast down their eyes, when they saw me coming'. Nevertheless, he went on to order his 'episcopal hat at Lock's', and underwent the 'humiliation' of being fitted for episcopal garments, gaiters and all.

> After lunch I walked to Atcheson Batchelor, 25 Margaret Street, who makes rings for bishops, and I inquired whether indeed it would be requisite to engrave arms on the ring. He said it was the almost invariable practice. My soul revolts against the grotesque snobbery of my having *now* to adopt arms, when I receive a character which might seem particularly incongruous with all that arms symbolise.

We see that this clerical wit took things too seriously, and was apt to make a mountain out of a molehill. But so also did others.

The wily, kindly Archbishop now put pressure on him. He 'indicated the possibility of his resigning office rather than proceed to consecrate me in the teeth of a really weighty protest from the bishops'. What was that but a polite kind of blackmail? Henson could not accept that.

The Archbishop now summoned him to Lambeth, carpeted him and presented him with a statement which he had drafted for him to assent to.

> In it I said that, while I repeated the statements in the Creed *ex animo*, I held that the method of the Incarnation might be conceived of otherwise than by a Virgin birth, as was the case in the Apostolic age, that with me the question was mainly one of emphasis . . . and that I had never found any satisfying alternative to the dogma of

the Virgin Birth. I don't like this kind of informal subscription, but the Archbishop appealed to me for the relief of his own conscience in performing a very difficult act.

A typical balancing act, and it was successful. It let both Archbishop and Bishop-to-be off the hook; the opposition bishops withdrew their protest, the ceremony could go forward, hat, gaiters, ring and all.

But Henson was enraged: it was put about that he had recanted – and he was the last man to recant anything he thought (at the time).

> I told the Archbishop that I deeply resented the way in which I had been treated, and I do. My relations with these abstaining bishops will not be exactly easy. They have done what they can to hinder my entrance on my episcopate; they have added enormously to my difficulties in starting my work; they have lent the sanction of their names to the campaign of calumny and insult. . . . All this it is impossible not to resent, difficult to forgive.

It is doubtful if he ever did forgive it. When, after he was safely consecrated, 'Fish' Cecil came up to him in the Athenaeum to make it up, he received an (episcopal) cold shoulder. Henson's explanation of the affair, 'the Hereford Scandal', runs thus.

> Probably this strangely violent agitation against me gives expression to a crowd of resentments, which have been accumulating for many years. There is always the fact of envy to be reckoned with . . . more than commonly considerable in the case of a man who is destitute of the recognised qualifications for success. I am a *novus homo*; I am a poor man; I have no party behind me . . .

The first words of his autobiography are: 'I belong to the middle class, and to the soundest part of it, namely that which from time immemorial has lived and worked in the country.' The family came from the parish of Morebath in North Devon – but his characteristics make one think of a stubborn North Countryman, rather than an easy-going Devonian. (They must have come from his stubborn Plymouth Brother of a father, never mentioned.)

For the rest of his life he regarded the day of his consecration as the unhappiest in it; and, whenever he thought of it, he was enraged – I suspect, at the thought that he had been made to climb down, or at least appear to. For he was a proud man – Warden Anson thought the proudest he had ever known (remarkable indeed in the far from humble establishment he presided over). But why should Henson be humble? A first-rate mind – an historian, not a theologian immersed in metaphysical nonsense – he had no respect for third-rate minds among the bishops. And in fact, paradoxically – everything about this plucky, cocky little man was paradoxical – from that time onward he had, though sitting on the bench with them, something like an anti-bishop complex.

What did Henson's wife think of the *fracas* – indeed of all the fracas that marriage to this fighting cock involved? There is no word from this poor, silent, unintellectual lady to tell us. Though he had *not* married for much money – she had a small private income – he had married for social position, into the Scottish upper class, with useful connections. He never brought her to All Souls; we never saw her: her photograph shows a dumb, not to say stupid, face. Early on she began to be deaf, later on impenetrably so. Was this in part defence-mechanism against her too voluble husband? It certainly was an additional cause for resentment, for, as Warden Pember said, the one thing that Henson wanted above all was that 'you should lend him your ears'.

The single passage he devotes to his marriage, in two long volumes, must be one of those that delighted the mischievous McFarlane.

Then I exchanged the unchartered freedom of singularity, for the salutary servitude of matrimony. Henceforward I had the strength and comfort of the most patient and considerate of colleagues. [How about that for 'male chauvinism'?] Indeed, it is impossible to overstate the merits of my wife. Placable and unselfish by nature, she was able to adapt herself to the successive and very different environments into which she was carried. I made great demands on her, and she never failed me. Her presence mitigated the resentments which my personal idiosyncracies and frequent controversies could not but provoke, and I enjoyed undeservingly a portion of the goodwill which she evoked.

And that is about all he says of the poor lady in 800 pages. She does not seem to have read it, and anyway she was not one to answer him back. That was something. I suspect that she did not accompany him to All Souls because he relished too much his return to the bachelordom where he had been so happy. He was Nature's bachelor.

He was not happy at Hereford, though proud to sign himself now 'H.H. Hereford'. The soft Western climate did not suit him, nor did a wholly rural atmosphere – as wise old Archbishop Davidson had seen. One historic achievement of his brief time there remains: he prevented the division of his diocese (he would), and the erection of a separate one for Shropshire, a bishopric of Shrewsbury. A Tory underneath his Radicalism – Warden Anson said 'a Jacobin varnished over to look like a Tory' – he did not like the breaking up of the ancient historic dioceses. Anyhow, the alternative was the break-up of Winchester into three, with a wholly new cathedral at Guildford. At Shrewsbury there was the ancient Abbey, which would have made a nice cathedral.

He was at Hereford only two years, 1918–20, when he was transferred to the grand see of Durham, with Auckland Castle to live in, and the splendid acropolis of Cathedral and Castle overhanging the Wear to play about in – Scott's description 'half-fortress and half-church'. Here there was a historic job to be done – to prevent Durham Castle slipping into the Wear: the historian rose to the occasion, tackled it manfully and successfully. He described himself, lying out there at Auckland on the edge of the coalfield – from which the see of Durham had formerly drawn such enormous royalties – as being 'like a whale stranded on the sea-coast of Patagonia'. (Actually, 'like a minnow' would have been appropriate.)

He took pride in the pomp and grandeur of his position there. He noted how curious it was that 'Fish' Cecil, brought up in a palace at Hatfield, refused to live in the Palace at Exeter and chose to live in a modest Georgian house in the suburbs; while himself, a mere middle-class man, preferred to live in a great, gaunt castle, with all its draughts and inconveniences. I suspect that this is where the sense of history comes in: the Bishop of Exeter had little – and hated being a bishop anyway. What he liked was pedalling around Hatfield, as Rector, on his old bicycle.

Not so Henson, who lived in some state. (Very kindly, he asked me twice to come and stay there; but I couldn't have stood the strain, rather invalidish, and too far north anyway.) He appreciated the historic privileges of the former Palatine bishopric; and one day at All Souls made the mistake of saying that, if this were the Middle Ages, his wife would have been a Princess Palatine. A better historian (E.L. Woodward) commented unkindly to me: 'Nothing of the sort: Palatine? – she would have been a concubine.'

Once more, his former colleague, Archbishop Lang, did not want him for companion in the Northern Province: too awkward a customer. However, it was Lloyd George again, as Prime Minister, who made the promotion. And it worked out very well. Henson already knew the diocese, and had been popular – at least, not unpopular – as Dean there, 1912–18.

He had learned from 'the Hereford Scandal', and was now set to behave himself. He gave no trouble to Lang as his archbishop at York, though he could not resist a famous little joke at his expense. Lang had had several portraits of himself painted – that splendid archiepiscopal presence, every inch an archbishop (he should have been a cardinal of the Curia). At last Orpen painted a telling portrait, rather

unfavourable, which aroused some discussion. Henson was
visiting at Bishopsthorpe, and Lang, not unnaturally, asked
him what he thought of it: 'they say it makes me look proud,
pompous, and prelatical'. 'And to which of these epithets
does your Grace object?'

No point in rehearsing the chores of a bishop's life – such
as made the scholarly Creighton complain that 'Confirma-
tions have set in with their usual severity', as if they were
the 'flu or measles. Or retailing the speeches Henson made
on dead issues in the Lords – for a bishop of Durham
automatically has a seat in that House.

> I succeeded in attending the debates whenever the
> subjects under discussion did, in my judgment, require
> that the Bishop of Durham should address the House.
> Thus, I came into sight and hearing of men whose
> names had long been known to me, whose experience
> in public affairs was wide and varied, whose ability was
> impressive, and whose personal attractiveness was in
> some cases irresistible.

He was not one to hide his light under a bushel; and of
course he became one of the best speakers in the House.

But his own attractiveness, the fact that he was likeable –
in spite of everything – was more in evidence in Durham.
He was friendly with everybody, particularly with the
miners; he was no Temperance fanatic like his Dean, one
Weldon whom he did not care for. Henson deplored his
'insatiable loquacity: he cannot keep silent with dignity, nor
speak with effect'. Here was Henson's own addiction to
antithesis. Dean Weldon was one day airing his teetotal
convictions during a Miners' Gala beside the Wear, when the
miners mobbed him and might have thrown him into the
river. They managed to throw his decanal top hat in, which
was seen to float buoyantly down the Wear.

Dean Weldon was prodigiously fat – since he was a
teetotaller I suppose it came from surfeits of cocoa. One day
Henson was asked if he had seen the latest popular review,
'Pigs in Clover' – 'No, but I have seen the Dean of Durham

in bed.' The Bishop's name for his Dean was 'Rhinobotto-
mus' – the young Princess Elizabeth's name for a rhinoceros
she had seen in the Zoo.

When the Hensons had occupied the Deanery they
installed the fine Chinese wallpaper in the drawing room
that had been the Prior's solar before the Reformation. Down
below was the huge 14th-century kitchen of the Priory.
When Alington, another All Souls man, succeeded as Dean,
Henson as Bishop swore him to use the medieval kitchen
'upon pain of excommunication'.

The Bishop had an odd way of *not* standing on his dignity
– Lang never got off it. Henson would chat with unemployed
miners on his walks in his great park, and wink at their
taking coal from the outcrops in it. Once, at a service after a
mine accident, when men had been killed, he broke down
and wept openly among their womenfolk. Warden Pember
told me of his confronting a mob of miners out on strike.
The old Tory in him disapproved of strikes. (What good did
they do?) He was returning from a Confirmation service
when his car ran into a crowd of miners, who might have
turned nasty, as they had done with Dean Weldon. Henson
stopped the car, and went back to talk with them; the talk
turned into an address, of course, and he spoke out his
convictions. He was heard with respect: the men could
recognise sincerity, when they saw it. Also courage: he said
to Pember, 'It never does to show the white feather.'

In the late 1920s the dominating concern within the
Church was Revision of the Prayer Book. It was needed,
and had been on the cards for years. The difficulty was to
achieve unity on the issue, for the Book was being revised in
a rather High Church direction, to please the Anglo-Catholics, and this displeased the Low Church Protestants. It took
years of work – or rather of negotiating and patching up
verbal compromises – to agree on a Revised Book.

Archbishop Lang took the effective lead in all this, behind
the revered front of the ageing Davidson, who had the
confidence of the Protestants, Lang of the Anglos. Somehow
they succeeded in recruiting Henson into the work: it would
never have done to leave him outside, to give his voice to

the Opposition. He was regarded as the best stylist among the bishops, the most useful for producing a pastiche of 17th-century style in writing new prayers. This appealed to his vanity: several times in his autobiography he notes the approbation he received for his 'beautiful English'. It is characteristic of the man – rhetorical, based on good 17th-century models, above all self-conscious, and out of date. (None the worse for that.)

When the Book came before Parliament for approval, it excited MPs no end. All the Prots of Ulster, and all the Noncs of the Celtic Fringe rolled up to do it in. This was the sort of thing that excited them, instead of looking after the long-term interests of the country, keeping their eye on the European situation, in particular the open rearmament of Germany. The leader in opposing the Revised Book was a third-rate lawyer, who signalised himself by his dictum that every day on which his name did not appear in *The Times* was a day wasted. (Baldwin later made him Minister of Defence – to confront the Germans' Rearmament! – when the only appointment that would have given them pause was Churchill.)

Henson was given the job of moving the Book in the House of Lords; and his speech was the most brilliant of all the absurd speeches wasting time on the issue. It did no good, the Commons were determined to vote the Church down. This made a sad end to Randall Davidson's long diplomatic career on the tight-rope; he took it badly and shortly went out into the dark. Lang, equally a politique, was not defeated. He saw at once that Parliament could not prevent the Church from using the Revised Prayer Book, legally or not. The bishops proceeded to introduce the Book in their dioceses all over the country, on their own authority, and no notice was taken. All the ridiculous fuss had been about nothing.

Lang was an ecclesiastical statesman, and he was right. Henson, with all his brilliance, was no statesman. He had the typical defect of the intellectual: he drew the logical conclusion in the abstract, completely at variance with the realities of the situation. The State had failed the Church, therefore let the Church cut the painter from the State. He came out then for Disestablishment, which was unnecessary, impractical and absurd. He had boxed the compass once more: from having been the leading Erastian in the Church, protagonist of the Establishment and its role in the State, he now became the advocate of dissolving it. He cannot have considered the consequences: an upset more catastrophic than Henry VIII's *via media* in the 16th century. Only a few doctrinaires followed his new lead in the opposite direction. Why didn't this clever man see what an ass he was? Intellectuals are usually too conceited ever to do so.

However, he did not develop his new campaign until the question of the leadership in the Church was settled. The succession of Lang to Canterbury was inevitable – even Henson, reluctantly, recognised that. 'The old Archbishop held up forces which his disappearance from the scene will release; and his successor, though an able and brilliant man, is on a smaller scale altogether and cannot expect to wield the same influence . . . However, I cannot suggest any better appointment.' Meanwhile, Henson was assuring the lay peers 'how little prospect there really was of the Establishment lasting much longer'. This was nonsense, of course.

But who was to succeed Lang as Archbishop of York? Henson was much the best-known figure to the newspapers, a favourite publicity-wise; his name was canvassed. Again nonsense, however – so much in public affairs is just nonsense. (As the sage Lord Salisbury had said: 'Few things matter much, and some things matter not at all.') One could not have *two* elderly men, both Fellows of All Souls, one of them unsound on the relation of Church and State, and much else, even apart from the Virgin Birth. The State made the right appointment, and appointed Billy Temple, a young man of the Left and a Labour man, as proper partner for the ripe Lang, more to the Right.

Undoubtedly Henson fancied himself for Archbishop of York, impossible as the idea was. *The Times* dismissed him politely as 'both too old, and as probably not desiring to leave Durham. . . . It *is* rather dismaying to find oneself put out of the reckoning as "too old".' The *Manchester Guardian* thought that his health was not good, 'which is news to me'. On the announcement of Lang's succession,

> He is certainly an impressive Primate to look at. The *Yorkshire Post* reproduces his last portrait, that by Sir William Orpen, and of course the papers overflow with eulogies and tributes. Yesterday, the proposals of the Archbishops were rejected with something like fervour. Today, their Graces are everywhere belauded as the best, the ablest, the wisest of men.

Henson might have consoled himself with the reflection of a disillusioned newspaper man, J.A. Spender: 'The longer I live the more I see that things really are as silly as they seem.'

However, he was not consoled. 'Why, then, should I wish to leave this great See? But do I wish it? I think that I desire the distinction of *refusing* a Primacy; and perhaps I resent the loss of consequence which my being passed over must needs involve.' In fact, there was not the least likelihood. Still, he noted resentfully that all three of the new promotions 'advance bishops who have been conspicuous as champions of the Revised Book. Probably, in the popular view I was myself the protagonist in that conflict, and now I am rejected as too old and too "cussed".'

The last word shows a little self-insight; why then didn't he profit by this piece of self-knowledge? All one can say is that people rarely do. The diary goes on and on chewing the cud of his 'rejection': he had not been rejected, he had not even been considered. He admitted that Lang and Temple would 'work well together' (as himself never would have done): 'They are both (in no bad sense, though inevitably not really a good one) men of the world, who are at home in the atmosphere of make-belief and compromise which Establishments create.' For himself, 'I had mentally decided to decline York if it were offered to me . . .' Anyway, 'the Establishment must be either mended or ended'. This was nonsense again – an intellectual's mere words: as Catherine the Great said of them, 'comme sur le papier, qui souffre tout'.

Henson did not let Lang off the hook. Both were present

in Chapel next All Souls' Day; Henson was preaching, and hissed (those ill-fitting dentures!) across at Lang, 'My predecessor, the great Bishop Butler, declined the Primacy because he would not be a pillar of a declining Church.' The Archbishop, hands over his eyes, gave not a sign that he had even heard – no doubt in his time he had had too many sermons to listen to, and knew what to expect from Henson. An observant young Fellow, taking notes, registered several things: (a) not very Christian, (b) rather childish. The historian reflected how sad it was for these men who had nailed their colours to the mast when it was not absurd for the ablest men to opt for a career in the Church. Today, no more: there are no longer bishops at All Souls.

Henson registered Lang's enthronement at Canterbury in his diary: 'His oration was, of course, very eloquent, and expressed in ample terms of sonorous platitude, which could neither wake criticism in the hearers, nor bind obligations on the orator.' In short, here was the right man for the job. 'It was, I suppose, precisely what pleased everybody and alarmed nobody. The framework of elaborated ceremonial annoyed me, and the copious eulogies of the newspapers even gave me offence.'

The first request from the new Archbishop was that Henson should give evidence, in the case of *The Well of Loneliness*, in favour of prohibiting it as an obscene book. This was an awkward one. In his reply he did not mince words.

> These disgusting abnormalities, which a former generation described as unnatural vices, seem now to have a kind of 'most favoured nation' treatment in the scientific or pseudo-scientific world, and thanks to the new psycho-analysis, which has replaced what we used to call morality, there are not lacking those who would claim from the State an absolute indifference to practices which must be regarded as highly anti-social.

But are they? – in a world where excess population is the greatest threat to the human race, and congested populations at the bottom of the troubles in the trouble-spots around the world. He declared himself so far out of sympathy with the modern world, or of understanding a subject so 'disgusting to me', that he had 'no desire to be mixed up with it, even in the modest degree your Grace suggests'. The wife of a previous archbishop, Mrs Benson, could have helped him to a better understanding of the subject.

The Archbishop's address on the death of King George V was not wholly to Henson's mind: in spite of its being 'very effective', it 'aroused a certain repugnance in my mind. One gets the impression that, an unusually good opportunity for advertising religion having been provided by the fact that King George was personally religious [was he?], an astute Prelate was making the most of it.' But wasn't that the Archbishop's job? Henson had too acute a nose for humbug to be a bishop: he should have remained a dean, like the admirable Dean Inge.

The Bishop expressed his view on that subject in which humbug is at its maximum today – Education. 'All the fond delusions as to the beneficent potencies of education, which deceived the 19th century, are still living and dominant in the ranks of "Labour". No aphorism is more bitterly resented, and more habitually ignored, than that which affirms the melancholy and far-reaching truth, that *You cannot make a silk purse out of a sow's ear.*' He recognised the fact that most people are not very educable; only the few are, in any significant sense – say, up to university level. Even so, there are plenty who ought not to be there. So why all the bother and expense?

A far more reverberating moral issue than Miss Radcliffe Hall's Lesbianism now arrived, a headache for poor Archbishop Lang: the coronation of the new King, Edward VIII. A confidant of King George V, Lang must have known the unsuitability of the son's relations with Mrs Simpson. He can hardly have realised his obstinate determination to marry her. The Archbishop called on his suffragans for a renewal of dedication in religious preparation for the coronation. When the horrid truth dawned, could the Archbishop con-

scientiously crown the aberrant monarch? He prayed and
prayed. At last a *deus ex machina* in the shape of Mr Baldwin
solved the problem for him, by deftly manoeuvring the
unsuitable occupant of the throne off it.

The relief was tremendous, and reflected itself in the
Archbishop's spirits. 'He is in the best of spirits, "enjoying
the Papacy" with a vengeance.' (He had waited long enough
for it.) 'Moreover, in spite of his unintermitted labour, he
seems to be in abounding vigour.' The coronation of a King
and Queen could now go happily forward, Lang directing
the rehearsals like the born actor he was. Henson might have
recalled his forecast of long ago, as to Lang's 'first-rate gifts'.
'And yet I am not happy with this unprecedented parade of
pageanted piety. [Appreciate the alliteration!] What can it
really mean? And how long will it last? At least we may be
thankful for being able to maintain a show of decency. How
near we came to a hideous profanation.'

As Bishop of Durham he had some part to play in the
ceremony, holding the ampulla and spoon for the anointing,
'which was not easy, as I had my book under my arm'. At
the time of his disappointment over York, he had reflected
at early service in the chapel at Auckland, autumn sunshine
flooding in and making it 'extraordinarily beautiful – neither
Lambeth nor Bishopthorpe has anything so fair'. Now Lang
was making an elaborate transformation of the garden at
Lambeth, paid for by 'an anonymous friend' (that would
have been Pierpont Morgan). Lang gets a tribute for this:
'He has certainly made it very fine. He is a born actor, and
has the actor's eye for effect. The result is an extraordinarily
effective arrangement of the limited space and contents of
the garden.' At Bishopthorpe he had created a fine border;
wherever he lived in his various episcopal residences he filled
them with flowers.

On the crucial European issues that darkened the Thirties
Henson had a good record: an historian, he understood
them, and what was involved, better than most. He saw
Mussolini's rape of Abyssinia as the crime it was, if not as
the beginning of the breakdown of international order. He
spoke out against it, and so did Archbishop Lang – to be

rewarded with obscene abuse in Italy. Henson was shocked by the silence of the Vatican on the international crime the war on Abyssinia was. But Pope Pius XI had had a prime share in riveting the shackles of Fascism on the Italian people: he gave Mussolini the triumph of the Lateran Treaty, ending the dispute with the Church which it would never accord to a democratic government. (Musso was no believer . . . the motive was the same as in Britain – anything rather than Communism!)

Henson understood the true nature of Hitler's Nazi régime from the first – which is more than most people at the head of British affairs did, or would. He was quite early informed as to the treatment the Jews were beginning to receive, and recorded that it made it 'almost impossible to regard Germany as any longer entitled to be regarded as a civilised country'. *Verb.sap.*

On the German issue he had an open public controversy with his oldest friend at All Souls, Bishop Headlam. Headlam was a remarkable figure, a big gorilla-like man, given to champing and nervous contortions at the mouth – hardly surprising, since he was descended from both Oliver Cromwell and Peter the Great. Dermot Morrah said of him in College that he was neither High Church nor Low Church, not even Broad but *Hard* Church. But he was soft-headed about the Germans. The simple explanation was that he was under the influence of his nephew and niece, the Headlam-Morleys. Agnes Headlam-Morley was made Professor of International History too – regrettably, instead of the better qualified E.H. Carr. They had a German mother, with the predictable consequence that they were fanatically pro-German. An egregious Chamberlainite MP, Sir Arnold Wilson, attacked Henson for his condemnation of Germany's barbarous conduct. Wilson too late realised that he had been wrong all along, and in repentance, though over-age, gallantly joined the RAF. The Germans killed him.

Why did not the Archbishop speak out about the German horror, as he had about Abyssinia? Here again the explanation is simple. His closest friends at All Souls were Halifax and Dawson, both Appeasers. Dawson did the most damage

of the whole lot, exerting a prodigious influence as editor of
The Times, in those days when that newspaper enjoyed it.
Churchill resented Lang's silence, and regarded him with
disapproval as a Chamberlainite. Courageous and cocky little
Henson was his man: on his retirement from Durham,
Churchill wanted his voice to be heard once more as canon
of Westminster. Lang did not favour this move.

With advancing age Henson had done his best to behave
himself towards his junior, who had long by-passed him on
the way up. In discussions at Lambeth, 'I came into as much
of a collision with the Archbishop as is decently possible in
the case of a bishop.' In the privacy of his diary his judgment
remained as ever – ambivalent.

> The senior Primate has an astonishing command of
> sonorous phrases. He is never at a loss for a word; he is
> humorous; has a good voice, and a fine presence. His
> fault is a certain suggestion of pompous oracularity; he
> is more rhetorical than convincing; for, while his purple
> patches are many and finished, he does not give the
> impression of personal conviction.

Henson on himself is more friendly.

> It has been my misfortune in the course of my life to
> disappoint every person who has followed me, and
> every party that has allowed itself to build hopes on me
> . . . A kind of Quixotic honesty, a fatal trick of lucid
> speech, and a temperamental indifference to the impres-
> sions I make, may perhaps explain the embodied para-
> dox I seem to be.

Candid enough (which Lang could not afford to be), Henson
is kinder to himself than to his superior. A simpler judgment
would be that Lang was always disciplined, under control,
Henson not.

To the end he kept an attractive boyishness. When he
retired he was well enough off to betake himself to a roomy
manor-house in Suffolk (Headlam: 'I like a *large* house').

And he would sign himself 'H. Hensley Henson, Hintlesham Hall, Hipswich.' When Lang retired, he had nothing, and was given a grace-and-favour residence at Kew.

Henson allowed himself one last fling at him, which I thought unkind. He wrote a letter to *The Times*, hoping to take the Archbishop down a peg: since he was no longer Archbishop of Canterbury, he should be entitled Bishop Lang, like the rest of the order. Nobody took any notice.

When in the vicinity of Ipswich I took the opportunity to go and see Henson. He was delighted to welcome somebody from the old College, with whom he could have a talk. Vivacious and spirited as ever, there he sat upright in his chair, his desk piled with books. (He was a voracious reader, Lang not.) He was now suffering from a weak heart; I wondered whether he might not have been over-excited – he was easily excitable – for, within a fortnight, he was dead.

Though I had not gone to stay with him at Auckland while he was alive, I did pay the Castle a visit after his death – I suppose the historian's cult of the past (one has more sympathy with people when they are dead, their lives rounded up so that one can see the picture in perspective, unfolded at length). The gaunt, gloomy Castle, the tall, columned, light-filled Chapel where he had ministered – the whole place spoke of him. So did the faithful retainer, his butler – evidently devoted to him. He said simply, 'When he left he was a great man; he came back so *little* a man.'

Archbishop Lang of the Abdication

Cosmo Gordon Lang would not have liked to think that his name would be remembered, if at all, simply as the Archbishop at the time of the Abdication of Edward VIII. But so it is, in the popular memory. Actually, he had little to do with it, and certainly was not responsible for it. In his partisan book the Duke of Windsor expresses his dislike for this 'black beetle', confidant of his father George V. He deplored his presence at the death-bed of the old King. But what more proper? – that was in the course of duty. The Duke had a complex against what was proper – and so he lost his throne. To the Archbishop's immense relief: for could he have gone on to crown him, in the all-too-obvious circumstances?

We have already seen something of Lang, at various points of his career, where he coincided, or contrasted, with Bishop Henson's, since they were contemporaries at All Souls. But, from the beginning there was more contrast than similarity between these two birds of a feather. As an undergraduate Henson was unknown, and an unknown quantity. Lang was already prominent as an undergraduate – could hardly have been more so.

Coming up to Balliol, from Glasgow University, in 1882 when he was still no more than eighteen, he was a leading orator at the Oxford Union of which he became President unopposed. He was the Secretary of the Canning Club, nursery of bright young progressive Tories; a founder of the famous OUDS, the Oxford University Dramatic Society.

At Glasgow he had been much influenced by the philosophic Idealism of Edward Caird, another Balliol man (and great bore). This led Lang to undertake good works; he became undergraduate secretary for Toynbee Hall, a Balliol institution which went in for slumming in the East End of London.

All this aroused the concern of the worldly old Master, Jowett: 'Your business here, Mr Lang, is not to reform the East End of London, but to get a First Class in the School of *literae humaniores.*' In the event he got a Second; but made up for it by getting a First in Modern History the following year. This enabled him to compete for a Fellowship at All Souls – no point in entering that race with a Second. It was only at a further attempt that he was successful. This made him Henson's junior in College and partly accounts for his critical remarks at the time of Lang's election – and also the envy of his so smoothly getting ahead of him up the episcopal ladder.

Neither of them intended the Church at the outset. The character of the College was not clerical, but legal, and all for public affairs; nor was its atmosphere Tory, it was Whiggish, inclining to Liberal Unionist. Both of these bright young men thought of the law; Lang saw himself as a future Lord Chancellor. He committed the youthful indiscretion of writing a novel – a kind of *Little Lord Fauntleroy* of vapid Jacobite sentimentality. For his College research, he told me once that he considered writing about Thomas Cromwell. It would have made a contrast with Cairdian Idealism, an education in Machiavellian realism.

But, then, the neophyte received a call. Coming away from Cuddesdon church at Easter-time, he was walking across Shotover (those bird-haunted, echoing dingles!) when he heard a voice: 'Why should *you* not be ordained?' This echoed in his ears, and made up his mind for him. I find it quite as moving as Henson's dedication of himself, alone in Iffley church. Perhaps more so: for all through the welter and inhuman toil of his career, the Archbishop would come back to renew himself at Cuddesdon at Easter-time. When he ceased to be Archbishop of Canterbury he came no more. He was one for these personal commemorations.

Son of a Moderator of the Presbyterian Kirk of Scotland, his ordination into the Church of England – he had to be confirmed first – was regarded with disapprobation in his native land. A foretaste of the abuse he was to receive at various points in his career. Disapproval was registered as he went up the ladder to become Archbishop of York. He told me that all the congratulations he got from his Scotch gillie was – 'Weel, ye've a gran' fine kirk noo.'

His clerical career proceeded in orderly fashion, accumulating experience as he went along. For a couple of years he served as curate, under Talbot, at Leeds. Those were rough-and-tumble Victorian days, especially on drunken Saturday nights. He had, stalwart fellow, often to part fighting couples; the most difficult to part, he told me, were the women, once they had hold of each other's hair.

The saintly Talbot, a High Churchman, had a continuing influence upon him, giving him counsel at various junctures. When Talbot died, it fell to Lang as Archbishop to conduct the funeral at Winchester. A Wykehamist Fellow of All Souls described the scene to me: the Archbishop all in white, led out according to the Use of Winchester by a choirboy holding either hand, Lang in tears. Then, at the end, commenting to my colleague, 'This pomp!' – as if he deplored it.

That was like him: he had a sense of humour, and could see himself from the outside. Even at his consecration as bishop, looking every inch the part, the cathedral packed with old ladies, he commented *sotto voce*, 'And the sea shall give up her dead.'

Of course, he liked pomp – what more proper for an archbishop? Once at All Souls, when he came down to chair some conference of Churches, Warden Adams gave a dinner party for him. At the end he left, to don his academic scarlet over his episcopal purple, and came back to the drawing-room, unnecessarily, to make the round of the ladies. When his Grace had gone, Miss Adams, a forthright Scotch body, said, 'To think that *my* mother called *his* mother Hannah!'

For a couple of years he was Fellow and Dean of Divinity at Magdalen. Hence the celebrated apologue of his after-dinner speech (he was the best of after-dinner speakers), in which he would refer to 'Balliol, my nursing mother; Magdalen, my mistress; but All Souls, my lawful, wedded wife'. This was much appreciated, coming from a dedicated celibate.

Lady Oman, with a woman's romantic heart, maintained that there had been a woman in Lang's early life – a titled lady, of course. There may well have been someone stuck on him, for he was handsome, a mass of raven-black hair, good profile, long stride – a fine figure of a man. This was too much for some women. Once when he was preaching in Portsea church, to some 2,000 children, a woman came mincing up the aisle: 'I want to kiss that man.' The verger, with great presence of mind, said to her, 'Won't I do instead?', and arm-in-arm led her out. The handsome preacher was saved.

Old Queen Victoria responded to the young cleric's good looks, and suggested that a wife would do as much as two curates to help him. He had a ready answer to that: if a curate was no good at the job he could sack him, whereas a wife was a fixture. This made the old lady laugh at his 'poor view of matrimony'. The fact was that he never had any wish to marry. Celibacy was determined for him by his nature.

Marriage was not in Lang's line: his emotional inclinations were otherwise. At Magdalen he made a lifelong friend of a young Scottish laird, Moreton Macdonald of Largie. The homo-erotic element was entirely repressed; but every year he spent his August holiday in a cottage on his friend's estate. Here he passed the month in retreat from the worldliness of the rest of the year. With his instinct for self-dramatisation he called it his 'cell'. In the little oratory attached he spent much of the morning in prayer and meditation, trying to achieve the selflessness that escaped him.

He was perfectly self-aware, under complete discipline. People thought him a snob; but he himself called his annual trek to his Highland retreat through the Dukeries – stopping at Welbeck, Clumber or Chatsworth – his 'snob's progress'.

When he was attacked by a fellow Scot and fellow religionist as such (in the *New Statesman*), I wrote in defending him demurely, that he 'found interesting people more interesting than uninteresting ones. What was wrong with that?' Logically unanswerable, it won an apology from the candid critic.

It was that lifelong repression, I used to think, that made him an insomniac. He had to make do with very few hours of sleep. He trained himself to lie perfectly still in bed, empty his mind of all problems and worries; and in that way, he told me, he got almost as much refreshment as if he had slept. Sleeping in Oxford was difficult anyhow, because of the chiming of bells at night. But what self-discipline it showed to carry, with that handicap, such a burden of work all his life – a burden he described towards the end as 'incredible, indefensible, inevitable'.

I suspect that he got many periods of rest in choir during services when he did not have to perform, or just give the blessing at the end. Observant boys at King's School, Canterbury, would see him sitting in his stall, contemplating his episcopal ring. As for giving the blessing, that was no strain. When A.E.J. Rawlinson was made bishop – to me as undergraduate at Christ Church the friendly 'Rawlers', our chaplain – he was in a hurry to exert his new episcopal status and blessed the congregation as he passed down the aisle. The Archbishop was displeased at this breach of etiquette: 'When I am present it is for me only to give the blessing.' (What precisely *happens* when a bishop gives one his blessing?)

When old Mrs Bickersteth was on her death-bed, at Canterbury, the Archbishop had promised to bless her; but was late. He had a characteristic excuse: he was lunching at Buckingham Palace. Still, he arrived in time to speed the old lady's departure. He evidently *believed* in such things – contrary to what H.G. Wells thought: he wanted to write a novel about an ambitious prelate who, when he arrived at the height of his ambition, found that he had lost his faith.

Lang scored in these personal kindnesses and attentions: he had an acute sense of the individual and therefore a good

judgment of men. Unlike his successor, the mountainous
Billy Temple, whose forte was general causes and ideas – he
was a 'philosopher' and theologian – and, geared to the
masses, rather over-looked the individual. Not so Cosmo.
This I observed from my first meeting with him, on the
night of my election at All Souls. It is the custom to drink
the new Fellow's health at dessert in champagne. But I am a
teetotaller, and the Archbishop, by whose side I was placed,
noticed my hesitation. He said kindly, 'I am a teetotaller too,
but on special occasions like this, I give myself a dispensa-
tion.' The gracious condescension of this, only slightly in
inverted commas, was not lost on the churchy young
historian, and I was his man thenceforward.

Actually, he was not particularly popular in College,
unlike Henson. The more secular-minded thought him too
prelatical. But, after all, he had been a prelate since before he
was forty, and had the dignity to keep up. When he retired
from Lambeth, he became less reticent – would say more
freely what he thought and tell one interesting things. While
he was Archbishop he *had* to be careful what he said: people
were ready to jump down his throat at the slightest slip. He
had had two harassing experiences of that.

In the first German war, 1914–18, he made a statement –
it may have been at Easter or Christmas – of a Christian
character, reminding us that our enemies were fellow men
and that one day we should come to terms of peace with
them – some such platitude. He had let fall two unfortunate
words: he had a 'sacred memory' of the Kaiser. There was a
national outcry at this, whipped up by the yellow press, for
in the first war the Kaiser was as much of a bogy as Hitler
was in the second. (Kaiser William was a vain, neurotic
peacock, possessed with envy of Britain – in this fully
representative of his people; but, from the point of view of
European civilisation, he was a cut above Hitler, the man of
the people.)

Lang's phrase, which gave the impression of sycophancy
besides its challenge to jingo sentiments, really referred to a
specific event: when he had witnessed Edward VII and the
Kaiser kneeling together by Queen Victoria's coffin. At

worst it was only a bit of episcopal humbug. The Archbishop was put through purgatory for those two words, hounded by the popular press; and, a sensitive man – no tough like Bishop Headlam – he suffered agony. At the time of this crisis all his hair dropped off, that magnificent poll of raven-black which had so gone to women's hearts. He tried a wig, but nothing would do. He emerged from this time of torment looking an old man, with a foxy look, a cranium as bald as an egg, a tiny bit of fluff above the ears. A bad blow has its offsetting advantage, says William Shakespeare: henceforth Lang looked, more than before, sage and pater-nal, not only Primate but Patriarch.

He himself thought that he had picked up this distressing condition from using hair-brushes at some Club. I often think of it at his Club, and refrain from using other people's hair-brushes.

He was not a man of the Right. In early days, while reading for the law, he took an interest in those good Balliol institutions, the Workers' Educational Association and the University Extension Movement, lecturing for them both. Surprisingly, when Archbishop of York, he supported Lloyd George's famous Budget of 1909, raising money for social insurance by increasing taxation on the rich. He angered the Tories – who were in a bad temper in those days – still further by supporting Asquith's Parliament Act, which clipped the powers of the House of Lords. A cynic might say that he was Asquith's appointment to York – a surprise to many – and one good turn from a Balliol man deserves another. However, I expect his convictions were with the Liberals in the ascendant.

This, however, is to anticipate. He had already proved himself in parish work as vicar of Portsea, 1896–1901: an enormous parish of 40,000 souls. Here he lived in a clergy-house with a dozen curates – in his element in a men's community. Stories are told of his favourites: Dick Shep-herd, who later became a popular number at St Martin's-in-the-Fields and as a Pacifist propagandist, had been one of them. Lang had practically to hold down this volatile young man at his ordination, felt a special responsibility for him, and so put up with his pranks.

One of them took place at York, when Dick was bearing the cross before the Archbishop in procession, but kept badgering him for permission to play golf afterwards. No reply from the boss – until Dick said that if he didn't say Yes, he would lead the Archbishop onwards down into the crypt.

Lang had a far worse headache later, at Canterbury, with the 'Red Dean', Hewlett Johnson – a Ramsay MacDonald appointment. This man was touched with megalomania, and made himself the spokesman of Soviet Russia as the incarnation of Christ's kingdom on earth. What a fool! – As bad as the idiotic Sartre, who thought Soviet Russia the incarnation of human freedom. Already a wealthy man, the Socialist Dean made another small fortune out of his bestseller on Russia as *The Socialist Sixth* (of the planet). Abroad, the Dean of Canterbury was often confused with the Archbishop, and his fatuous pronouncements imputed to Lang. When the distinction was pointed out, peopled asked why didn't the Archbishop control the man, or get rid of him? But no archbishop could control the rogue elephant, nor could people comprehend that, in the Anglican Church, a dean is virtually irremovable: he has what used to be called the 'parson's freehold'.

It was at Portsea that Lang won the favour of old Queen Victoria, always sentimental about Scots. He only once talked to me about her – some story I have forgotten, but mentioning the old lady's beautiful, rather deep, voice. This was Lang's introduction to the notice of the royal family, continued and consolidated with her grandson, George V. Once, having to preach before him when Prince of Wales, he had prepared a sermon on Missions, but received a message beforehand that the Prince disliked sermons on Missions. Nevertheless, he proceeded to preach it, as planned. I registered that this was to show that he was no sycophant: I was meant to approve of his standing up to royalty. With me it was hardly necessary. But with others? C.R. Cruttwell, who was not under his spell, told me of his bringing the young Prince of Wales (later Duke of Windsor) to dine in Hall, and sweeping up to the dais with the lad, bypassing the younger company with a gesture, 'these are the Junior Fellows'. I see no harm in that: for some carpers he could do nothing right.

He was Bishop of Stepney 1901–09 – we have a 'Spy' caricature of him as such in the smoking-room at All Souls, an 'energetic young prelate'. Half-Highland Celt, he had a psychic gift of which he was proud. One day he was being shown round a church in the diocese, when the clergyman came to a hideous west window, and wished that someone would throw a stone through it and break it. The Bishop agreed, and put a curse on it. Not long after he got a letter from the clergyman reminding him, with the news that a thunderstorm had shattered the offending window. Clearly, of this among his 'first-rate gifts' he needed to be careful.

An effective raconteur in his slow and stately way, he told me the following story. Opening his post at Bishopthorpe one morning, he got a letter of warning from a Noncon-formist minister, who had had a dream about him. He saw the Archbishop, in motoring cap in his car, going down a steep declivity to a narrow gorge, with a bridge across a stream and a sharp U-turn. There an accident happened to him. Lang recognised the spot: it was on the very route he had to go to a Confirmation service that morning, the place precisely described in the letter. Pause. 'So what did you do?' I asked, youthfully tensed up. 'I rang the bell and ordered my car.'

Those were years of intense activity, of genuine enthusi-asm, in which he exerted leadership in Church causes and, preaching all round the country, became a national figure. In those days before wireless it was much more strenuous, hard work. He was Chairman of the CEMS, the Church of England Men's Society, which I remember in its prime. He travelled the country pleading for his East London Church Fund. He served on the Royal Commission on Divorce and Matrimonial Causes, taking the minority line along with Warden Anson. (I fancy that on this Henson took a more liberal line.) He made a marked impression at the Lambeth Conference of 1908.

Then came the 1914 war, and the howl of rage at his asserting Christian values in an unfortunate phrase. Undeterred, he led the National Mission of Repentance and Hope, which answered to a need, in the discouragement and depression of the time: 1916, the year of appalling casualties at the Somme. Worse was to come in 1917 and 1918: I remember as a choirboy the lengthening list of our young fellows being killed, read out in church – would it never end?

His tour of the United States and Canada gave him an audience on the other side of the Atlantic – over eighty speeches in forty days. He was welcomed by the famous financier, Pierpont Morgan, the start of a friendship over many years. It would be easy to call this making up to the Mammon of Unrighteousness. But Pierpont Morgan was a good friend to Britain during the war, when she badly needed it; and, an Episcopalian, he was a good friend to the Anglican Church. The Church's provision for the upkeep of Lambeth was never enough; annually Morgan met the deficit. (And what would Vatican finances be without the USA?)

The post-war period was dominated by the remarkable partnership between Randall Davidson and Lang: the Church of England was ruled by those two canny Scots. Randall Cantuar had the confidence of the Protestants, Cosmo Ebor of the Anglo-Catholics. At a grand London party one night a devout young lady genuflected to Davidson and kissed his ring; he turned round to Warden Pember with a grimace of distaste. Lang, on the other hand, welcomed such symptoms of devotion.

A Church Assembly was added to the chores of bishops and clergy, somewhat unnecessarily, when there were already the historic Convocations of the two Provinces, Southern and Northern. Both Scots were past-masters as chairmen; at the Assembly Davidson would occasionally say to Lang, 'Get up and put that donkey right.' Lang himself was chairman of the Commission on Ecclesiastical Courts and of that on Cathedrals. Then came the prolonged and delicate business of getting agreement on revision of the Prayer Book. Lang favoured a return to the 1549 Book, as did the Anglo-Catholics, for it was more or less a translation of the Sarum Mass. But on this he gave way to the majority, which proceeded on the basis of the 1662 Book. Was this a strategic move on his part? It enabled him to appear in the favourable light of being willing to make concessions. Thus it was he who steered the long discussions through to an agreed Revised Book.

All this involved constant journeys between Bishopthorpe and Lambeth, where he had his rooms in the Cranmer Tower (appropriately, but *absit omen!*). Not that he neglected the affairs of his vast York diocese. He had made it more manageable by detaching South Yorkshire for a new see of Sheffield, and then the Pontefract area to add to that of Wakefield. (Would Henson have consented to shortening his arm?)

These were the years in which we saw most of Lang in College. After a week's work at Lambeth he would often take refuge in the privacy of All Souls for the weekend. Here he continued to function as Lord Mallard at gaudies, and to sing, in his beautiful voice, the Mallard Song. Very good of him, I thought, for it is the most awful 17th-century doggerel.

This goes back to the folklore that, when the College was founded in the 1430s, a mallard flew up from the marshy spot. So a mallard is the College totem and appears everywhere, on dinner-plates, china, silver, etc. – like the Cardinal's Hat at Christ Church. I suppose Lang took on this chore when young, to show that he was a 'good fellow'. I could not have borne to sing the words – and, though I dutifully joined in the chorus, made one of the two or three who watched the rest throwing themselves, heartily and unselfconsciously, into the jolly row they kept up. The words ran,

> Gryphon, Turkey, Bustard, Capon –
> Let other hungry mortals gape on,
> And on their bones with stomachs fall hard,
> But let All Souls men have the Mallard.

Then we all joined in the chorus, shaking the rafters:

> by the blood of King Edward,
>   O by the blood of King Edward,
> It was a swapping, swa-a-apping Mallard.

I do not know which King Edward this refers to – surely not the unsuitable, though martyred, Edward II? More likely young Edward VI; for at the time of the Reformation All Souls was recalcitrantly Catholic – and the tune to which we sang the chorus sounded to me like a parody of the Litany.

The third verse was always omitted, 'in deference to the Cloth' of the Lord Mallard, and I never heard it sung:

> Swapping he was from bill to eye,
> Swapping he was from wing to thigh;
> His swapping tool of generation
> Out-swapped all the wingèd nation.

> O by the blood of King Edward, etc.

At the beginning of each of the last three centuries, in 1701, 1801 and 1901, a Mallard procession around the roofs of the College took place. The Lord Mallard was carried in a chair by a couple of hefty Junior Fellows, and on a pole before him the symbolic dead mallard. Medals were struck to commemorate this idiosyncratic ceremony; we possess those for 1701, 1801 and 1901 when Lang (not then a bishop) was so chaired. (Will the absurd procession over the roofs take place in 2001?) Lang himself has left an account of this venerable nonsense. 'It was my glory to hold that office in the College for some thirty years. It is, indeed, a strange office. The holder of it is not appointed: he *becomes*: he takes his place by the informal assent of the College.' The assent could be taken for granted in his case, for his clear tenor voice was the best. No one could sing the Mallard song as well as he did – and he had other favourites in his repertory also for gaudy nights. The last time I heard him sing it was in 1945, only a few weeks before he died, when he gallantly performed for us in that voice still clear, though a little quavering.

In 1901 he had been carried around the roofs of the College at dead of night, the proceedings lit up by the torches of the Junior Fellows carrying staves. The participants give one an idea of the character of All Souls in the good old days. The procession was headed by the Warden, Sir William Anson, the constitutional lawyer venerated as almost a second Founder. Then came seniors like A.V. Dicey, and Sir Thomas Holland, whose portrait greets one on the grand staircase of the Athenaeum. The Lord Mallard was borne by two couples of Juniors. The athletic Sir Arthur Steel-Maitland became a Cabinet Minister in Baldwin's government, 1924–9; Sir Maurice Gwyer, Chief Justice of India; tall Sir Philip Baker-Wilbraham, an ecclesiastical lawyer who was chancellor of half the dioceses in England; Sir Foster Cunliffe, a fine young baronet killed in the First German War.

Lang tells us that 'the whole strange ceremony had been kept secret; only late workers in the night can have heard the unusual sounds' – which went on for a couple of hours. And, loyal to such memories, he faithfully kept the Mallard totem-pole.

Years later, when he condemned Mussolini's criminal war against Abysinnia, the Archbishop was held up to execration in Italy. (The Vatican kept audibly silent.) Happening to be in Italy at the time, I encountered a young friar who was able to assure me that Archbishop Lang had sacrificed the body of a dead woman on his own altar. Astonished at this information, I assured the cleric that anything of the sort was out of the question with the respectable old gentleman, whom I knew. The Italian was polite and courteous, but evidently disbelieved me.

It was only afterwards that the explanation occurred to me. Some distorted version of the Mallard ceremony had been relayed to credulous Italians, as part of anti-British propaganda. Ordinary humans will believe anything, the more nonsense the better: they find it more difficult to credit sense. That all too friendly young friar had swallowed what he had been told (Tertullian: Credo *quia* impossibile), and my rational disclaimer had no effect whatever.

We do not need to go over the silly Parliamentary excitement over the Revised Prayer Book again. Suffice it to say that poor old Archbishop Davidson went out a defeated man. Not so Lang: the politician in him saw that the Book could be introduced into the dioceses, by the sole authority of the bishops, without the Yea or Nay of Parliament. And Parliament would not dare to prosecute the Church for doing so. So that was that – all that fuss about nothing.

What threatened Lang was his health. Shortly after his 'inevitable' succession to Canterbury he was struck by a succession of illnesses. He developed duodenal trouble, then the somewhat mysterious neuralgia of the fifth nerve, rackingly painful; acute fibrositis, and finally shingles. All these were in part nervous complaints, owing to the intolerable strain of overwork to which he had subjected his body for years (plus, perhaps, sexual repression).

Still he did not give up, and his friend Pierpont Morgan came to the rescue. He took the Archbishop for long Mediterranean cruises both in 1929 and 1931 – Lang said the happiest times in his life. He peregrinated the Mediterranean in purple and skull-cap, like a cardinal. Or perhaps as an alternative Pope, *alterius orbis papa*. He once spoke of himself as the one through whom God chiefly speaks to the English people, evidently thinking of himself as another Vicar of Christ. He by-passed Rome, unfriendly to the Anglican section of Christianity in those days. But he cannily made the most of his time making friends with the Greek Orthodox ecclesiastics, in Athens, Jerusalem, everywhere he could; and ultimately exchanged counsel with the Patriarch in Constantinople, the new Rome itself.

His health completely recovered and he was able to carry on for the next ten years at full stretch as before. What mostly occupied his mind were his ecumenical plans, which demanded, and received, his full powers of statesmanship – outlined in his 'Appeal to All Christian People', the highlight of the Lambeth Conference of 1920, upon which he had stumped the country.

No space here to go into his elaborate and friendly negotiations with the Free Churches, the Church of Scotland, the Greek Orthodox Church. He had the satisfaction of welcoming the Old Catholics, a break-away from Rome, into full communion with Canterbury at the Lambeth Conference of 1930. He left relations with the Lutheran Churches, of Finland, Latvia, Estonia, Scandinavia, to his old All Souls colleague, Bishop Headlam, who also took an interest in relations with the Churches among the Southern Slavs. (For a memorial to himself he fancied a large statue by Mestrovich outside the west front of Gloucester Cathedral.)

The more touchy subject of relations with Rome, the Malines Conversations under Cardinal Mercier, elicited Lang's cautious sympathy and co-operation. Later in the Thirties the Patriarch of Romania rolled up at Lambeth; conversations in Belgrade, Sofia and Athens proved co-operative – all these Churches ready to recognise Anglican sacraments and orders. Rome could wait. It looked as if the Lambeth Conference planned for 1940 would set the seal on Lang's twenty years of ecumenical work. The outbreak of war, again, shattered his hopes.

We must descend from these giddy heights to the personal and more intimate. He had good relations, in fact, with Cardinal Hinsley at Westminster, largely conducted through the medium of Hinsley's coadjutor, my friend Archbishop David Mathew. It was he who arranged for Lang to propose Hinsley, a new-comer to London, for membership of the Athenaeum, in those days a haunt of bishops. David Mathew much enjoyed his contacts with Lang, a familiar Curial type. His hope of succeeding Hinsley at Westminster, for whom he had been a factotum, was defeated by his too obvious Anglican sympathies. Instead of him, a safe third-rater was appointed.

In my first years in College we had daily Chapel services, which I found rather a chore, especially in the mornings. Only a handful of Fellows attended, daily services were petering out, and eventually ended by resolution of College Meeting. Lang accepted this gracefully, with a tribute to

Warden Pember's exemplary attendance. Pember was no believer, but an old-fashioned Whig Rationalist, like his friend Asquith. Chapel services continued at weekends, with a *very* old-fashioned Use going right back to the Regency. Our prayer-books in those early years contained prayers for the Dowager Queen Adelaide; and the Communion retained the Low Church Northward position. (I longed to hear a full-scale High Mass sung in that resonant Chapel, Palestrina or Byrd. Sometimes, youthfully on my own, I would try out the ordinary plainsong, 'Credo in unum Deum, patrem omnipotentem', etc. Once in a sermon Lang recommended our continuing to go to Chapel, even if we did not believe. At the time I thought this rather questionable doctrine; now I see that he was right: it can do no harm, and may do some good.

I used to watch him at College meetings, sitting at high table, from my junior place below. He never wasted any time, or any words. He sat there writing his letters; if anything affecting the interests of the Church came up, he rose, said his few words, sat down and went on with the endless correspondence. The pile of letters grew higher and higher. Years later I took to following his example, and, instead of wasting time on the argy-bargy that forty or fifty clever men can think up, took to writing my letters too. Of course there were amusing moments to distract one; I do not remember Lang ever being distracted – a lesson in concentration.

Since handwriting is an index to character this is the place to say that Lang's was almost illegible – and yet he carried on an enormous amount of correspondence in his own hand. When he became Archbishop of York one of the Fellows visiting him noticed the piles of hundreds of letters stacked in the hall at Bishopthorpe, which Lang was slowly ploughing through answering. Henson's missive was characteristic: 'I am, of course, surprised that you go *straight* to an archbishopric.' Not yet in sight of even a bishopric, he was plainly jealous; 'but you are too meteoric for precedent. I am sorry, of course, very sorry that you are so stiff a High Churchman.' But Lang wasn't stiff: he was a pliable High Churchman, and his forte was sound judgement, precisely where the more intellectual Henson failed.

People found Lang inscrutable, like his handwriting. He found himself 'perhaps too reserved'; but he had good reason to be reserved – which I came to understand. Ambivalence is a great advantage, it doubles one's sensibilities and perceptions. Lang could not let himself go, except very occasionally with one of his young men, like Dick Shepherd, for whom he had a paternal, perhaps even fraternal, love. (He put up with a good deal in the way of Dick's antics.) He understood himself very well, if nobody else did – saw all round himself as few people do. One can see this in Orpen's celebrated portrait of him. I do not think it 'cruel', as people said. True, there is a sly look in the eyes, understandable enough in a Curial ecclesiastic – he would have made a remarkable cardinal, a good pope. But also those are eyes, if you look carefully, that understand *everything*.

He was very introspective, constantly examining himself, accusing himself of falling down on his duty (absurdly, in my view, when he drove himself so relentlessly) – of not coming up, I suspect, to his expectations of himself. Year after year in his 'cell' in the Highlands, and in Holy Week at Cuddesdon, he would examine himself, go over his faults with unexpected humility. Hardly anybody knew this side to him, perhaps only his chaplains who would catch him alone in prayer.

Devotional notes remain from those quiet times at Ballure or Cuddesdon – I find them strangely touching, that reserved, secret man baring his soul.

O Lord, I give myself to Thee,
Thine ever, only Thine to be.

'Those simple words of the hymn I repeated so often to myself just before ordination that they always come back to me bearing the associations of that happy time with them, recalling me from the dryness and dullness of work to the freshness and fullness of the first consecration.' (This was written to encourage Dick, before his ordination.)

He constantly came back to the revelation he felt he had received that Easter at Cuddesdon and coming away across Shotover. 'What must have been His purpose, when all those years ago He changed my life and revealed something I had never known before – "the joy and peace of believing", the sense of His Love and the peace of His Presence? When in a way I cannot doubt He called me to His Service? . . .' Here, in a secret way Henson and he touched hands after all: for it is like Henson's dedication of *himself* to God's service, laying his hand on the altar, alone in the church at Iffley.

When he moved to Lambeth, he became official Visitor of the College as Archbishop of Canterbury: it had been founded by a predecessor, Henry Chichele, whose tomb at Canterbury we keep up. Hence Lang, regretfully, ceased to be a Fellow, and we did not see so much of him again until his retirement. His official reception as Visitor was a small, family affair. I remember only Warden Pember's speech, with its dig against 'the divine right of presbyters' – not very tactful, I thought. The Archbishop took no notice: he must have been used to such flouts.

It fell to E.L. Woodward, as Domestic Bursar, to send Lang's few sticks and chattels of furniture to Lambeth when he ceased to be a Fellow. Woodward had at one time intended to be a cleric himself – hence in College we called him the 'Abbé', for he had consorted with other *abbés* in Paris. Then he had reacted into anti-clericalism, and made a point of sending the archiepiscopal cracked chamber-pot after him. I don't know if he sent Lang's comfortless iron bedstead.

The curious thing is that those Victorian Fellows had no idea of comfort: 'public splendour and private squalor' might have been their All Souls motto. The iron bedsteads and hard mattresses! When Hailsham as a Junior Fellow, then Quintin Hogg, made a speech of protest in College Meeting, he was denounced as a 'sissy' – Quintin of all people! – by old General Swinton as Dean. He told us, for good measure, how he was brought up to run naked across the barrack square to the cold pump in the mornings. Maynard Keynes found our attic bedrooms of an Arctic spartanism after the luxury of King's, Cambridge.

When Lang died he left us his fine grandfather clock, with special intention that it was to remain in the Common Room. This was to remind Fellows not to remain there too long, swilling port at dessert – in particular, to remind Warden or Senior Fellow in the chair to get up and go after a decent interval, to release other Fellows to go about their occasions. I dare say Lang, who had an acute sense of time, had suffered as I have done, from imperceptive wine-bibbers hanging on. Myself, I don't put up with it: I break the rule and march out. Bad for them anyway. But the clock has been relegated, against Lang's intentions, to the Warden's Lodgings.

At Canterbury, when the Archbishop took time off to show guests around the cathedral, he made a regular pause arriving at the tablet inscribed with the names of his predecessors: 'Here is the place of my humiliation,' he would say, with typical self-dramatisation. Among the long roll of eminent names were the martyrs: Becket, Cranmer, Laud. I fancy he would not have minded joining the 'noble army of martyrs' himself. When war came again in 1939 he was at Canterbury, which was proclaimed a danger area. But he would not leave: he would rather be martyred 'on the steps of my own cathedral'. He evidently saw himself in the rôle of Becket. In the event a couple of Army officers were sent down to fetch him away.

He himself told me that he had received a handsome American offer to rebuild Becket's shrine, there on the pavement desolated by Henry VIII. (It occurs to me now that that would have been Pierpont Morgan again.) Lang did not favour this: that issue had been settled, said he. Evidently it would make another subject of controversy, of which he had had more than enough. All the same I wish Canterbury would restore the high altar to its original position below the shrine – too many steps up to it now for convenience – and then the goings-on at it might be visible through the choir-screen from the nave.

As for controversy nothing could exceed the furore raised by the Abdication of Edward VIII and the circumstances surrounding it. In fact the Archbishop had not so much to do with it – though crowning the King, in circumstances of which he was well aware, would have presented him with an appalling problem. Poor Lang was unjustly blamed, for his minimal part in the affair, by the Duke of Windsor in his book later. When the affair was over the Archbishop was asked 'to speak for Christian England'. Once more a couple of words – as when he had referred to Edward VIII's cousin, the Kaiser, years before – caused a great outcry and made Lang unpopular for a time. He deplored the 'exotic entourage' of the Windsors. I should have thought that a mild term to employ for the rackety lot with whom the Windsors chose to consort, a questionable Franco-American financier, and the pro-Hitler socialites ready to curtsy to Mrs Simpson.

The sentimental heart of the British people thought that this was 'kicking a man when he was down' – we really didn't know the full facts of the case at the time. (A statue might be put up to Mrs Simpson for ridding us of an unsuitable monarch.) Wicked expression was given to this sentiment by A.P. Herbert, who had his own reason for disliking episcopal views on divorce:

> My Lord Archbishop, what a scold you are!
> And when your man is down, how bold you are!
> Of Christian charity, how scant you are!
> And, auld Lang swine, how full of cant you are!

One may well conclude that the Archbishop was more deserving of sympathy than the infatuated King. Again, while Archbishop he could never say all that he thought or knew, or even defend himself: he had to resort to periphrasis, as when he described George V's language as 'vivacious' – it was in fact quarter-deck.

When I think back over it all, I am surprised at how many things he did tell me, one way and another (far more than the loquacious Henson did). One could hardly expect him to approve of my *Cornish Childhood* when it came out – very nice of him to have read it at all. David Mathew found him reading it, and asked what he thought of it. 'Very – very interesting,' was the non-committal reply.

But my local Bishop Hunkin asked specially for a review copy to mount a personal attack on it on home ground in the *Oxford Magazine*, though I had gone out of my way to be friendly with him in Cornwall, when he was not my cup of tea at all. An ex-Nonconformist, he had been appointed as the result of a round-robin from the profiteers of the panic election of 1931 asking the PM not to send down another Anglo-Catholic Socialist. Bishop Frere was no socialist, but a scholar, a saint, and a gentleman. Hunkin was none of those things; he signalised himself by saying prayers on the Nazi pocket-battleship visiting Falmouth harbour (what was it *for* but to sink British sailors?).

He should never have been made a bishop: he should have remained at Cambridge, where he made an ass of himself over the comic Sex Viri affair. J.B.S. Haldane, a university professor, wanted to marry, and to obtain the necessary divorce had to plead adultery – it transpired that it was pure collusion *pro forma*, and no adultery took place. Hunkin as Proctor took it upon himself to cite Haldane before the Sex Viri, an extinct body which he resuscitated for the purpose. No case lay against Haldane, but it gave Cambridge amusement at Hunkin's expense. Lang told me that Hunkin would never have been made a bishop if it had rested with him. In his time the custom was for the Prime Minister to submit three names to the Archbishop, in case he had any objection to raise. He could not fairly raise any objection to Hunkin. So we were saddled with the fellow for the rest of his life in Cornwall.

I never spoke to him again: he fitted in well with the Chamberlainite Appeasers who had complete sway – in those years when I was so bitterly opposed to them – right up to the war they brought down upon the country.

Lang once asked me what the religious situation was in Cornwall. Well up in Marxism, I was able to tell him that the moneyed middle class were Wesleyans, in politics Liberals; the lower classes apt to be Primitive or United (more

precisely dis-United) Methodist, many of whom were
Labour. My sympathies were all with the Anglo-Catholic
Socialists, very much in the minority, but an élite. 'Just as I
thought,' said the Archbishop sagely, committing himself
no further.

The apogee of Lang's career was the coronation of George
VI in 1937. After all, his prayers had been answered – by Mr
Baldwin – and the unsuitable couple, the Windsors, sped
abroad. When the Archbishop had discussed the coronation
with Edward, when King, the only interest he showed was
that the service should be shortened. He then called in his
brother Bertie – as if he had some presentiment, Lang
thought afterwards, that it would concern his brother rather
than himself. People close to the Duke of Windsor, like
Chips Channon, thought that he had an inner feeling that he
would not be able to stand the strain of the job. With him
and Mrs Simpson out of the country, solid people felt that
the *opéra-bouffe* was over.

For the Archbishop it was an untold relief – or rather, a
told one, for on the subject of the coronation he was
unwontedly explicit on paper. 'It was indeed like waking
after a nightmare to find the sun shining. No words can
describe my relief, my burden, like Christian's, falling from
my back.'

His preparation of the new sovereigns for their ordeal was
much in contrast. At Buckingham Palace, 'after some talk
on the spiritual aspects of the Coronation and of its spiritual
meaning for themselves, they knelt with me: I prayed for
them and for their realm and Empire, and I gave them my
personal blessing. I was much moved, and so were they.
Indeed, there were tears in our eyes when we rose from our
knees.'

'The rehearsals of the ceremony in the Abbey began early
in the year. There were about eight fixed rehearsals. I
attended them all. It was not easy to bring what at first
seemed chaos into order. The ordinary Englishman will not
take ceremonies seriously when he is in his ordinary clothes.'
But Lang was not ordinary, nor even an Englishman. In this
business he was in his element: not for nothing was he a

cousin of Matheson Lang the actor, and his early training as a founder member of the OUDS showed his bent. As Henson had reported of him at All Souls, he was not an intellectual, but his gifts were pre-eminent – and all through his life he had made the most of them.

Now, 'I had perforce to take the leading part in these rehearsals, for the Earl Marshal, though always in command, was too quiet and modest to be sufficiently peremptory and decisive.' Not so the Archbishop: he took over command. Quintin Hailsham told me how his voice would come clearly down the aisle of Westminster Abbey, 'Lord Salisbury, you are out of line!' Knowing the absent-minded harlequin Cecils, I bet he was straggling well out of line.

However, 'the final full dress rehearsal went well; and on the great day there was not a single hitch, and everyone from the King to the smallest page played his or her part.' One sees how much he savoured it all as drama; he himself wrote, 'It was said afterwards with some truth that the Archbishop "produced" the Coronation.' 'Once I saw it was going well, I enjoyed every minute,' he said. 'Thank God that is over!' said Lumley Green-Wilkinson – evidently an ordinary Englishman – as they got into the car to leave the scene. 'Lumley' – a name out of Belloc – 'how can you say such a thing!' said the Archbishop. 'I only wish it was all beginning over again.'

One wonders if the Windsors saw the performance on film, wherever they were.

For the first two years of the war Lang remained at Lambeth. On nights when bombing was bad, he would sometimes descend to the basement of Lollards' Tower. Headlam told me that he encountered him on one such night on the staircase, descending in purple dressing-gown and clutching his chamber-pot: 'When you are old you have need of this utensil.' In the Blitz of May 1941 four bombs fell in the courtyard, one of them nearby felled him to the ground; the great hall was gutted, and the Palace rendered uninhabitable.

Next year he made way for William Temple, born in the purple, for his father had been archbishop. Lang had trained him up to succeed him; after evening prayers in the chapel,

Lang would say, 'Come along, William', and lead him into the study. Billy Temple, a mountain of a man, stayed the pace only two years; he died of over-eating – he would scupper a whole plate of cakes – with a weak heart. Lang said, 'If I had known this would happen, I would never have retired.' He took his successor's funeral service at Canterbury.

His own time was not long. When he retired, he had no money – all had gone in service to the Church. Of course he had lived in style befitting a prince of the Church: there were some eleven retainers at Lambeth. He was granted a grace-and-favour residence at Kew, and once more Pierpont Morgan helped him out.

The last time I saw him was on the pavement on his way to a meeting of the Trustees at the British Museum. I had the pleasure of presenting to him my companion, a congenial Signals-Serjeant in the American Forces. The old Archbishop was all benignity, no doubt would have given us his blessing, if asked.

Not long after, he died; he was on his way to the British Museum when he collapsed in the street, his last words so characteristic: 'I must get to the station' – duty impelling him to the last.

His ashes were taken to Canterbury, to be buried near the tomb of Archbishop Chichele, founder of the College he had loved all his life.

I find a sad little note in a pocket note-book of that time.

10 December 1945, 11 a.m.: the bell of St Mary's tolling for the memorial service to Lang. I sit here in the room that once was his, hear him saying, 'Won't you come and pray for me? Yes, there's a good lad – do.' Yet, all the same I sit on idly in my chair, tired with all the fatigues of travelling about the country.

I know I ought to go. I see him very distinctly: that gracious, deliberate, silvery presence, with all his kindness to me. I think of meeting him outside the British Museum earlier this term, when sauntering about London with Don; or on the pavement in the High,

with Dick, my Canadian nephew; or on his last visit to
College, when he told me various things 'that remarkable old lady', Queen Victoria, had said to him.

In a way I knew him better than all the people in St
Mary's this morning. Yet I sit on here till the bell ceases,
the hour strikes, and I must move on to my work.

Two Foreign Secretaries: Simon and Halifax

Two Fellows of All Souls who were prominent in the public eye in the deplorable 1930s were Sir John Simon and Lord Halifax. They had bad luck in being Foreign Secretaries in that evil time – Simon 1931–5, Halifax 1937–40, but they certainly did not make the best of a bad job. In fact an historian may fairly say that they made it worse. The historical record will not let them off lightly: they bear a heavy responsibility for the confusion of British policy in dealing with the criminal aggressors against European peace, first Mussolini, then Hitler.

On the other hand, there were better aspects to their public record. I suppose that Simon was at his best as a law-officer, at the Home Office, and a good Lord Chancellor. He should have stuck to the law, but he fancied politics more: he would always sacrifice a several-hundred-pound brief for a miserable political meeting. Earlier he had certainly meant to be Prime Minister; fortunately Providence disposed otherwise. Halifax's service to the state was as Viceroy of India, where he had a remarkable record – best Viceroy in this appalling century, along with Curzon, another All Souls man. Eventually, after an unpromising beginning, he did well as ambassador in Washington.

Both men, it is only fair to say, were public-spirited, imbued with a sense of duty. But that is not enough to pass the test of history, even of contemporary politics. Both of them failed the country in the crucial tests of defending its interests, safeguarding its security, against the obvious, increasing danger from its enemies. From the point of view of history there can be no graver condemnation.

How to account for it? What is the clue to the failure of these two very different men? And to the men themselves?

Their origins could not have been more dissimilar: Oxford brought them together, in particular All Souls. John Allsebrook Simon was born in 1873 at Manchester, the son of a poor Congregational minister, and therefore hereditarily Radical and rather a Puritan. Edward Lindley Wood, son of Viscount Halifax, was born in 1881 at Powderham Castle, seat of his mother's family the Courtenay Earls of Devon, one of the oldest of European stocks. On his father's side Yorkshire industrial money made the Woods rich – several estates and grand houses: Hickleton, Hemsworth, Garrowby. Halifax eventually inherited from an aunt Temple Newsam, the splendid Jacobean palace which he handed over to Leeds for a museum.

He gave me an amusing description of this formidable aunt, the Hon Mrs Meynell-Ingram, for whom Bodley built the wonderful church of Hoar Cross, near Burton-on-Trent. (After I saw it, I could think of nothing else for a week.) The old lady was a *dévote*, had a sure sense of beauty, and of her own importance. A hunting accident left her crippled. She would process into church on her stick, a footman before her bearing her prayer-book on a cushion.

Simon was well educated at Fettes College, Edinburgh, a good classic, head of the school; Archie Campbell used to say in College that he was the typical Fettes prize-boy, who had to win all the prizes. I see nothing wrong in that – what his contemporary and rival at Wadham, F.E. Smith, called 'glittering' prizes. They have lost all their glitter in the society of today, in which nothing is worth while. Asquith used to call Simon the 'Impeccable' – rather derogatory, for it meant that he was without the little weaknesses that recommend us to our fellows. Abstemious, always under control, nature's Nonconformist, he did not have a popular nature: nobody really liked him. He *said*, 'Shyness has always been my trouble, though I have learned to conceal it.' But was shyness the trouble? – I should have thought conceal-ment more like it.

It was a revealing fact that in College he had no group of friends, as most of us had. Even Lang had a group that were close to him – Geoffrey Dawson of *The Times*, Dougie Malcolm, and Halifax. Simon had no one, always a lone bird. He did not wish to be, he had a pathetic longing to be liked. And I am sure that he really loved All Souls – which did not respond. The *Dictionary of National Biography* says of him, 'To the companionship of All Souls, as exacting intellectually as undemanding emotionally, he owed much throughout his life.' (What do they know about emotional lives? Much more interesting than they know – as my Aubrey-type 'Private Lives of the Fellows of All Souls' may reveal to the next century.)

He won enough scholarships to come up to Wadham, where he achieved two Seconds to begin with. Donnishly, I find something significant in that. Was there something second-rate about that efficient, well-oiled filing-cabinet, his mind? I never once heard him say anything striking or original: he had no touch of genius – it was all efficiency. Typical of him was this. My mate, Roger Makins, was making a speech at College Meeting when we were young – a nerve-racking experience before all those lawyers and public figures. He made three points – always a mistake to enumerate, for when he came to sum up he forgot what the third had been. Simon automatically put it in from high table, though he had not appeared to be listening.

Clem Attlee summed him up – 'a lawyer, could argue anything, believed in nothing'. That was rather unfair, at least of the earlier Simon. Characteristic of him as an advocate, his fellow lawyer, Donald Somervell pointed out, was the extreme simplicity in which he would put the case – and then slip a fast one in, when nobody was noticing. Of course he was a target of envy from colleagues at the Bar, especially his juniors, for he was undeniably a 'leader' there, making a very large income when the going was good. I remember someone asking what brought him down from

London in the middle of the week, and the reply, 'To advise Morris [the great motor-car manufacturer who ruined old Oxford] how to get out of tax.' I'll bet that brought a huge fee. In those days he had a big Jacobean-style house out at Frilford – where he asked us all out to lunch – to be near the golf-course. A Nonconformist, he was no aesthete – and set store by winning some absurd prize on the golf-course at St Andrew's.

At Wadham he got his First in Greats, was President of the Oxford Union in 1896, was elected to All Souls in 1897, along with Leo Amery. Again there could not be a sharper contrast than between those two mates. Though Wadham was a small college, Simon was one of a group of promising men. Outstanding was F.E. Smith, to become Lord Birkenhead, 'Galloper Smith', of Chesterton's devastating poem, Tory Secretary of State for India, and Lord Chancellor. Rivals at the Bar and on opposite sides in politics, Simon and he retained friendly enough relations. F.E., an insolent character, would come into our buttery, where he did not belong, order himself a beaker of All Souls ale, and have it put down to Simon. F.E. was wildly extravagant; I don't think Simon was mean about money. Another of the group was the Liberal economist, F.W. Hirst, who later became an arrant advocate of Appeasement.

A Liberal of the promising days of 1906 (they thought that the future was with Liberalism!), Simon got a long lead of F.E. Smith. Solicitor General in 1910, Attorney General in 1913, he was offered the Lord Chancellorship in 1915, which would have skied him in the Lords. Evidently Asquith did not think that he was Prime Ministerial timber; Simon thought otherwise, and accepted the Home Office, to remain in the Commons. At the outbreak of war in 1914 he at first favoured remaining neutral – as if Britain could, against the menace of Germany! This showed that he had no real grasp of European realities, and – 'coming events cast their shadows before' – indicates why he made such an ineffective Foreign Secretary when Germany started on her second attempt, under the popular leadership of Hitler.

Then in 1916 Simon made a crucial mistake: he resigned

from the Liberal government over conscription, when it was absolutely necessary if the war was to be won. It was already belated, and its absence imposed far too heavy a strain upon France. Henceforward he was out of office for fifteen years, in the prime of his life. Stafford Cripps commented to me that Simon, having once lost his footing on the ladder, was not going to make that mistake again.

In 1926, at the time of the Trade Unions' futile General Strike, he made a most influential speech in Parliament arguing its illegality. This may well have been correct on legal grounds, but to Labour people it was obvious politically that he was working his passage towards the Tories. He got his reward in 1931, when both the Tory and Liberal Parties ganged up against the Labour movement to form a 'National' government, which retained an immense majority throughout the Thirties. It could have done anything necessary to defend the country's interests; it could have led the country to take the necessary action; it could have alerted the bemused and easy-going British as to Hitler's aims. They were obvious enough, all set out in *Mein Kampf.*

In 1931 Simon formed the 'National Liberal' section of the former Liberal Party, now divided, to co-operate with the Conservative Party, really dominant in British politics from the fall of Asquith's government in 1916. Simon's reward was, at last, to reach office again as Foreign Secretary, the office for which he was least fitted. A good classic, he knew no modern languages, he knew no modern history: it would have alerted him as to Germany's record, though it should not have been necessary after the experience of 1914–18. He did not know Europe; he had had no training in foreign affairs. He might have accepted, reasonably, the Home Office, which he had left in 1916.

Simon is not to be blamed for the feebleness of Britain's reaction to the Japanese invasion of Manchuria, and the beginning of Japan's career of aggression against China and the Far East. The United States was shut up in its hopeless Isolationism, which left Britain exposed. As Simon observed to me, the United States would take no action. That ended the matter: Britain could not move on her own in the Far East.

Europe and the Mediterranean were another matter, nearer home. Mussolini's aims were obvious enough, and at the Stresa Conference in 1935 the ageing MacDonald and the agile Simon could have clarified them. In fact, no mention was made of them, and Mussolini assumed that he had the green light to go forward with his war of aggression on Abyssinia.

This led to an explosion of sentiment in Britain. This was partly a genuine reaction at the breach of the peace and of the post-war settlement in Europe; partly an outburst of sentimental idealism, out of keeping with the facts of life, politically speaking. What was odd was that this was joined by the far from idealistic opinion of *The Times*. Geoffrey Dawson, its powerful editor, was one of Milner's Kindergarten and had served his apprenticeship in South Africa. At All Souls one day I dared to say to him, 'Can't you let up on your attacks on Italy? It is not Italy, but Germany that is the danger – far more powerful.' Dawson replied, 'If that is the case – mind you, I am not accepting your argument – but if Germany is so powerful, oughtn't we to throw in our lot with her?'

I found the obtuseness of this stupefying. He had no idea that the guiding principle of British policy through the centuries, the sheet-anchor of Britain's security, was to form a Grand Alliance with other nations threatened by any dominating aggressor – the Spain of Philip II, the France of Louis XIV and Napoleon, the Germany of the Kaiser. This was the only way of dealing with Hitler's Germany. In the absence of the United States as counter-weight, it meant coming to terms with Russia. The British governing class would not accept the necessity, even to save their country from Hitler – though Churchill grasped the life-line at once, when Hitler attacked Russia in 1941.

Why would they not see this? The Foreign Office understood it, and is not to be blamed for the confusion and collusion that brought the country face to face with a

Germany more powerful than in 1914 – by 1940 in control of most of Europe. This was the result of making concession after concession to Hitler. Anyone who had read *Mein Kampf* would know that any concession would only be made the basis for a further demand. I wrote at the time that no concession whatever should be made to Hitler's Germany – only a Grand Alliance, as in earlier centuries, and as in 1914, would have any effect.

In the case of Mussolini's Italy the British governing class was confused. It did not want to see Mussolini making an empire in East Africa, on the borders of Egypt and the Sudan and the sea-route (crucial in those days) to India. On the other hand, it did not want to see Mussolini fall and Italy topple over into Communism. This was their logic throughout the Thirties, and exposed them to the blackmail of both Mussolini and Hitler, who went on happily bidding them up to the end.

What policy could they have pursued towards Mussolini, in the circumstances?

A policy of *Realpolitik* would have aimed at keeping him in the ring against Hitler's Germany. This would have meant coming to an agreement with Mussolini over Abyssinia – some compromise, perhaps a condominium or a partition of spheres might have been arrived at. Alternatively, a decided push might have toppled him over, and a democratic Italy would have allied with us as in the 1914–18 war. That would have been the better course – and have avoided the terrible sequel.

The 'National' government did neither, and fumbled the issue. Why? The simple answer was given by Simon himself – a complete give-away – at All Souls. Sir Reginald Coupland asked him why a ship couldn't be sunk in the Suez Canal? It was then under British control, and a ship even temporarily blocking the Canal would have stopped Italian reinforcements to Abyssinia.

Simon replied, we couldn't do that. 'It would mean that Mussolini would fall.' There was the clue. The British governing class followed their class-interest, against the interests of their country.

The consequences were disastrous. The half-hearted and ineffective propaganda campaign against Italy alienated Mussolini and threw him into the arms of Hitler. His intelligent, earlier mistress, Margarita Sarfatti, told me that he did not like Germany or Hitler, – probably truly: he had been strongly pro-Ally in 1914–18.

Hitler drew his conclusions from the ineffectiveness of Britain and France – that he could go ahead with impunity, and did. Hence the militarisation of the Rhineland, and the deliberate breaches of the Peace settlement. So long as Italy remained with the West, keeping a watch on the Brenner, Hitler would not have been able to proceed with the annexation of Austria. Now he could, and did, assuring Mussolini with heartfelt gratitude, 'I will never forget you for this.'

He kept his word: the two international gangsters remained true to each other to the end. The Berlin–Rome Axis was formed; the Spanish Republic overthrown; the annexation of Austria turned the flank of Czecho-Slovakia; the way readied for Germany's renewal of war in far more favourable conditions than in 1914. Germany owed that to the Führer and – as David Cecil used to say to me – to the ineptitude of the opponents he had to deal with. Hitler himself expressed his contempt at their inferiority.

There were those in the Foreign Office who foresaw the malign course of events. Wigram foresaw it with absolute clarity, and secretly informed Churchill of the mistakes until, worn out by it all, he was struck down and died. Vansittart understood Germany and Hitler, and what to expect completely – and was disconsidered and maligned for being right. The fatuous *New Statesman* crowd coined the concept 'Vansittartism' to justify their pro-German sentimentalism; that paper was the only one, along with *The Times*, to advocate the break-up of Czecho-Slovakia even before Munich. When the consequences came home to them all in 1939, Cadogan – with whom the ineffable Chamberlain replaced Vansittart – admitted in his diary: 'It has all come about as Van said it would, *and I never believed it.*' There is no point in further argument: it settles the matter.

Simon himself told me that he often had to defend

Vansittart in Cabinet. Think of it! – having to defend the correct insights of a real authority (and first-class brain) against the fumbling, complacent second-raters of the 'National' government. In 1935 Simon left the Foreign Office for the Home Office once more, where he was certainly much more at home. Everybody recognised that he had no 'feel' for foreign affairs. When he asked plaintively in College what he should do, Sir Charles Grant Robertson – who had a good record all through this miserable decade – shouted, 'Resign!'

When Neville Chamberlain – who had resisted Rearmament as long as he could, in the interest of 'favourable' Budgets – took control in 1937 he promoted Simon to succeed him as Chancellor of the Exchequer. And he remained one of the inner gang of four who opted for appeasing Hitler more persistently than ever: Chamberlain, who believed that he could do a business deal with Hitler, Simon, Sam Hoare and Halifax.

They thought, and even went so far as to *say*, that they were 'indispensable': they could see no alternative. Even when it was all over, Hoare had the hardihood to defend, in his book, the course of concessions, conceding each one of Hitler's demands as it came up, Austria, Czecho-Slovakia, the Polish Corridor and Danzig (castrating Poland), Memel – did it never occur to them that the end of that process would be a Germany dominant in Europe, Britain at her mercy?

Sam Hoare had not made it when he sat for the Fellowship at All Souls – thank goodness we did not have that little pipsqueak to add to the other Appeasers. Neville Chamberlain, in his ignorance of Europe – Czecho-Slovakia, 'a country of which we know little' – had for intimate adviser Horace Wilson. This ignoramus was of enormous influence as *éminence grise*. It was not beyond his capacity to carpet Con O'Neil, a young Fellow of All Souls in the diplomatic service, who knew the situation in Berlin all too well, for daring to disagree with the fatuous course being followed.

Simon himself said, 'We must keep out of trouble in Central Europe *at all costs.*' The *DNB* comments mildly on this blindness, 'by the time Simon left office the aggressors were well away'. The whole balance of power pivoted on Central Europe: Hitler understood that, and meant to dominate Europe from the Centre. '*At all costs*' – the price that Britain paid for the decade of 'National' government was her defeat in 1940, when Germany overran Europe.

At that crisis, when Churchill took over with the men who had been kept out – Eden, Cranborne, Amery, Attlee, Bevin – he got rid of as many of the 'indispensables' as he could. Sam Hoare was sent off to Madrid to earn the reward for his pro-Francoism; the plausible Lothian, propagandist for Appeasement, was sent off to the Washington Embassy, where, said his friend Lionel Curtis, 'Philip died in the knowledge that he had been wrong'. What was the good of that? These men ruined their country. Simon was kicked upstairs to the Woolsack, where he could do no more damage: he was kept out of Churchill's War Cabinet, and of anything to do with the direction of the war. It was the end of his political career.

Naturally in those later years we saw more of him in the College to which he was devoted, where nobody loved him and some people took positively against him. Personally I did not, much as I disagreed with him politically. As an historian I was interested to pick up any scraps of information – such as academics, less interesting, cannot contribute. When he was first at the Home Office, a court case had to be arranged to quash the unfounded rumour that George V, as a young prince, had contracted a clandestine marriage in Malta. Queen Mary said to Simon at Balmoral, punctuating her words with her parasol, 'George has many faults, but not *that one*'. And Simon described to me the scene of the old King's death-bed at Sandringham: he was beyond speaking, but with regal courtesy nodded to each member of the Privy Council as he filed out.

Once only Simon tried to recommend Neville Chamberlain to me – as no reactionary, but a progressive in social matters, etc. I recognised that he had done good work in local government, and agreed with Churchill's estimate: 'A good Lord Mayor of Birmingham in a lean year.' But nothing on earth would recommend Neville Chamberlain to me. On another occasion Simon made a point to me about railways, where he was quite right. As against nationalisation he thought it better to retain the four main groups, with some element of competition, some incentive to keep up standards. I felt that there was justice in this observation. Halifax, as Chancellor of the University, made Simon its High Steward (as Birkenhead had been), and this gave him much pleasure: I am glad that he had that consolation prize at the end.

His first marriage had been blissfully happy, but his wife died after only four years. This was a deep source of grief: a full career of happy married life might have released some human spring – as it was, it shut him up further within himself. In the long vacant years he became a close friend of rich (brewing) Mrs Ronnie Greville (Edward VII was a closer friend). Cyril Radcliffe – one of our anti-Simon lawyers – used to have a story of Simon humiliatingly on his knees before the little millionairess, at her house in Charles Street, beseeching her to marry him. However, it *was* true that, at one of her grand luncheons, she indited a note to the butler, 'You are drunk. Please leave the room.' He staggered across and carefully placed it before the abstemious Simon.

Rather late in life he made a second marriage to a woman who made a song-and-dance about slavery. Douglas Wood-ruff's sister, who was her secretary, said, 'Talk about slavery – it's nothing to being secretary to Lady Simon.' Whether from over-exertion or not, the poor lady's reason gave way. (She became an alcoholic – to me incomprehensible.) One used to see Simon nobly leading her by the hand round the lawn at Encaenia parties. I suppose it was affection for the College that made him once repeat, word for word, the concluding paragraph of an essay of mine on All Souls, a kind of prose-poem, which I never reprinted.

He took it quite well when the College removed his portrait from the Hall, where it had previously hung – he made a graceful little speech on the dismissal. But John Sparrow as Warden made it up to him by having his coat-of-arms placed high (beyond a stone's throw) on one of the towers in the front quad. There they are, with their ungainly penguin supporters, and the ludicrous motto thought up for him by the Heralds' College, 'J'ai ainsi mon nom'.

He lacked the human touch, and was rather accident-prone in personal relations. There are many stories of this – one of them he told me. When young he and his wife were invited out to their first political dinner-party by Leonard Courtney, Radical MP and pro-Boer. They duly arrayed themselves, and arrived – to find that they were not expected: they were inside the house of W.L. Courtney, editor of the *Nineteenth Century*. At an Encaenia Luncheon Simon was ploughing away in halting French to a *vis-à-vis* whom he took to be the French Ambassador: it turned out to be Sir Frederic Kenyon, head of the British Museum.

One Christmas, at an hotel in Switzerland, he thought to imbue his family with the Christmas spirit. He dressed up in a tall clown's hat to visit them in their bedroom, threw open the door with a 'Peek-aboo', to the surprise of an unknown couple in bed: he had got the right number, but was on the wrong floor. When someone asked tactlessly if the story was true, his reaction was characteristically the wrong one: 'Do you mean to insult me?'

He certainly tried hard to be a good fellow – to most people it comes easily. In early days in College one finds him frequently in the Betting Book, usually winning. His first bet, in May 1898, with Amery – that Balliol would not go Head of the River – Simon won. He lost to H.W.C. Davis, who bet that the 'explorer' of unknown North Australia, Rougemont, would prove to be an imposter: the historian's judgment was better. In 1903 he lost over two by-elections, where his Liberalism made him too optimistic. He won two bets over the Fashoda incident in 1898, lost one over a Sydney Smith quotation to a fellow lawyer (and country gent) Wilbraham, but won against the excellent Latinist, Malcolm, over a quotation from Horace.

Henceforth he won all his bets. One was against Raymond Asquith, that Haldane would not be Lord Chancellor before Reid. Asquith's father was not yet Prime Minister, and the

son had no inner knowledge. He also had a rather disillusioned view of politics:

> He loathed affairs, he hated the State:
> He wrapped his lunch in Livy;
> He threw the Great Seal into the grate,
> And the Privy Seal into the privy.

Simon won his bet against Cunliffe over the surrender of
Port Arthur, and against young Douglas Radcliffe over
Home Rule. This Radcliffe was killed by the Germans, as
were Raymond Asquith, Cunliffe, Shaw-Stewart and Anderson among the Junior Fellows. Barrington-Ward avoided
service and was discountenanced in consequence.

In 1914 Sir William Anson, Warden since 1881, who was
venerated as almost a second Founder, died, leaving Grant
Robertson, who had served the College handsomely, as his
favourite to succeed him. It was said that Simon, as Sub-
Warden, ran him too hard, on Party lines. The College
thought otherwise, and elected a harmless candidate, a
combination of lawyer and classic whom Oman described as
a 'Returned Empty'.

A worse fate befell me as Sub-Warden, with two dying
Wardens on my hands in succession, Sumner and then
Hubert Henderson; having to administer the College with
no authority, and with a hippyish lot of junior Fellows
returned from the second German war. Isaiah Berlin termed
them the 'Sans Culottes'. The senior College officers wanted
me to take on the Wardenship; privately, I did not want to
spend my life on committees as to who should cook, or cook
up, what. Ironically, Simon and Halifax – Appeasers both –
wanted me for Warden; when Simon saw which way the
election was going, he characteristically went over to the
majority. I was really rather grateful that, in those awkward
circumstances, Simon as Senior Fellow should have taken
the conduct of the election out of my hands. Henderson was
fatally ill, and never came into residence; the College made a
mistake, as I had realised, in electing him. I had wanted Eric
Beckett, of the Foreign Office and a good anti-Appeaser –

the younger generation were against. But I was surprised at the firmness with which Simon took in hand Henderson's resignation: it was inevitable – but I could not have fixed it, and was relieved that Simon took it upon himself.

Naturally I had much less contact in College with Halifax – he was there much less; but he did ask me to stay at Garrowby (I could never have got up to those moral altitudes, daily chapel and all). When I reported to him the disrepair and vandalism at Strafford's old church at Went-worth Woodhouse, he got on to it at once – Yorkshire patriotism – I think he was President of the large Yorkshire Association. My old Headmaster at St Austell went thence to start a new school at Hemsworth, in what had been a mansion of Halifax's family – again he was kind enough to present the prizes at their School Prize-giving when I asked him.

His father was a connoisseur of ghost-stories and published two collections of them. So was the son, who followed his father in everything – never can there have been a closer father-son relationship. My ghost-story, 'All Souls' Night', was a favourite with Halifax – perhaps from the title, though it had nothing to do with the College. It was about Wardour Castle in Wiltshire, where I had stayed with the last Lord Arundell of Wardour. (He was in a prison-camp in Germany the whole of the war, and died the week of his repatriation.)

Halifax said that he regarded the College as 'a second home for more than fifty years'; but we never saw so much of him as of Simon. This was partly due to his service taking him abroad, as Viceroy of India 1925–31, and Ambassador in Washington 1941–6. Much more it was due to his love for Yorkshire and what he liked best – riding to hounds there.

It was surprising that he should have had such a good seat, for he was immensely tall – about 6 foot 4 inches – which made it a question to provide a bed long enough for his comfort. Secondly, he had an atrophied left arm. He was very stoical about that, and would say bravely that its chief inconvenience was in lighting a cigarette while holding a coffee cup. I wonder whether it had not some deeper psychological effect? – certainly the Kaiser's withered arm had. And wasn't Halifax's extreme religiosity – Anglo-Catholic sacramentalism was the centre of his life – a defect rather than an advantage, in politics? Lord Hugh Cecil would say, in the absurd terms common to both, that 'Edward has no sense of Original Sin'.

This meant that he had no idea how evil human beings could be – a Calvinist would have known better. It was a disadvantage for a Christian gentleman in dealing with gangsters in politics: Bill Astor reproached me, à propos of my *All Souls and Appeasement*, with overlooking that his father and Philip Lothian were Christian gentlemen committed to peace. Waldorf Astor and Lothian were both Christian Scientists, so I suppose crude matter was not 'real' to them. It is obvious that giving way to peace-breakers is no way to ensure peace.

After his visit to Hitler Halifax said, 'He struck me as very sincere.' Of course he was sincere: the real point was, what was he sincere about? He meant Germany to be on top in Europe – he was sincere about that, as anyone could have seen from reading *Mein Kampf*. But the Foreign Secretary of Great Britain had never bothered to read the work until, it is said, lent it by the present Queen Mother.

There is another, more general, defect I diagnose among these representatives of a declining governing class in the last days of Britain's historic greatness – that is their superciliousness. They should not have been so superior about the lower-class types they had to deal with on the international scene – such people may well be abler as well as more unscrupulous. Halifax said of Goering, that he might have been 'the head-gamekeeper at Chatsworth'. He was a criminal thug, largely responsible for the murders of July 1934 – of colleagues as well as opponents. But at Nüremberg he turned the flank of the American prosecutor so effectively, attacking the American record over the Indians, slavery, the Civil War, etc., that it took the British Attorney-General, Maxwell Fyffe, to put him in his place. If I may put in a good word for Harold Nicolson – when he was interrupted by an American woman, one of those would-be do-gooders going on about the British treatment of Indians, he asked sweetly, 'Do you mean our treatment of our Indians, or your treatment of your Indians?'

The *DNB* says of Halifax's discussions with the Nazi leaders, 'The squire of Garrowby could well discern their social inadequacies: the Christian failed to detect their wickedness. . . . Halifax believed that the Nazis were reasonable men whose ambitions could be modified by patient and persuasive discussion.' Fatal ignorance of what men are like and are capable of! When we asked him at All Souls what Molotov was like, he replied, 'Rather like a buttoned-up secondary school-master.' No doubt that was what he *looked* like, but he was also (a) a man of great ability and will-power, and (b) what Ernest Bevin, who understood such people, always regarded him as being – a murderer.

Even with Stalin, after the war, the watchword was appeasement. Halifax disapproved of Churchill's Fulton speech, warning the West – especially the United States, which needed it then – against Stalin's intentions (witness Poland, Romania, Czecho-Slovakia, Hungary) – and wanted Churchill to moderate his warning. Churchill's comment, even more forceful in his accent, was '*Grovel, grovel, grovel*, first to the Indians, then to the Germans, now to the Russians – nothing but *grovel*.' He has an amusing phrase somewhere about Halifax being loaded with honours and decorated with every integument of state, and then gaily awarded him, somewhat superfluously, an OM. Halifax described this to me, I think genuinely, as 'absurd', but accepted it.

Apart from his physical and religious handicaps he started with every conceivable advantage – everything was his for the asking. At Eton he was bored by the cult of the classics, and took to history instead. It seems that he was easily bored: later he found work at the Board of Education and at the Ministry of Agriculture both boring. At Christ Church he read hard, got a First in the History School and was one of the few from that background to win in 1903 a Prize

Fellowship at All Souls. His mate was H.H.E. Craster, to become Bodley's Librarian, who later edited Halifax's speeches for him.

As a young bachelor living in College he fell easily into its ways, hunting regularly twice a week, sometimes with the Chaplain, Arthur Johnson of the silvery voice and disagreeable manners. (I did not like him, though it appealed to me – when he found me, ill in hospital, reading Renan's *Souvenirs d'Enfance et de Jeunesse* – that the old man had heard Renan lecture in Oxford.) The young Fellow paid for his hunting expenses by taking three pupils – one of them Neil Primrose, Lord Rosebery's son, who 'not infrequently lapsed into dreamless slumber while I discoursed'. Typically, his only recorded bet was a riding one, that Maurice Gwyer would be thrown from his hireling horse next day: this Wood lost. He recorded a scrap of conversation at dinner. 'Last night I was narrating the story of the fox on the roof and saying that he had probably known his way about the farmyard for some time, when one of them nips me with "You would infer then, Wood, that he had been accustomed to browse on Chanticleer."' This left him speechless. I recognise the idiom: that would have been Edgeworth, the economist, who talked just like that.

The piece of research he undertook is represented by his biography of Keble, his only book, for he had no aptitude for writing. Nor did he have much response to poetry or natural scenery. Newman described poetry as 'the refuge of them that have not the Church': Halifax, under his father's aegis – a national figure as President of the English Church Union and lay head of the Anglo-Catholics – had religion, not poetry.

Next came a world tour. In South Africa he met several of Milner's Kindergarten, including Dougie Malcolm. Dougie introduced him to Lady Dorothy Onslow in the refreshment room on Berwick-on-Tweed station, when they were all on their way to some grand Scotch ball. There followed a happy marriage, then Member of Parliament for a Yorkshire seat, unopposed. In spite of his disability he served for a time in France, with the Yorkshire Yeomanry, before being recalled.

Everything went well with him until he came up against Hitler.

It must be emphasised that he had courage; indeed, it was said that he was without nerves – he was a cool, passionless, unemotional man. The reason for his failure in dealing with Hitler and the Nazis, or even understanding them, was his instinctive belief in compromise, in moderation and persuasion.

This had worked, up to a point, with Gandhi in India – which makes Halifax's term as Viceroy the brightest spot in his career. Those two understood each other; both were religious, both were gentlemen, and each a *rusé* politician. Halifax was not an obstinate man, like Chamberlain – merely mistaken. Halifax reached an agreement with Gandhi, after interminable discussions with the prophet. When someone asked whether Gandhi was not tiresome (which he was), the Viceroy replied, 'Some people found Our Lord tiresome.'

I remember only one All Souls story from that time. He said that he had suffered only two sleepless nights in his life; one when uncertain whether to pardon an Indian terrorist condemned to death, the other when Simon asked him to call him 'Jack'.

One of Simon's best efforts was the prolonged work he put into the Indian Statutory Commission from 1927 onwards. For this he gave up all his lucrative work at the Bar, and devoted his powers of assimilating information, assembling and analysing it, as the basis for further devolution of powers and constitutional progress towards dominion status. The good work was rendered nugatory by the failure to include Indians on the Commission. This mistake was owing to Birkenhead, who as Secretary of State, was sold to the Indian Princes. It led in the end to a breach between Halifax and Birkenhead. Nothing that Halifax could do – and he tried hard enough – stopped the idiot communal hatred between Hindus and Moslems. It has become far worse and more murderous since the British left India to its own vices. Humans in the mass *are* idiots. The only worthwhile result of the Simon Commission was the education it provided Attlee in Indian affairs. When his time came, he recognised the sad necessity of Partition between an India and a Pakistan. The disagreeable task of working out the details and drawing an impossible border line fell to another All Souls lawyer, Cyril Radcliffe. The mutual murders now continue on a larger scale.

Perhaps this is the place to note the contribution that All Souls men have made to India historically, from Bishop Heber of Calcutta, who died young there, onwards. Three Viceroys: Curzon the most notable of them; then Chelmsford of the Montague–Chelmsford Reforms; then, nearing the end, Halifax. F.W. Bain lived his life there, wrote up its folklore and legends in many books, and returned a poor man. Sir Maurice Gwyer went out as Chief Justice and, requested to reform the university of Delhi, spent his best years as its Vice-Chancellor. Sir Reginald Coupland served on the Cripps Commission, and devoted several books to Indian subjects. Lionel Curtis invented 'Dyarchy', the devolution of powers to Indians in the provinces while maintaining control at the centre – a transitional phase. On the takeover of power, Sir Penderel Moon became Nehru's righthand man in economic affairs. The first President of India, Radhakrishnan, was for several years a Fellow of All Souls. I recall his shutting himself up for a four-day fast on Gandhi's assassination by his fellow Indians. The British had merely awarded him occasional, comfortable detention – evidently safer for him.

Arthur Salter wanted me to write up this promising subject, All Souls and India, after my *All Souls and Appeasement*. I told him briskly that he could ask his chosen Warden Sparrow to write it.

Halifax is to be blamed for coming to Chamberlain's help when the old man got rid of Eden in 1937 in order to conduct his own foreign policy unhampered. Eric Beckett said to me, 'It is not Eden, but the Foreign Office that has been defeated.' Chamberlain had used Mussolini's emissary, Grandi, to counter the arguments of Britain's Foreign Secretary, and rejected President Roosevelt's proposal of a Conference at which the dictators might be confronted. The suggestion should at least have been taken up, the possibility of getting the United States into the case not neglected. Halifax's accession positively strengthened the infatuated old man and gave him a free hand.

Halifax did not accompany Chamberlain to Munich, but he thoroughly agreed with what was done there. Britain's Foreign Secretary made the public statement, 'Herr Hitler has had a great triumph, and I for one would grudge him nothing of a triumph which he knows to be accorded, not only for what he has gained, but also for the contribution which he made to a settlement through agreement.' The 'agreement' was of course utterly empty. Churchill stated the truth when he said that it was the greatest diplomatic defeat in Britain's history, at any rate since the loss of the American colonies.

Chamberlain preferred 'to trust Herr Hitler's word', rather than the democratic President of Czecho-Slovakia; and, 'he has given his promise to me' – the scrap of paper he had signed with Chamberlain abnegating the use of force. Hitler was, among other things, a good mimic and gave his entourage comic imitations of the old man he meant to cheat – Adam von Trott told me that Hitler's polite word for Chamberlain was the 'arse-hole'.

After Munich Halifax did give him the advice that he should broaden his government and make it truly 'national' – bringing in Churchill, the only step that would give Hitler pause. Subsequently people have defended Munich on the ground that it 'gave us time'. We now know (a) that the German Army was not ready, and made a poor show when taking over Czecho-Slovakia; (b) the Germans made far more use of the interval in preparing for war than Britain did.

Halifax himself had been at the War Office in 1935, when Hitler began operations with the Remilitarisation of the Rhineland. Geoffrey Dawson on this: 'What has it got to do with us? It is his own back-door' (sic). The slick phrase had come from the plausible Lothian. The DNB comments that Halifax's brief time at the War Office 'revealed to him the paucity of our defences, but did not impress him with an urgent need for rearmament'. There was then yet time to stop Hitler in his tracks, and avoid what Churchill always called 'the unnecessary war'. The clue to this was – as was eventually proved – an understanding with Russia.

A friend of these people at All Souls, Lord Brand – brother-in-law of Waldorf Astor – understood the case and condemned them.

> Baldwin, Dawson and Halifax all had this in common, they were all English country gentlemen, all good Public School men and all good Churchmen. They seldom visited Europe, or knew what Europeans were like. None of them could have the slightest conception of the enormity of Hitler. [They should have listened to those who had – Vansittart, for instance, or their own Military Attaché in Berlin, Mason Macfarlane, who gave them accurate information, of which they took no notice.] Their whole upbringing conspired against understanding that such people exist, and that the Nazi State was a lunatic State.

They understood well enough the truth about Stalin – why wouldn't they hear the truth about Hitler? The answer is simple: *they did not want to.*

The historian is impelled to the sad conclusion of a foremost statesman of the 17th century, Oxenstierna: 'Do you not know with how little wisdom the world is governed?' I am also impelled to think that these men were second-rate intellectually, certainly wanting in imagination and knowledge of what men are really like. Bob Brand – that ice-cold intellect – was very far from second-rate.

Sent off to Washington, Halifax got a bad Press at the start: American democratic humbug objected to his daring to hunt, and in a red coat! Opinion came round as people realised how bravely he bore his personal sufferings and grief: one of his sons killed, a second brave young fellow having both legs smashed by a German bomb, which failed to explode. The Ambassador plodded on with his uncongenial work – I suspect that he never found anything so congenial as his work in Delhi. His fine figure and distin-

guished bearing fitted in well with the pomp and circum-
stance of Viceroyalty in Lutyens's vast palace – last
monument to the glorious Raj, that unique experience in
history.

In Washington Halifax assembled around him an able team
to help to win the war – some half-a-dozen All Souls men
among them. Lord Brand dealt with the crucial financial side
of things; Sir Arthur Salter did a manful job in shipping (as
he had done in the first German war); Sir Harold Butler and
Isaiah Berlin helped with the Press, John Foster on the legal
side. They made an effective team.

However, Halifax remained consistently an Appeaser even
when war was on. In May 1940, at the crisis of Britain's
existence, when Europe lay toppled over at Hitler's feet,
Halifax was in favour of a compromise peace. It would have
been fatal – it would have left Hitler in possession, and
meant that he had won. This is the worst blot on the record
of the Christian gentleman who did not believe in Original
Sin.

It has been suggested to me that I have been insufficiently
critical of Halifax's record at the Foreign Office, particularly
in regard to Germany and Hitler. I dare say that that is so,
and that the case is stronger than I have dared to say. For it
now transpires that Halifax and Chamberlain were in favour
of a compromise peace with Hitler, even when we were
already at war, as late as May 1940. Churchill had just come
to power, with the backing of the Labour Movement, to
save the country when it was in the gravest peril: all had
been thrown away during eight years of Tory rule and it
might have given in to Hitler. For that is what a compromise
peace would have meant: Hitler's Germany on top in
Europe.

It appears that at that fearful moment when France had
fallen, the Netherlands and Scandinavia been overrun, the
Foreign Office was prepared to make an offer of accommo-
dation, through Mussolini, with Gibraltar, Malta, Suez as
pawns, i.e. giving up the Mediterranean. Churchill had come
in only just in time: when this defeatist proposal came up, it
was turned down by the narrow majority of only one vote.

Churchill, and the two Labour men, Attlee and Greenwood, against Chamberlain and Halifax.

What *did* they think they were doing?

Of course it was the logical end of their policy right along: the betrayal of their country, selling out its interests and its future to the enemy.

An historian cannot but conclude that the whole conduct of Britain's interests, its very security, was betrayed in the nerveless hands and confused minds of these people in control between the two German wars. An historian, looking back over the astonishing achievement of the small island power, from the Elizabethan to the end of the Victorian age, cannot but feel that its governing class – once tough and *vorsichtig* in its defence of the country's interests – had lost its touch. The touch of Elizabeth I and the Cecils, of Cromwell and the Pitts, of Nelson and Wellington, of the great Lord Salisbury (another Cecil) at the turn into this deplorable century. That is to say, except for the heroic years of Churchill, 1940 to 1945, when Britain's arc of achievement as a great power went out in flames.

When Churchill was gone from the scene the nervelessness came to the fore again. No doubt the time had come to hand over in India, though strategically it left a dangerous vacuum for the United States (so anxious to see us out) to fill – and, while we were in India, the Russians were not in Afghanistan. Then came the hurried scuttle from Africa . . .

The objective, historical case against Germany – even apart from Hitler – is that her recessive, barbaric recourse to military aggression and war in this century *speeded up the processes of history*. No doubt colonialism would have tapered off, however, but for Germany's two wars, we should have had more time to develop services in Africa – educational, medical, civil, governmental – which would have given the black states a better chance when they came, more slowly and gradually, to take over. No doubt nuclear fission would have been discovered before the end of our hideous century, but we should have had more time.

In Britain the decline continued needlessly in the fiasco over Suez, which advertised it to the world. Never was the failure of touch in what was the governing class, its instruments the Conservative Party and Whitehall, made more disgracefully evident. The Foreign Office should have thought out a coherent policy towards Egypt: it is now known that an agreement could have been reached over Suez with Nasser. It should have been reached.

Britain could have entered Europe on its own terms after the war. So far from that, the Foreign Office not only missed the chance and left France – France, after the experience of 1940–5! – to take the lead, but positively obstructed the achievement of a European community. So that when Britain was eventually allowed in, after several supplications, it was humiliatingly on *their* terms.

Even in internal affairs the touch had gone. In an already over-populated small island it was deeply irresponsible to allow unrestricted immigration for so long. An Under-Secretary for Colonial Affairs at that time (who happened to be a Fellow of All Souls, and certainly no racist) sent a memorandum to Macmillan's Cabinet each year urging that, if no measure of control was taken, it would mount up in time to an almighty problem. There was no forethought, no foresight; no notice was taken – and we are left with a permanent (and quite unnecessary) problem, as those responsible now for public order in our cities know all too well.

Even in dealing with the Trade Unions – so essential to the economic well-being of the country – we now learn that there was in those earlier years a good opportunity of introducing the secret ballot before strikes, with the good will of the Unions. Vetoed by Walter Monkton! (friend of the Duke of Windsor – another symptomatic figure of historic decline).

It has been left to a woman, but one with a Churchillian touch, Margaret Thatcher, to curb the Trade Unions for the good of the whole society. It is evident to an historian, if not to many people, that she thinks ahead in the long-term interests of the country. Now all too late.

Sir Harold Acton:
Citizen of the World

How happy I am that both Harold and I are alive to enable me to pay tribute to him on his eightieth birthday! It makes me a little sad, too, to remember those far-off days when we inhabited neighbouring staircases at Christ Church, when our lives and all that would happen in them were before us, when all was promise and hope. We lived in Meadow Buildings, with their outlook on the marshy, cow-strewn spaces of Christ Church Meadows – which Alphonse Daudet took one look at and declared, 'C'est le rheumatisme vert.' Harold's sitting room on Staircase V was a high, rather sunless room with its own stark balcony. Mine on Staircase VI was more modest but, a floor higher up, had a better view.

How many of us in that undergraduate generation have stuck to our last and accomplished anything? Where are ——and —— who spoke so ardently at the Union, for whom everybody foretold careers in politics? Where are —— and —— who were so much to the fore in undergraduate papers, the *Cherwell* and the *Isis*? Not to mention *Oxford Poetry*, which Harold edited, *Oxford Outlook*, or *The New Oxford*.

It does one more good to remember those who held on and did fulfil their promise: David Cecil certainly; Evelyn Waugh and Graham Greene, after uncertain beginnings; Cyril Connolly, Peter Quennell and John Betjeman. Richard Pares, among those friends, was struck down early, but not before he had shown himself the best of our 18th-century historians. Robert Byron was a sad loss from the war, but Evans-Pritchard fulfilled himself as anthropologist, Anthony Powell as novelist, even Graham Pollard as bibliographer – and Sir Harold Acton has richly fulfilled his genius, an exotic bird of brilliant plumage in our grey domestic aviary.

In those days he was to the fore as a poet; he was our leader, virtually the uncrowned king of Oxford writing – or perhaps crowned, for he certainly carried a nimbus along with his inseparable umbrella. That umbrella! – I shall never forget it: a very useful implement for brandishing at Hearties. In those days there was a war between Hearties and Aesthetes, of whom Harold was the most conspicuous and challenging specimen.

The tale went that there was a confrontation on neutral ground, Worcester College, where a team of rugger-men awaited a bevy of Aesthetes, led in by Harold, smiling and saying, in his inimitable Italian accent: '*They* are so in-no-cent, and *we* are so de-ca-dent.' That conquered them.

Apart from his natural distinction Harold had that of publishing *books* when still an undergraduate. This was a matter for envy when we looked in at Blackwell's shop-window to see the multi-coloured binding of his first volume of poems, *Aquarium*. Harold tells me that his Muse deserted him, when paradoxically it never has this historian: I have kept writing poetry all my life with one hand, almost secretly, while writing history with the other.

Harold used to welcome my early, ingenuous ventures in verse, and publish them in the kindness of his heart – his own then so well-publicised and, as I thought, so outrageously sophisticated. It was on that modest literary footing that I occasionally penetrated Harold's rooms – to be astonished at the Victoriana, the waxed fruit, the glass domes, perhaps even antimacassars.

I was not sure, from my proletarian background, that such sophistication, membership of the Hypocrites Club and what *that* meant, was not rather wicked. There was I, wasting my time on Labour politics, actually marching up and down St Aldate's, a sandwich-board man saying 'Vote for (Kenneth)

Lindsay' – feeling rather a fool. Meanwhile, Harold was spending his time more sensibly, going to Spain with the cultivated Beazleys.

Why then, austere Leftist as I was, did I give him the benefit of the doubt? – Because he was the best-natured man in the world. He had a golden nature, serene and unperturbed – exceptionally so, when so many of us were perturbed about politics (what wonder?) – happy in himself and the source of amusement in others. If I had to cap him with a title from literature I think of Goldsmith's *The Good-Natured Man*.

Shortly after taking our Schools, I became a Fellow of All Souls, Harold, wings outspread, sailed out into the world, and our ways parted. With a result that is again enviable: Harold's experience of the world – America and China, Italy and France and all the fascinating people he has known and written about, where I have observed some of them, but from the margins: a true *Citizen of the World*. (Goldsmith again: how odd! – one can imagine no greater contrast among writers.) In all this he has kept true to his mistress – Writing; and how distinguished his accomplishment has been in various forms.

Not much of a novel reader, I cannot do justice to his novels. Sooner or later everybody comes to history. His historical books on the Bourbons and Medicis would have shocked me when young; now I suspect that Harold has the right of it, and I have come to share his distaste for modern 'progress'. As for him as autobiographer, I regard his two volumes of *Memoirs of an Aesthete* as among the most original of the century, well able to hold their own with the comparable four volumes of Osbert Sitwell.

Though he has given up the poetry of our young days, I greatly admire his prose, into which he has put the poetry of his nature: polished and elegant, beautifully turned and exquisitely phrased, humorous and smiling, so true to himself, above all urbane.

This tribute to Harold, for the Birthday Book in his honour, needs amplification and even a little excuse. He has achieved so much, and so remarkably, which we could never have guessed in those innocent days. I confess that we did not understand him, even misunderstood him. Among our generation of Evelyn Waugh and Graham Greene, Anthony Powell and John Betjeman – Harold Acton is an under-estimated writer, a more considerable one than is generally realised. There are reasons for this, which I hope now to explain.

First, there is his desertion of the literary scene at home for China: he was absent throughout practically the whole of the Thirties. It reminds me of Montherlant's desertion of Paris for Spain and North Africa – with the result that Sartre, a writer inferior to him, moved to the centre (which hap-pened to be on the Left), and captured the gullible public. China was a world of experience in which we could not follow Acton – even now we learn of his contribution to literature and scholarship in that field, without being able fully to appreciate it. However, it will come more clearly to the fore as the years go on – as China comes to the fore on the planet – as it is bound to do: one-fifth of mankind occupying the largest area under a continuous civilisation for the longest period of time.

Secondly, we did not realise how serious, and consistent, his Occidental campaign was for the arts, which he was ultimately to bring to fruition and describe in his *Memoirs of an Aesthete*. It was an aggressive campaign on all fronts: he arrived in Oxford with it already formed in his mind.

> Elsewhere the poet and the artist were widening their fields of observation, but the contents of *Oxford Poetry* were indistinguishable from those of *Georgian Poetry*. I was determined to clear the ground of linnet-infested thickets, to crush chalcedonies and chrysoprases, to devastate the descendants of Enoch Soames with mock-ery and, if need be, with violence. . . . My poems made many friends. I was prolific and none too critical, and scattered them on the Oxford breezes. I read them from my balcony to groups in Christ Church Meadow.

I recall that megaphone.

We thought this was all fun, as indeed it was. How could

we embryo-dons be expected to see the serious side, or foresee that Harold would carry forward his artistic campaign all through life, and into so many fields?

When he left the scene, his place was taken by a group much in contrast. One has only to think of the contrast in appearance with its apostle, another Christ Church man, Wystan Auden: dirty mackintosh, shabby ill-fitting clothes, tobacco-stained finger-nails. There was Harold, handsome and well-groomed ('Nature has been good to me'), well-off and well-dressed, looking, as he has said, too prosperous. And the advantages he had! – that cosmopolitan background, Florence and the United States, all that nice American money plus the beauty of La Pietra, bilingual in English and Italian.

It was altogether too much, a source of envy. Harold is the only contemporary writer of whom I am envious – along with David Cecil for the marvellous historic background *he* enjoyed. No envy of my middle-class contemporaries: compared with them this proletarian had some advantages, as D.H. Lawrence had. Harold was not merely a decade ahead of us, but a whole generation – thus we lost sight of him, vanished over the horizon.

Actually he was seven months my junior – who would have believed it? – hair already thinning above that candid forehead; born on 5 July 1904 at La Pietra (the 'milestone' – and what a milestone!), the elder son of Arthur Mario Acton, of a cadet branch of the famous family to which both the Prime Minister of Naples and the historian Lord Acton belonged. His mother, Hortense Mitchell, brought in the Chicago money, which enabled the artist father to recover the beauty of the villa, of which the son has given us the history, and to recreate the wonderful Italian garden, formal terraces and statues, from the informality of the English garden, all the rage in the later 18th century, which had taken its place. As Harold wrote to me, its beauty is architectural, as against the romantic landscape at Trenarren. He expounds one advantage of the Italian idiom, in that it retains its attraction all through the winter, when flowers and borders diminish.

What an education it already was to grow up in that

historic villa, with an artist father's collection of Italian Primitives. Some of these have recently been burgled, such is the deplorable society we have survived into. And think of the cultural vistas of the city below, Duomo and churches, palaces and villas and galleries, the art collections! He grew up with the sense of the Medici he was later to write about; their presence still everywhere, the boy familiar with their pictures, portraits, sculpted busts.

Though all this was there for the taking, food for the imagination, he was evidently not spoiled. In the background was discipline, a touch of paternal strictness in the family; Harold grew up essentially controlled, a disciplined mind, for all the luxuriance of his temperament, the hedonism of an aesthete. The malice-tipped pen of Evelyn Waugh noted that Harold, even after his return from the war in the Far East,

> lives a life of great severity. His parents will not permit his going out when they have guests or his staying at home when they are alone, so half his time is spent in being polite to aged American marquesas. . . . He will treat me like an aged American marquesa, bows me in and out of doors, holds umbrellas over my head and pays me extravagant compliments. But he knows everything about ART.

He has always had good, rather elaborate manners – Evelyn not; however he goes on to admit, 'La Pietra really is very fine. Much more than I ever expected.' Later, 'La Pietra is grand but very uncomfortable. . . . I had a bedroom as big as the throne room at the Vatican and not unlike it. Light switches indistinguishable from bells concealed behind tapestries. Whenever I woke in the night to take my poison I rang by mistake and troupes of servants of all ages and sexes charged in crying "Il bagno adesso?"'

Eton followed, with the companionship and stimulus of some of the cleverest boys in England, a few of whom I was to come to know later. David Cecil introduced Harold to Donne. Eddie Sackville-West could play Debussy (I don't suppose he had been heard of in Cornwall, except by the

Cathedral organist, Guillaume Ormond, Sargent's nephew). Harold did not much care for Connolly – too vulgar – nor would the bleak and squalid Eric Blair (George Orwell) be his cup of tea, any more than mine. He made a salutary sensation with the *Eton Candle*, devoted to the arts, produced along with the talented Brian Howard, who was to waste his talents. Him I encountered only once when, crossing Canterbury Quad, those long, outrageous eye-lashes gave me an appraising leer. Aldous Huxley was a beak for a bit – and had an influence on Acton's novels: Mrs Mascot in *Peonies and Ponies* is pure Huxley.

At Oxford he came into his own, became a public figure and made literary history. Where I went so far as to invite Robert Graves from Islip to address the Christ Church Essay Club, Harold invited Gertrude Stein over from Paris, accompanied by Alice B. Toklas and a bevy of Sitwells. That was an event, a University occasion. He hired an extra-large room, which was packed. The large, squat sybil, looking like an Aztec idol, had no difficulty in putting down the clever boys, like David Cecil, who thought to embarrass her with their questions.

> I had started sweeping away *fin-de-siècle* cobwebs with a paper called *The Oxford Broom* . . . *Aquarium*, my first volume of poems, was published during my second term, and its red, black and yellow striped cover met me everywhere like a challenge. For a book of poems it had a prompt success. Since I was free from false modesty, as from everything false, and possessed a resonant voice, I never faltered when I was asked to read them, but shouted them lustily down a megaphone. Nor would I tolerate interruptions. The megaphone could also be brandished as a weapon.

He got that from Edith Sitwell, another influence.

What we took to be frivolity was already a mature confidence; he knew his aims and intentions. We were not yet sure, except for someone like Peter Quennell, a schoolboy genius who had already published a volume of poems, and was beyond Oxford undergraduate life.

> He had come up to Balliol too late. He should have come up at the age of twelve or thirteen. By now he was pining for the *vie de Bohème*, the Café Royal . . . A new school of poetry was in gestation, and I boldly undertook to be its local midwife. I was aware, however, that Peter Quennell's poems excelled mine as did his critical acumen.

Together they edited a volume of *Oxford Poetry*; 'but so lofty were his standards that I feared *Oxford Poetry* would ultimately be limited to a poem or two by himself. I had to reject many poems that appealed to me personally, including a few by Day Lewis.' Peter just froze them out – however, my modest poems got through the mesh. Eventually, he froze himself out, as a poet, into silence – such critical self-consciousness is bad for a poet. Harold was more catholic, enthusiastic and generous, perhaps the American element freed him.

The Oxford chapters of the *Memoirs* give one a more truthful picture than *Brideshead Revisited* – as I heard François Mauriac sum up, Waugh was essentially a *fantaisiste*. He appears in the *Memoirs* – 'an almost inseparable boon companion . . . a little faun', and Harold appears recognisably in *Brideshead*. I hear his idiom at once in describing someone, 'sip-sip-sip, like an old dowager'. Waugh's 'period of medieval tutelage drew him into a circle of Chestertonian friends, to Christopher Hollis and other robust wits already steering for Rome. They assembled in his rooms for what they called "offal".' That was out of C.R. Cruttwell's comic vocabulary, to which Richard Pares proposed to compile a guide – Cruttwell being Evelyn's tutor at Hertford, whom he detested and proceeded to use his name for caricature in several books.

Pares, who was Waugh's 'dearest friend' as an undergraduate, was my dearest friend (if not in the same sense) at All Souls. So many of these clever boys, whom I knew only marginally, appear. Desmond Harmsworth Harold considered 'more innately poetical than my other contemporaries: he had the "innocent eye" which was lacking in Peter Quennell'. A man of honeyed charm, he was a gifted poet, whose poetry, Harold considered, was sacrificed on the altar of matrimony.

How many of those characters were variously gifted! One of John Sutro's inventions was the Railway Club – and what original fun it gave them. I knew Graham Pollard better, already a Communist and a learned book-collector and bibliographer; but scruffy, beery and smelly, with his red handkerchief round his neck and his not getting out of bed in the mornings. Harold has veracious portraits of them all – Robert Graves in the squalor of domestic life and all those kids at Islip; Boar's Hill in those days occupied, not by business executives, but by 'artists, musicians, writers, where they lived as on the hills of Tuscany, giving concerts, theatricals and poetry readings which I often joined – to the horror of Peter Quennell'.

Within Christ Church were the Beazleys. Harold has a vivid portrait of the exotic Marie, more sympathetic than mine: 'very black oblique eyes, a long Oriental nose and the curved lips of an archaic goddess; she wore a black and white checked skirt with a black velvet jacket.' She talked an awful lot of twaddle; no wonder Jacky took to those freezing silences and would disappear from the room. Up on St Giles's they shared the beautiful Judge's Lodgings with an enthusiastic amateur archaeologist, 'Wee Pricie'. One summer vacation they all went off to Madrid together, for the Beazleys to study the Greek vases in the Prado.

Harold gives as his recreation in *Who's Who* 'hunting – Philistines', as Osbert Sitwell used to describe his education as 'in the holidays from Eton', with more than a grain of truth. For all his taking the offensive against the Hearties, Harold was not unpopular. Christ Church was rather proud of him as an original 'character'; the Junior Common Room even asked him to design a new College tie instead of the dreary piece of black-and-white check we sported. He suggested something so arty, in which purple predominated, that we retained the old, looking more like a duster than a tie.

He intended to set the seal on his career there with an Early Victorian exhibition, for which he and Robert Byron had collected a variety of domestic ornaments and secured promises of loans. They prepared an illustrated catalogue, for which Lytton Strachey was to write the introduction. The Proctors, dull dogs of academics – who knows who they were now? – banned it without a word of explanation. Thus we missed something that would have been really educational as well as amusing.

In a lifetime at Oxford I can remember no undergraduate who made such an impact: tribute not only to an original personality but of an evident capacity for leadership.

And so 'bursting with bonhomie' and armed with complete self-confidence, he departed for the life literary, social, artistic in London and Paris, where all doors were open to him. He takes the offensive against denigration of the Twenties as frivolous and superficial, in particular citing the work of his friends, the scholarly books of Robert Byron, Quennell's literary criticism and biographies, Waugh's social satire. In fact the Twenties, as Maurice Bowra used to point out, were a time of prodigious literary creativeness. Hardy, Kipling, Yeats, Shaw, George Moore were still writing; Wells, Arnold Bennett, Maugham were in full flow; so too Belloc and Chesterton; to these were added a new generation of D.H. Lawrence, Joyce, Eliot, the Sitwells; along with all the Cambridge–Bloomsbury contingent, Forster, Strachey, Virginia Woolf.

We need not bother with the evanescent social figures of the time whom Harold knew, the Cunards, Emerald and Nancy, Lygons or Mitfords. More worthwhile were those creative in the arts, Christopher Wood and Cedric Morris, whom I did not know, though I bought their paintings when I had the money, as later Piper and Coldstream, John Aldridge, Minton, Felix Kelly. Bonhomie did not prevent Harold from speaking up for himself in the literary snake-pit. I was out of it, buried with Richard Pares in historical research. There was Connolly, all affability at luncheon parties, yet when Harold's novel *Humdrum* came out he 'proceeded to demolish it. . . . Such was the treatment I had learned to expect from literary friends.' *Humdrum*, 'my single excursion into what I imagined to be the realm of popular fiction', went rather against the grain, and is not a favourite with its author.

As for the Left poets of the Thirties, who were not only in the main intellectual current of the decade but good at publicising themselves as such, 'Poetry had fallen into the hands of hot gospellers more interested in their gospel than in the form it assumed. Auden and his followers were struggling with ideas and leaving the words to look after themselves.' We must make an exception for Louis Mac-Neice here, best craftsman of them all, but Acton scores when he observes that they wrote a great deal of prose without knowing it. How much more self-evidently is this true of the uncooked 'verse' that presents itself as such today!

I respect his independence of judgment, going his own way without making up to the popular trends of the time. Of the American writers who were attracting such publicity:

> Their biggest business was discovering America, admonishing America and pepping her up about her creative impulse. Most of them were paraphrasing Walt Whitman. John Dos Passos, Sherwood Anderson, Carl Sandburg were all contained in Walt. They were passionate yes-sayers to life, whatever they might pretend. They wallowed in the crude squalors of the mid-West or of New Jersey, the hurly-burly of Chicago or Manhattan, the drabness of Main Street, and their excitement about the vast scramble was contagious.

I once encountered the last of these, Carl Sandburg, on his own stamping-ground in Illinois, and listened to his denigration of Henry James, who 'could not make up his mind whether he was a citizen of the United States or a subject of Great Britain'. When asked how I took this flout, I replied

that Henry James would be remembered when Carl Sandburg was totally forgotten.

With Harold's own American inheritance, we may leave it
to him to ask: 'Since when has a new spirit *not* dawned in
American life? Since when had America *not* had a sense of
wealth, of confidence, and of power? Ever since I could
remember she had been conscious of these possessions.' He
must have found this constant self-concern, the continual
harping upon what America means and is, not only adolescent but positively masturbatory. 'The most voluble of them
was at that time Carl van Vechten.' Who has heard of him
today, or remembers Carl Sandburg with his voluminous
self-identification with Lincoln? (He also had a scunner
against Eliot for leaving the US.)

Acton had the independence of mind to call in question
the most conspicuous of the 'shrewd literary self-advertisers',
Hemingway. 'It was considered essential to look tough, to
simulate the cowboy, to make a cult of the hair upon your
chest. I was suspicious of this vaunted virility, and I saw just
enough of these bogus Broncho Bills to shun them.' This
was in their Paris days, but 'how little they assimilated from
their sojourn in France! They were utterly alien to France
and, had they possessed the power, they would have
destroyed the culture inherited from classical antiquity.'
Stylistically Hemingway had picked up a trick or two from
Gertrude Stein, and he 'called now and then in clumsy
homage, but he was afraid of her. Her eye saw through his
matador poses; besides she had called him yellow.' From
French literature and art, if they had understood it, they
could have learned discipline; 'whereas writers like Henry
Miller lack discipline of any kind: they work themselves up
into a delirium tremens of words.'

Nor was the young Acton taken in by Pound,

> the flamboyant mandarin of Montparnasse and Rapallo,
> bursting with bumptious magniloquence. . . . Pound
> was like his name: he pounded on the table and thumped
> on his chest. He simply had to have something to shout
> about, never mind what. Much of Pound's own verse

was stilted unsayable jargon and he had shouted it to
deaf ears. Then he took a tip from Mussolini: he would
shout about Fascism.

Sacred cows from the homeland were not immune from
Acton's shafts, though encountered in faraway China. There
arrived from Cambridge the pedantic Empson (*Seven Types
of Ambiguity* a sacred text), to teach the Chinese Basic
English: that Cambridge nostrum, 'the beauty of which he
descanted on with a fervid eloquence incompatible with his
doctrine. He told me that the Basic version of the Gospel
according to St Mark was one of the incontestable master-
pieces of English literature. His own poetry must have
welled from within, for I noticed that he hardly glanced at
his surroundings.' It is the business of the historian to record
the sillinesses of *littérateurs* no less than of politicians.

Acton was no more taken in by the politicians of the time,
and their vaunted professions, than by the pedantic professors of literature, and from his vantage-point of La Pietra
had a sharp eye for the early braggarts of Fascism, and a
sound judgment of where it would lead.

> Florence had grown more garish, owing to the greater
> influx of bright uniforms. Their triumphs over the
> Abyssinians, despite the organised opposition of the
> plutocracies, had persuaded my young Italian friends
> that they were in very deed the heirs of the ancient
> Romans, and they sported their rows of medals like
> peacocks' tails. . . . The *Duce* would lead the world yet,
> and with Hitler imitating him, Bah! democracy was
> doomed.

Acton saw exactly where it would lead – complacent asses
of political 'leaders' in Britain, some of them disingenuous
sympathisers with Mussolini, did not. 'The walls of houses
were scrawled all over with slogans which were meant to
persuade one that "*La Guerra è bella*" (War is beautiful).' Did
they find that when finally they came up against the consequences of their folly? How well I remember the aftermath

of the Abyssinian war, and Mussolini himself prating from the balcony of the Palazzo Venezia – the convict face, the heavy, ill-shaven jowl – while I looked on from my nook in the square, with Machiavelli's *The Prince* in my hand. Everywhere one saw the slogan on the walls, '*Il Duce La sempre raggione*' (the Duce is always right). He turned out to be right over the half-hearted opposition to his criminal war on Abyssinia. He himself confirmed to Marshal de Bono, who had bombed the unarmed Abyssinians from the air: 'the English attitude has helped instead of injuring'. Acton puts, patriotically, the very point which Simon, as Foreign Secretary, would not face. 'To me the disturbing question was: how far had we connived at Italy's aggression, and how genuine was our "collective opposition". *It must have been known outside Italy that an oil embargo would stop the campaign.*'

The British Government would not take that effective step, and reaped the worst consequences. Mussolini was given his triumph, when he might have been toppled. Hitler drew the obvious conclusions and went ahead. The Rome–Berlin Axis practically closed the Mediterranean in his war: it meant the death of thousands of good fellows – including Harold's friend, Robert Byron, who was drowned there.

Acton observed the Fascist deformation of the friendly old Italy he had grown up in. As in demotic Germany there was a campaign to get rid even of foreign words and their associations – product of an infantile inferiority-complex.

> *Autista* replaced chauffeur, *albergo* hotel, and half the hotels in Italy had to be re-baptized in Fascist style, all the Eden Parks and Eden Palaces, since the very word Eden had fallen under a blight; besides the countless Albions, Bristols and Britannias, as well as public squares and streets, shops that had called themselves 'English Tea-rooms', 'Old England', 'Merrie England'.

All this is characteristic of the lower-middle-class mentality that dominates popular urban society, in contrast to the taste of an aristocracy. Nor is it really proletarian. The country folk were more sensible.

> The peasants, who formed sixty per cent of the population, were less elated than the townsfolk, and in the farms round La Pietra the genuine Fascists were few. They may have been impressed by the battery of propaganda, but they asked what they had gained from Tripoli in the past. Were they likely to get more out of Abyssinia? The cost of the campaign had been terrific . . . Now they had to watch their words, for denunciations were frequent.

These country folk were the people who, when war came, protected Jews and hid hundreds of Allied airmen fallen from the skies. It is *country* life that remains sound in the drugging and mugging and thugging of the cities, the over-populated conurbations of today.

In Shanghai Acton was to meet Mussolini's daughter, the egregious Edda, and son-in-law.

> I was introduced to Count Ciano and his wife, whose button eyes and massive jaws gave her a striking resemblance to her father, Mussolini. She was trying to behave like royalty, surrounded by attentive myrmidons. Ciano himself had not yet developed into his father-in-law's ape. He was a very ordinary young Italian, not a whit different from the lounge-lizards who loitered in front of Doney's, criticising the points of passing women on the Via Tornabuoni.

He could not have guessed that he would be executed by his father-in-law, nor could the daughter have foreseen the squalid end, the Duce in a square in Northern Italy, hanged upside down.

What wonder then that Acton should turn away from the crass and vulgar Fascist Italy to the cultured past, and devote his first historical work to *The Last Medici*? There had been plenty of books on the early Medici; he knew as well as any professor that 'the Renaissance is admittedly the most interesting period of Italian history, Florence the most typical state, Lorenzo de' Medici its most typical citizen.' There is in fact a rich Anglo-Italian literature, from Byron and Shelley and earlier, onwards through the Brownings to Acton himself; we may include the American contribution, from Hawthorne and Henry James to Iris Origo and Mary MacCarthy.

We did not need yet another book on Lorenzo the Magnificent and Michelangelo, or Leo X and Raphael. Here was a more original inflexion. Acton scores with a telling point for historians, if capable of appreciating it: 'The political history of Florence is of minor importance; what matters supremely is its culture. It is as inspiring patrons of art and literature that the Medici will live, not as Machiavellian manipulators of Italian diplomacy.' Nothing is so stale as stale politics, and this is what ordinary history books are about – understandably, because their writers have no visual sense and little culture. Even a master of political history, Sir Lewis Namier, never once looked at the splendid collection in the British Library of prints and engravings of the 18th-century people he wrote so much about – when they are so revealing of personality.

Acton is aware of all this, having lived among these portraits and sculptures, and puts it to proper use in writing history. With the later Medici, 'the Bourbon has intruded. There is no longer the same austerity: instead a ponderous sensuality becomes more and more apparent, loosening into a thicker voluptuousness, curdling into flaccid folds, until finally a terrible senile lust asserts itself. Decay sets in.'

He need not apologise therefore, 'if I have sacrificed much of the outer to that inner history which describes the individual and desires the unique: a twisted nose . . . a preference for satyrs to sylphs, etc.'. Of course he could have regaled the reader with 'hair-raising anecdotes about Gian Gastone for the benefit of sexual psychologists, or quote from his brother's correspondence with famous painters and musicians for the benefit of art historians and musicologists'. Instead he has restrained himself, and gone for 'those facts and details which, in a single sentence or anecdote, explain the secret of a whole age or people better than do all the pages historians and philosophers ever wrote'.

This is strong language, but makes its point. We have more than enough political history: cultural history is the thing. Acton has made his contribution – as I have done my best with four volumes on the Elizabethan Age. Again he scores when he points out that biographies of the Medici have tended to become treatises on Florence. Even in their last days the Medici were patrons of the arts, of painting, sculpture, music, theatre; and the last princes of the house left their supreme art collection for posterity.

> The Grand Prince Ferdinando, who predeceased his father in 1713, was a more enthusiastic and discriminating patron of art than Cosimo III. Alessandro Magnasco's *Hunting Scene* is an eloquent example of his taste in reaction against the pietistic preferences of his father. . . . Magnasco must have appealed to Gian Gastone, whose *penchant* for the bizarre was more acute than his elder brother's.

This striking artist, so odd and recognisable, whose idiosyncratic vision has an affinity with a modern eye, was more appreciated by the last Medici than by his native Genoa. Hence their collection in that small room in the Uffizi, which I have not forgotten after fifty years.

He did not have much luck with this first of his history books any more than with his early novels. It came out at an unpropitious time in England for books about Italy. People read Trevelyan's books on Garibaldi and the Risorgimento, for he was a bestseller; but Keith Hancock's book about Ricasoli did not sell, and was never completed. 'In Italy, on the other hand, my book would give official umbrage, for only the heroic achievements of the past were meet to be recalled. . . . What chance had I to obtain a hearing with a chronicle of decadence?'

However, he was no less capable of perceiving and understanding the greatest of the Medici.

Lorenzo had been a paragon of pacificism in a period of extensive petty warfare – no less petty for the peasantry whose fields were ravaged than for the citizens burdened with taxes to pay for the bands of mercenaries. As the leading citizen who struggled to keep the peace of Italy his merit was outstanding. But his cultural significance transcended his age. He was a cosmopolitan Italian with a sense of the fundamental meaning of existence, enriching the minds of others as well as his own.

The same may be said for Acton, who has enriched us.

Not everybody thinks so, those who are not up to it, and they are the losers. A Cambridge professor tells us that Lorenzo the Magnificent is 'not today a favourite with "democratic" historians'. Why not? – too subtle a mind, too creative a spirit, too sparkling for dullards, their uniform monochrome. By the same token he tells us that 'Sir Harold is (I fear) read by fewer undergraduates (or "students" as they are now known) than he should be', and that there are reasons for this. We need not look far: they are just not up to it. As for the opinions of 'democratic' historians, occupying their chairs their brief hour, what matter what they think? They recur – and are as soon forgotten. It is the work that stands, and is an end in itself – just as it is art that lasts, politics not.

'One writes for one's own delectation', he says – as I do myself. 'To be candid, I was fascinated by the prodigious pageantry as well as by the ferment of fine arts of 17th-century Italy, whose virtues were being rediscovered after the usual cycle of neglect.' He was rediscovering the Baroque, which was then something new. And I am delighted – though it would have surprised us in the old Oxford days – that he discovered for himself the esoteric joys of historical research.

In the 1920s the Florentine Archives were far less crowded than they are today. I was privileged in this respect, for I enjoyed the luxury of a little table all to myself, piled with old Court diaries and other docu-

ments from which I made extracts more copious than
would ever suit my purpose under the spell of their
pulsating actuality.

There speaks a true historian. 'With the aid of direct quotations I tried to let my readers see Cosimo III and his family
as they were seen by their contemporaries.' His moral
detachment from their goings-on was considered rather
shocking, especially by the regiment of women who had
made rather a corner in Florence, or by such an old lady as
E.M. Forster, who took up a public stand about morals (his
private ones not imparted to the public). Harold wonders
now at his fixation, 'for I had plenty of other temptations to
distract me'.

  I find it rather affecting to think, now that we are old, that
when young, while Harold was day after day at his table in
the Florentine Archives, Richard Pares (long dead) and I
were buried all day and every day similarly in the Public
Record Office in Chancery Lane.

We come to the central question of Acton's life: his relation
to China or, rather, to Chinese culture. Several reasons must
have combined to make this decisive break with Europe.
Disillusionment with the way things were going with us –
which he foresaw all too clearly; disappointment with the
frustration of his literary career; the desire to cast free from
the leading-strings of La Pietra and to find himself in a new
world of experience. All these entered into it, but the
fundamental reason I do not fully understand. He says,
'Until I went to China my life could not be integrated and I
knew it.'

  This is strange; I discern something American in it. I
cannot think of any of my English friends needing China to
integrate themselves. But several eminent Americans have
had a love-affair with China – until the Communist Revolution shattered the idyll. (President Nixon did an historic job
to repair some of the damage.) I find Acton's relationship
with China somewhat akin to Eliot and Pound's magpie
attitude to European culture. But it was emotionally

stronger, an obsession – 'an innate love of China beyond rational analysis, and an instinct that I had some vocation there'.

But 'would I get there in time? I was haunted by misgivings. I had seen one war and dreaded the certain prospect of another, which might prevent me from achieving integration. It is not agreeable to be aware that one is an unbaked mould.' I think that that places it in the category of Eliot's remove to Europe, rather than Auden's option for America. It was some instinct that made him say, in the middle of his London literary frolics, 'I knew in my bones that I would go to the Far East, and that once there I was likely to stay.'

The nearest I can get to an explanation is that his was a Mandarin nature, which was seeking its home. Was he indeed in time? He was just in time to acquaint himself with the relics of a once transcendent culture that was on its way out, to imbrue himself in it as far as any Westerner could, before its destruction. He immersed himself in it, took to a Chinese way of life like a duck to water, he became the Mandarin he was. In that sense the mission for integration succeeded: he found himself. Here is something exceptional, if not unique.

I am quite unqualified to follow him in this realm of experience – realm? – continent, world rather; for the Chinese had achieved a universe of culture when we were but barbarians. I must rely on what Acton himself tells us, and others bear witness. 'My emotions on entering Peking were similar to Gibbon's when he entered the Eternal City.' He at once set out for the Imperial Palaces, those relics of the immeasurably more cultivated, more creative past.

> Neither Versailles, nor the Pitti, nor any aggregation of palaces I had seen or imagined, with the exception of the Vatican, had the magnificence of this extensive city of courtyards and pavilions. Within our time no handiwork of man has achieved such a dignified and spacious harmony of buildings. For once the sky was part of the architectural design. The sweeping curves of the golden roofs held the blue sky like jewelled chalices. Massive

though the buildings were – half shimmering roof, half pillared portico and marble balustrade – they had an aerial lightness and grace. Thus the whole plan had an aspiring spiritual quality. Huge ramparts, of a colour that varied with the time of day from pale rose to deep coral, separated it from the outside world. Many of the doors had remained sealed since the Emperor's departure: the peacock blues and greens of the woodwork were flaking off; the crimson lacquer on the colonnades was splitting . . . The Olympus whence China had been governed was as deserted as a pyramid in the desert.

Such was a monument, an achievement, that only a mandarin culture could create. I suppose that in the West, or half-West, one might compare it with the sparkling and coloured complex of the Kremlin. And think of the appalling taste of their demotic successors!

Not only Peking, but the open country outside the city walls, was so beautiful and calming to eye and nerves that I longed to discover the secret of this beauty, unapproached by anything I had seen before. I had seldom, if ever, found such peace in Christian places of worship: the Crucifix alone recalls scenes of agony, and death and tears are always present. Impatience, the most marked characteristic of all modern modes of thought and the curse of all our lives, was banished by the light of Buddha's smile.

Here we come close to the religion that has sustained him in our grievous time. 'Self-control seemed easier to practise where everything expressed self-control.'

He felt himself as much at home with Chinese art-relics of the past, of course – the scrolls with their calligraphy and painting. 'To me their traditional quality was delightful; the evolution of a noble culture; and the diversity under their apparent uniformity was more subtly original than the stews and fricassees served up on European canvases as landscapes and naked women and still lifes. I was surfeited with Western painting.'

No lack of human sympathy, or compassion either. There were the rickshaw men: 'I could never get accustomed to the plight of these human beasts of burden . . . Yet their cheerfulness was as striking as their poverty. They were always ready to smile. No education had disenchanted them.'

Mr Cyril Birch tells us, 'Harold Acton spent the years from 1932 to 1939 in China. By so doing he missed Hitler's assumption of power, Mussolini's invasion of Abyssinia, the Spanish Civil War and the Munich agreement. He caught, by the same token, the aftermath of the "Manchurian Incident", the Long March of the Chinese Communists, the weekend kidnapping of Chiang Kai-shek and the first two years of the war against Japan.'[1] In these circumstances it is remarkable that he should have been able to achieve the peace of mind he had sought, give himself up to the dual task he set himself, and meanwhile enjoy and observe the variegated social life he describes in *Peonies and Ponies*. I suppose this to be his best novel, the life described with an amused smile.

The inner life was two-fold. As lecturer in English Literature at the National University, he set himself to interpret the best of Western literature, particularly the modern poets, English and American, to his enthusiastic neophytes. Dressed as the mandarin he was, he made friends of them, welcoming them to the beautiful house he inhabited, with its courtyards, where he lived in Chinese style, collecting around him the art objects he loved as well as the people.

More important is his work in the realm where I cannot follow him – irremediably Occidental as a Cornishman must be – in translating and interpreting modern Chinese poetry and, in collaboration, some of the classics of Chinese drama. He was not concerned with contemporary fiction: 'He relished the young poets, heirs of Baudelaire and Mallarmé as well as of the Tang masters . . . and for the classical

[1] *Oxford, China and Italy. Writings in Honour of Sir Harold Acton*, ed. E. Chaney and N. Ritchie, 3 foll.

theatre of China Acton developed a passionate and enduring love.' Hence the publications *Modern Chinese Poetry* in 1936, *Famous Chinese Plays* in 1937; and *The Peach Blossom Fan* years later in 1976.

'From the start his responses to new experience were those of the informed scholar rather than the tyro.' He equipped himself for his new life with a mass of relevant reading in translation from the philosophers, the Confucian classics, and his friend Arthur Waley's renderings from Chinese into English poetry. He well understood the precariousness of the situation in which he lived, in 'an ivory tower surrounded by munitions factories'. Still, 'even as late as the 1930s the patterns of everyday Chinese life retained enough traces of traditional ways to delight the eye and mind of a historian.' For the more complete re-creation of the vanished world of scholars and beauties, courtiers and warriors, Harold Acton turned to the storytellers of the past and to the representation of their themes in the classical theatre. He rejoiced in the great chronicles, the *Three Kingdoms* and *Men of the Marshes*, their colour and pageantry brought to life by actors of the Peking Opera then enjoying a heyday. He was able to appreciate 'the consummate grace and artistry of this gener-ation of actors whose great days Acton was just in time to witness', not only the male leads but the female imperson-ators – 'a triumph of art over nature, rarely to be found nowadays and soon will be seen no more'. Undoubtedly not, under the repressive triumph of Puritanism character-istic of demotic revolution, Chinese as well as Russian. More sophisticated natures can appreciate the ambivalence that is as true to life, as well as more subtle.

Another expert in this field enlightens us as to the unique-ness of Peking at this time: 'the only city in the world where physical and social traditions a millenium old had survived into the 20th century'.[1] What a unique opportunity for a historian! 'It was the overall *ambiance* of traditional Peking that Harold readily responded to, and understood better than any foreigner I knew in China. Harold's natural affinity with

[1] Laurence Sickman, ibid, 69–70.

poets, painters, writers and scholars assured his entry into
the intellectual ferment of the New China, centred in Peking
University.' This was accompanied by a no less intense
interest in Occidental literature, in which he could teach and
lead.

In his traditional house he gathered his collection of art
objects eloquent of the creative past: scrolls, paintings,
screens, wood carvings, bronze mirrors which 'illustrated
the fact that no other people have lavished so much talent
and ingenuity as have the Chinese on decoration limited to
the circle'. An important part in the collection consisted of
paintings and calligraphy of the 17th- and 18th-century poet-
painters. One album of these Harold gave, with typical
generosity, to an American museum. It was as well, for
most of the collection was destroyed in the catastrophe of
our time.

He had no illusions about the Japanese, the barbaric cruelty
that underlay the veneer of politeness. Nor need we, when
we consider the barbarism of their most distinguished writer,
Mishima, publicly disembowelling himself in the traditional
manner *pour encourager les autres*. Perhaps Harold has suffered
some disillusionment too in his love-affair with the Chinese?
We read more recently that 'in the summer of 1966, at a
Peking school for girls from high-ranking intellectual families, the students forced their headmistress, one of China's
first Western-educated women, to crawl through an underground drain. Then they beat her to death. "These teenage
girls, ordinarily shy, mild and gentle, had somehow become
capable of unimaginable cruelty".'[1]

We see that the Chinese are humans after all.

So much of Acton's life has been lived outside England that
we lose sight of him for whole periods; I suspect that this is
the chief reason for his underestimation as a writer, when
early friends soared ahead. His war-service in the RAF was
varied and interesting; others have made successful books of

[1] q. *Times Lit. Supplt.*, 22 Aug. 1986, 909.

their experiences, while he embedded his in *More Memoirs of an Aesthete*.

It was patriotic of him to come back to England and pull every string to get into the forces. This aesthete had notable courage – that often surprises people (it surprised people among the gilded youth around William Rufus). The *Llangibby Castle* in which he was sent overseas was attacked and nearly went down in the Atlantic – it would have been like the loss of Robert Byron in the Mediterranean, whom Harold missed most in the post-war years. In India he was desperately ill, had a kidney removed – and recovered after Extreme Unction. Typically no very good use was made of his specialist knowledge: he longed to be sent to Chungking, then the capital of Nationalist China. But some dunderhead in the Foreign Service delated him – I cannot think for what, as he was no Leftist, unlike Burgess, Maclean and Philby the vipers whom they foolishly nourished in their bosom. Perhaps they suspected Harold of the vice of Confucianism.

He got on well with his mates and in the mess – unlike Waugh, who yet put his experiences to good use in his war novels. Harold saw plenty of suffering, which he does not dwell on, though the compassion comes through. In the course of a variegated, somewhat vagrant, life he came up against rascals, of different sorts in different classes, but 'curiosity always got the better of me, though I never liked people *en masse*'. Aesthetes can always insulate themselves, and have inner resources denied to Philistines.

Meanwhile, at home in Florence, the Germans gave the usual evidence of their pretty ways. Harold's father and mother were driven to take refuge in Switzerland, leaving La Pietra exposed. Berenson as a Jew had to go into hiding, some of his splendid collection of pictures lost when the *Herrenvolk* wantonly blew up the historic bridges over the Arno. Ghirlandaio's 'Adoration of the Magi' they used as a tabletop; when the curator of the Museum asked them to remove bottles and glasses, they knifed the picture. Much of the Acton collection was dispersed, except for the Tuscan Primitives, statues in the garden damaged. Of the Airborne

Corps Harold knew, who were parachuted into Lorraine, all but one were murdered by the Gestapo.

Sent into Germany during the Occupation he was surprised by the sullen hatred among the people, while 'their slavish obedience to a Hitler remained an enigma. . . . What a superhuman faith in Hitler when hardly any building was intact!' This need not have surprised him: he did not know German – 'a regrettable deficiency' – or German history: credulity is their occupational disease. Hitler knew all too well: 'Germans do not know how they have to be gulled in order to be led.' If the masses were not such idiots they would not have been gulled by the slogans with which Nazis, Fascists, Communists alike treated them.

After the war Harold's father gave himself up wholly to tracking down and trying to retrieve the collections dispersed from the five other villas he owned. The son returned to the life of culture, quoting Flaubert: 'the only way not to be unhappy is to shut yourself up in art' – that speaks half for me too, only I would not put it negatively: it is a way to be positively happy. He quotes Pascal, no less relevant today: 'Tout le malheur des hommes vient de ne savoir pas se tenir en repos dans une chambre.'

Before Mussolini entered the war Acton had paid a visit to the sage Croce, insulated in his library at Naples, which the Fascists had raided. Curiously enough, in that defeatist time, Croce remained convinced that the Allies would yet win. Mussolini thought that Hitler was winning the war and hastily jumped on the bandwagon. We recall the view held of him before the war by Sir John Marriott, Tory MP for Oxford: 'His was the idealism of Mazzini, combined with the practical statesmanship of Cavour and the heroic temper of Garibaldi.' What fools these people were! Acton sums up Croce: 'the life of culture was his religion, his remedy for human ills'. That again half-speaks for me – since there seems no remedy for humans' idiocy.

After the war Acton gave himself up to several years of research into the Bourbons of Naples for his major historical work. What could be more appropriate? His distinguished cosmopolitan family had produced a historic figure in

General Sir John Acton, leading minister of Ferdinand II for many years before and after 1800. Of the ancient Shropshire stock of Aldenham, but with a French mother, this Acton made a memorable career, building a navy and re-creating an army for the awkward dual kingdom of Naples and Sicily. It was too large to be disregarded in the politics of Europe, too small to weigh in with effect; difficult to govern, with a feeble governing class and a frivolous population, with their childish cult of San Gennaro and the regular liquefaction of his blood.

The General made the best of things in the circumstances. The British ambassador, the famous connoisseur Sir William Hamilton, wrote of 'the general want of good faith at Naples, every department of state is more or less corrupted'. Constant cabals against Acton, whose influence permeated the whole government; he ended up as Prime Minister. He had the confidence of the King, for his judgment was sound, himself an honest, cool head, always exerting a moderating influence – a recognisable English temperament in that excitable merry-go-round. He instituted a number of reforms, but could hardly be expected to reform the monarchy out of existence. The ferment let loose by the French Revolution was the affair of a small minority of doctrinaires; the people at large remained loyal to the monarchy to the end.

One may see Acton's book as written in reaction against the cult of the Risorgimento – which produced other reactions in the course of time and considerable disillusionment with the naif expectations of literary ladies like Mrs Browning, besides that against the historiography of the Trevelyans in our time. Acton did not fail to draw the moral. 'The liberal Nemesis overtaking Bourbon tyranny had been overtaken by an anti-liberal Nemesis which made the Bourbon tyrants look like gentle lambs.' His anti-Fascism had been as outspoken as it was courageous – rather to his father's apprehension.

It was natural that he should have been drawn to Bourbon Naples, with his family associations. The Acton Palazzo on the Riviera di Chiaia now belongs to the State, but his cousin the Prince of Leporano could still produce family archives from his war-battered Palazzo Cellamare. The old General had not been addicted to women but, succeeding to the English baronetcy, at sixty-four he married a niece of fourteen to ensure progeny. One grandson was the famous historian, Lord Acton, another a saintly Cardinal.

Harold was drawn to Naples too as 'a spectacle of voluptuous enchantment, as powerful in its masses as it is sumptuous in its detail'. His aesthete's eye conjures up for us on the page the 'prodigal colour' which distinguishes Neapolitan from Roman baroque; he responded to the Berners-like cult of romantic decay, the unfinished palaces, the grandeur concealed in slummy back-streets, the unparalleled *mise-en-scène*. And, 'no other city in Europe has been ruled by so varied a succession of foreign dynasties' – Angevin, Austrian, Spanish, Bourbon, finally the House of Savoy. Naples preferred the Bourbons, whom it regarded as its own; after the take-over the Piedmontese needed 120,000 troops in the South, and a civil war of sorts rumbled on till 1865. I suppose a united Italy was inevitable, and things might have been better if only Cavour had lived. There remained a permanent problem of the South.

Acton's interest, as in his book on the Last Medici, is in the culture, the arts and personalities, as when in the 18th century Naples was the musical capital of Europe. One appreciates an historian who is not only literary but literate, who can quote the English memoirists and Goethe, along with Baudelaire and Blake; who can describe the tiresome Louise Colet as 'one of those illiberal liberal dames of letters', like Mrs Browning, whose dreadful *Poems before Congress* provided pabulum for politicians. Then there are Daudet, in *Les Rois en Exil*, and Proust in *La Prisonnière*, describing the last Bourbon Queen, sister of the beautiful Empress Elisabeth, both superb horsewomen, riding in the Bois de Boulogne.

Lest I be thought incapable of criticism, perhaps I may express my reservations. The two books on the Bourbons of Naples are too long; Harold's opulence of temperament, his very enthusiasm, led him into frequent quotations from original documents and letters. A good fault – but it always improves a book to slim it (American academics please note!). Over *The Last Medici* he 'pocketed his pride' when his publishers made him cut 30,000 words. Similar surgery would have improved later volumes. A lifelong don, perhaps I may suggest that he would have done better with the History School at Oxford – good training – instead of wasting time on PPE.[1]

Strangely again he had no encouragement for his writing from his family. His father, wrapped up in his own visual aestheticism, with social life only for outlet, would reproach him with the Hanoverian 'Scribble-scribble-scribble'. A kindlier American aunt would say, 'Why not write about something other than those old Bourbons?' (pronouncing it in the American manner, like the drink).

Well, he did. I can only single out a few among his later writings. *More Memoirs of an Aesthete* offers something of a contrast with the earlier volume: one comes closer to the inner man in it, in one way it is more realistic, in touch with a wider spectrum of life, war service and all, with less reserve about himself. We learn that he places courtesy first among the virtues. We might have guessed that from his books, which exemplify not only politeness, but *politesse du coeur* – again a contrast with so many writers; but then, he is not only an aristocrat born, but a great gentleman. Even on the subject of snobbery he scores: 'I am only a snob in so far as I often want better company than my own.' A strain of ruthlessness often goes with pure aestheticism: here what is exceptional is the humanity that accompanies it. I put that down to the credit of the American side in him: his mother had a good heart.

His splendid volume on *Tuscan Villas* has all his gifts – what he was born to write (*pace* Father). The whole landscape lives for him, its beauty, improved by (elect) man, its buildings, folklore, memories. From the lofty square tower of Il Trebbio,

[1] The School of Philosophy, Politics and Economics.

The view over the Mugello in every direction has scarcely changed since Dante took the winding road to exile, and its neat garden still has a medieval accent reminiscent of Pietro Crescenzi's treatise *Opus Ruralium Commodorum*, which had circulated over a century in manuscript before it was printed in 1471; and of such delicate miniatures as illustrate the 'Romance of the Rose'.

Here we have all his qualities in one sentence: the visual and historical, the literary, the learning worn with grace and lightness.

And then, for our own time, the country houses of Siena and Lucca in their poetical situations, in secluded corners or on solitary hilltops.

Many are forsaken, their closed shutters wrapped in cobwebs, the plaster peeling in patches from their mottled walls, their gardens running wild, their fountains dry, their armorial gateways rusty . . . haunted by owls and nightingales . . . Alas, the flimsy bungalow and prefabricated cottage are becoming more popular than the fine old Tuscan farmhouse with its solid walls and noble proportions . . . and ancient castles that might still be made habitable are slowly collapsing.

Such is the society that has taken the place of Medici, Chigi, Bourbons.

Such is demotic society everywhere. In England too, country houses and town houses that were its glory – the expression of an elect society – have been destroyed in hundreds, many of them needlessly, their contents emptied out, scattered abroad. Many could have been rehabilitated, as Arthur Acton saved and revived La Pietra. Country-house life, with its sense of proportion distributed between country and town, its patronage of the arts and literature, its deliberative improvement of the landscape, park and plantations, its responsibilities in the social life going on around, set a better example of civilised life than any the world has known. In his *Memoir of Nancy Mitford*, a sparkling depiction of that vanished life of his friends – Sitwells, Mitfords, Waugh and Norman Douglas – Harold has a revealing word about 'that embarrassing self-consciousness which is peculiarly English. The constant muzzling of emotion tends to freeze the heart.' And not only the heart, I may add. But why whould we subject ourselves to *their* standards, Harold any more than I, a pure Cornishman, not English? A real writer should never set himself to meet the expectations of the conventional.

Among his last books have been a research work on the Pazzi conspiracy against the Medici, and an enchanting little volume, *Three Extraordinary Ambassadors*: Sir Henry Wotton, Sir Horace Mann, Sir William Hamilton. They span the peninsula – Venice, Florence, Naples – and the centuries from the late eighteenth to the early nineteenth. Harold Acton now joins their company, as the best cultural ambassador between Italy and England in our time. Italy has recognised that with the signal tribute of conferring on him the honorary citizenship of Florence, a rare recognition. Difficult as it is to define a place for so rare a bird, with such variegated plumage, we may place him alongside such kindred spirits as the Sitwells and Norman Douglas, and perhaps Berenson, though he was less catholic and more specialised. We may say for him also that, in his eminent cosmopolitan family, he takes his place alongside the General and Prime Minister of Naples, and Lord Acton the historian.

Graham Greene: Perverse Genius

What a contrast there is between Harold Acton's world and Graham Greene's – Greeneland, as he himself describes it! And between their lives – except that we three contemporaries at Oxford have lived on (improbably in my case) into our eighties. Who could have foreseen the way things would work out for each of us? Harold was wholly given to poetry, yet has fulfilled himself more as historian and autobiographer. Graham was a promising poet, but became the most professional of novelists, a Somerset Maugham. A Scholar in English Literature, I was pushed by the dons into history, though I held on all my life, like a secret vice, to writing poetry, into which I could put my inner life.

Yet there were indications. In an early poem Graham wrote, in terms recognisable in his later work, almost prophetically:

All these belong to youth; all these I hate:
The constant dreams that change and interchange . . .
Yet creeping up to bed when it grows late;
And short-lived loves that yet are over-strong,
When all the mind is one old weary faction . . .

We see that a potential poet was lost in him. These public school boys were so much more sophisticated than I was; if not yet mature, they had lost their innocence.

Graham went on, with almost psychic foresight,

> But age is like a wreck within a bay –
> [as it might be Antibes]
> The sails are down; they do not feel the wind:
> There comes no whisper from a foolish Spain.

He was to write a good deal about Spain and the Spanish world, Mexico, Central America, Habana, Cuba.

It seems that *Public School Verse*, in which we appeared, was Graham Pollard's idea. In 1919–20 we find him from Shrewsbury, Peter Quennell from Berkhamsted, Wilfrid Blunt from Marlborough. Next year (I have Raymond Greene's copy) four poems from Peter, another from Blunt, and I appear from 'St Austell's (sic) County School', propelled by my headmaster, for I had no idea of such possibilities, hidden away in a small Cornish school. In 1921–2 came four more from Peter, our top-boy, one from Isherwood at Repton, and Graham makes his first appearance from Berkhamsted, along with a second poem from me.

At Oxford Harold Acton comes to the fore in *Oxford Poetry* 1923 with three poems, with David Cecil, 'Puffin' Asquith, Christopher Hollis and me; two poems by Graham. In *Oxford Poetry* 1925 three by Acton, two by Graham and me, and my later close friends, Rosalie Mander and R.W. Ketton-Cremer, make their appearance. What happened to all the rest? – those promising names not heard of since.

If coming events cast their shadows before there are evidences enough of the future Graham Greene in his schooldays. Born 2 October 1904, he was the son of the Headmaster of Berkhamsted School – a good school, while his father was a liberal-minded, long-suffering man. As a young man Graham deliberately set out to shock his father's ideas (like Evelyn Waugh, who treated his father abominably) – to his 'misery and remorse' when his father died. He detested school, and in *A Sort of Life* rubs in unnecessarily the smell of farts in the boys' lavatory; as a boy of six he had done a coloured drawing of a 'bit of shit' for the family gazette. He regularly played truant up on the Common, hidden among the bushes reading the books he had stolen from W.H. Smith's bookshop, as he tells us.

It is all in the autobiography, on the principle of whose writing I am in agreement with him. It is direct and without irony; anybody can see that to treat one's past with irony is a mere ploy of self-defence to forestall criticism, but 'it falsifies history'. I was typically criticised by a middle-class literary critic for writing mine without irony: I took no notice – one has no need to defend oneself against the third-rate.

Suicide attempts loom lugubriously in the account. Once he attempted to cut his right leg open with a pen-knife; another time he swallowed hypo (whatever that is), then twenty aspirins before swimming in the bath. He then took to a revolver. 'I put the muzzle of the revolver into my right ear and pulled the trigger. There was a minute click, and looking down at the chamber I could see that the charge had moved into the firing position.' This dangerous addiction was repeated at Oxford: 'the revolver would be whipped behind my back, the chamber twisted, the muzzle quickly and surreptitiously inserted in my ear, the trigger pulled'.

I find this extremely distasteful – this ingratitude for the marvellous gift of life – and incomprehensible after my happy schooldays, deplorable compared with the struggle I had to get to a university at all. I can suggest only that with his fortunate middle-class upbringing – with those clever brothers, Raymond and Hugh Greene, his mother a first cousin of Robert Louis Stevenson – he must have been spoiled. In my working-class background he would have been disciplined, given a regular hiding – instead of that he was psycho-analysed. Really, at sixteen! He admits that the excuse for being away from school, reading on his own in Kensington Gardens, probably did more good.

Then came Oxford. He failed twice to win a scholarship, but his 'overburdened father' gave him an allowance of £250 a year, and got him into Balliol. (The three scholarships I had such a struggle to collect made £200 a year in all.) I didn't see much of my contemporary, though we contributed to the same literary papers and went in for the Newdigate – neither Graham nor Evelyn Waugh getting a mention. (I was vexed at winning a *proxime accessit* to a much senior

Rhodes scholar.) It was Graham who organised a session of 'Oxford Poets' in those early days of the BBC at Savoy Hill, with Harold Acton and others forgotten now. He records that I was the only one to receive a fan-letter – from an old lady who found my verses 'consoling'. I had completely forgotten that, and remembered feeling rather a fool, being emotional into the mouthpiece of a machine.

We did not see much of Graham at Oxford – he did not appear at the Labour Club, where I was intensely active as Secretary, then as Chairman. But, like Acton, he precociously published a volume of poems, *Babbling April* (now an expensive collectors' item), and was writing a novel. Kenneth Bell – a boisterous, roaring Fellow, a fellow Berkhamstedian – took him under his wing and got him an exhibition of fifty pounds a year, which he more than spent on drink. He tells us in his autobiography that for one whole term he was drunk every day from breakfast to bed. When it came to appearing before the dons at end of term, Kenneth Bell steered him in and out.

As a lifelong don, and a teetotaller, I cannot be expected to approve of that – or of Kenneth Bell either, whom I came to know well. He was a former Fellow of All Souls, and when I first joined the College I was intimidated by his rough tongue and crashing manner. He had a generous heart, and I came to terms with him, once I stood up to him; but he was a roaring Philistine and a drunk too – *not* my cup of tea. A member of the distinguished publishing firm, Bell's, he should have known better; but he was not under control, perhaps a little 'touched', and the end of his career made a strange story. Still, Graham was lucky to have him as protector; he says that, in the event, he got a moderate Second in the History School. I thought it was a Third, like Evelyn's.

Thence to Nottingham, for an apprentice job on the *Nottingham Journal*. Here he lived in cheap lodgings with his dog, Paddy, which was frequently sick on his diet of tinned salmon. The editor was Cecil Roberts – another point of contact, for later Cecil latched on to me and became a familiar acquaintance. He was a successful middle-brow novelist, whose novels I did not read; having made a fortune he was driven to live abroad by our penalising taxation, like Graham himself when he became successful.

From the provinces he graduated to *The Times*, where the editor, the notorious Appeaser Geoffrey Dawson, was kind to him. Barrington-Ward, a still worse Appeaser for he was sure he was right, was not: 'a cold complacent man', who reminded Graham of Pecksniff. When Graham made the mistake of resigning and tried to return, he received a cold snub from him. Of someone else who perceived all too clearly what Hitler was up to, Barrington-Ward said, 'We don't want any hot-heads here.' From being an Appeaser of the Germans, after the war he became an Appeaser of the Russians; altogether he was a very bad influence on *The Times*.

Meanwhile Graham was writing novels, with no money and no success – except for adventitious luck with *Stamboul Train*. He had married Vivien and started a family: when one thinks of the hardihood, the hardships they endured, the perseverance, one can only say how much he deserved his eventual triumph. It does not seem to have made him any happier. All through his work there is this expression of a perverse preference for death. Can it be sincere? Here he envies Radiguet and Alain-Fournier their early deaths. What a loss to literature those young men of genius were! And what a perverse denial of the glory of life, for which one should be grateful – especially a Christian, ungrateful to his God. Perhaps he would have more gratitude, if he had had such a struggle to hold on to life as I endured for years. Even today he says, 'perhaps it is only desperation that keeps me writing'. Is that true, or sincere? If so, it is at the least ungracious for the gifts he has received, his genius, greatest gift of all.

Vivien was a Catholic, so he became a Catholic. He claims, as did Evelyn Waugh, that this was a matter of intellectual argument, not of emotional leanings. Today he writes, 'with the approach of death I care less and less about religious truth'. An historian is concerned above all with what is true. A philosopher, like the Master of Graham's old college, Balliol, and an ex-Catholic, knows that no rational arguments can prove the existence of God. Even if there is a God behind the universe, it would not mean that Catholic dogmas were any other than myths. When Pope Pius XII proclaimed the dogma of the bodily Assumption of the Virgin into heaven, he stated that it was 'not a terrestrial fact, but a celestial fact', i.e. not a fact at all, just a myth. When the archbishops of Canterbury and York protested against this new dogma, the Jesuit theologians behind it were able to reply that it rested upon the same grounds as the Incarnation and the Resurrection. That is, they were all equally mythical. J.H. Newman, cleverer than any of them (equally credulous), realised that it could only be a matter of faith, not reason. So Greene and Waugh should base their faith on faith: I am not impressed by intellectual claims from inept intellects – their forte is otherwise.

Father Gervase Mathew, of Blackfriars at Oxford, to whom *The Power and the Glory* is dedicated, was a close friend of both of us. He used to tell me a good deal about Graham; that he would forget the intellectual arguments that had persuaded him, and Gervase would have to remind him what they were. Simply mumbling the 'Rock of Peter', as in that book, is mere mumbo-jumbo.

On the plane of common sense there is much that I can agree with. On the personal element in literature, for example. He knows that there is an element of the author, the creator, in the created characters of his novels. 'There is no spark of life in *The Name of Action* or *Rumour at Nightfall* because there was nothing of myself in them.' Real writers know that truth; critics often do not, and resent being told, with regard to Shakespeare, for example.

On the other hand I have no sympathy for the disease of Boredom, with which both Greene and Waugh were afflicted – it used to drive Evelyn to a local cinema three times a week. Graham says that it has been with him all his life, and has driven him to escape to all those horrible places, Liberia, the Congo, Kenya during the Mau-Mau horrors; Communist Cuba, Mexico during the religious persecution, Viet Nam. What was he seeking? – I suspect the squalor of

Greeneland. As against the beauty of the world and nature, such an inspiration to Harold Acton and me – Graham admits that psycho-analysis affected, if not atrophied, his visual sense.

So many points of contact in our so contrasting youths: collecting cigarette cards, and the addiction to reading Henty. Graham even read Q.'s novel, *Foe-Farrell*, three or four times. And he makes the good point of how important the early influence of books is upon one – at least upon the intelligent who read. But I do not share his idea of living today, 'like most of my contemporaries, an apartment life between bedroom and sitting room'. With all his money he could rescue a beautiful country house, and live in it – even in England.

He prefers the cult of squalor. I had enough of that in the working-class village where I was born and brought up, on its way to becoming a slum. I suppose it is the charm of the old folk ways of life that attracts people in *A Cornish Childhood*. But I could write an account of it that would give the other side of the coin. From one end of the village to the other: at the farm at the end, madness, the farmer cut his throat in the lunatic asylum; a few cottages along, an old widower hanged himself in the spence; next door, a sun-struck ex-soldier drove his wife to prostitution and would beat her, the two little kids were starved to death (the woman stole my mother's only gold brooch, gift of her friend). The dreadful life next door to us I did describe, the impoverished family of the rogue under the name of Jack 'Loam'; but not the fact that round the corner a poor single woman, with two children, earned her living as a prostitute and died of syphilis. In the cottages above her, a poor little boy was murdered by a lout from the next village. A nice young fellow at the end – I went to elementary school with him – died of syphilis picked up in the town.

No wonder I preferred life at All Souls, and country-house life at Trenarren. Edith Wharton was such a *grande dame* of letters that everybody wondered whether she had ever experienced sex. When she died it transpired that she had written a perfect piece of pornography, to show them. I have sometimes been tempted to write up the other side of village life from *A Cornish Childhood*. It would show that one need not go to the Congo or Central America, the Mau-Mau Reserve or Viet-Nam for horrors.

Brighton Rock (1938) was Greene's first undoubted master-piece: he still thinks it one of his best books. I am not sure that it is not his very best; it is certainly a *tour de force*. It makes for breathless reading, and yet what a nasty world it depicts – the little 'mob' of gangsters with their ready razor-blades and face-slashing, even murders, led by an utterly amoral, evil boy Pinkie (is the name suggested by pink-eye?). He is a lapsed Catholic, which gives us a little convenient Catholic flavouring now and then – an utterly incredible character, yet Greene succeeds in bringing him to life. The mastery is in the dialogue, and the gangster-lingo is certainly convincing. So are some of the other characters: the heroine, the good floozy Ida with her big breasts (much insisted on) and her regular habit of belching stout (ditto).

The Brighton depicted is hardly the Brighton I recognise. The sea there is glimpsed at the end of the street like common washing hung out in the square of a tenement. A child limps by, leg in an iron brace, while an old man, licking a sore lip, rootles among the seaweed for cigarette ends and rubbish on the beach. The smoke rises from a crematorium, which has had a busy day; the body of the murdered man had ingrow-ing toe-nails. A gangster drains the whisky out of himself into the movement below the piles. He then treads in a dog's ordure. After copulation with the generous Ida, Phil has his mouth open, showing a gob of metal filling; he is yellow with sexual effort.

Pinkie marries the girl Rose, to shut her mouth about what she knows. She works in Snow's squalid restaurant, where a cinema organ plays, 'a great *vox humana* trembled across the crumby, stained desert of used cloths: the world's wet mouth lamenting over life'. Rose's home is of indescrib-able squalor, the passage stinks like a lavatory. For Pinkie to marry is 'like ordure on the hands'. Since both are, or rather were, Catholics, their registry office marriage does not count, their copulation a 'mortal sin', with Pinkie 'trying to taste God in the mouth'. (Ugh! a horrible image.) A proper marriage would of course have the couple before the altar with the priest and the Host.

No wonder the Brighton Council took exception to the depiction of their beautiful town – those splendid Regency squares and terraces fronting the sea; the remarkable Victorian churches, one of them, St Bartholomew's, tall like Albi cathedral, one of the finest in England. Let alone the unique Pavilion, with its domes and minarets. True, when I was last in Brighton, it was swathed in scaffolding for repairs from a fire started by a vandal – quite sufficiently typical of the filthy society we have survived into.

Graham is self-conscious, and on the defensive, about Greeneland, but he derives inspiration from seediness and squalor. About the time of *Brighton Rock*, I commented to Vivien about his remarkable eyes – opened wide and magnetically as if he saw the world with horror, as I suppose he does. I cannot approve: I immeasurably prefer Acton's vision, seeking for beauty wherever and in whatever it may be found. Why? One must always give a reason: the one is an enhancement of life, the other is a degradation.

About this time too I recall a meal in Oxford at Graham's. There was already a strain in his marriage, which I will not go into, though I know the other side. I remember the furniture, the elegant, uncomfortable Regency window-seat Vivien had picked up, but little of the dinner-party. Martin D'Arcy, the Jesuit, another friend (within limits) was there. Conversation did *not* flow; Graham was silent, I felt a fish out of water and had nothing to contribute. Martin was reduced to filling in with snobbish talk about his old Irish family. There was a sense of desolation. Not long after, Graham left Vivien.

Meeting him a year or two after, I said to him squarely, 'I don't much read novels. Tell me which is your best one, and I'll read that.' He very kindly gave me *The Power and the Glory* (1940). Dutifully, I ploughed through it, put off from the beginning by the squalid scene, a seedy settlement on the coast of Mexico. A few vultures, searching under their wings for parasites, look down on a poor dentist, Mr Tench (stench?), who is not carrion yet. The sharks look after carrion on the other side, the sea. Mr Tench spits out the heavy phlegm in his mouth, three spits in two pages, then spits out the gathered bile – five spits in four pages. 'We should be thankful we cannot see the horrors and degradation lying around our childhood, in cupboards and bookshelves, everywhere.'

A stranger arrives on this delightful scene: he is a hunted priest, in the time of religious persecution, who is to be martyred at the end of the book. He is, of course, not an attractive character – O no: that would be too easy game. He is a whisky priest, a drunk, and he has had an illegitimate child in his dubious past. Nevertheless, 'I can put God in man's mouth all the same' (that distasteful image again!); and he has 'given God' to the faithful. Nor is he an attractive specimen to look at: his dark suit and sloping shoulders remind Mr Tench of a coffin 'and death was in his carious mouth already'. He felt a reluctant hatred of the sick woman and child ahead of him: 'he was unworthy of what he carried', i.e. he could perform the Miracle. Everywhere was pain in 'the huge abandonment', i.e. Greeneland.

Depreciation is a form of recommendation – like the unattractive Irish priest who reconciles the Marquis on his death-bed in Waugh's *Brideshead Revisited*. An intelligent person is not taken in by this ploy; nor by the popular objections to Catholicism made by the kindly Lutheran couple, only to show how silly they are and how absurd are their objections to the Faith. Another Catholic, Flannery O'Connor – heroic woman and splendid writer – as a born Catholic objects to the converts, Waugh and Greene, subjecting art in their novels to preachment, pushing their proselytising. She considered that it deformed their work: nothing of that in hers, thank goodness. Actually Waugh did not always approve of the inversion of moral sense in some of Greene's books; and Acton, a fellow Catholic who never drags his nostrum under one's nose, has a comment to the point: 'Morals mattered more to Evelyn Waugh than to certain other religious novelists of our age.'

The squalor is continuous. 'It was the hour of prayer.

Black beetles exploded against the walls like crackers. More than a dozen crawled over the tiles with injured wings.' The Communist lieutenant is a sincere, rather a 'good' man, only he believes that human beings have evolved 'from animals for no purpose at all'. (The answer to that, Graham, is that men find their own purpose within themselves, or simply fail to do so.) We come up against the perversity about death, which we noticed in the author's account of his early life. 'Fear and death were not the worst things. It was sometimes a mistake for life to go on.' The priest excuses the American gangster: 'He only killed and robbed. He hadn't betrayed his friends.'

Now killing *is* worse than betraying one's friends, for there is no rectifying it. If one betrays one's friends there is a chance of redeeming it. This is only common sense. Greene's ploy is to invert common sense – like the perverse Sartre, with his 'Soviet Russia is the incarnation of human freedom.' So Greene tells us that pity is corrupting, that a sense of innocence goes with sin, that it is *treachery* to be more afraid of the pain of bullets than of 'what comes after'. No one knows what comes after. All this is inversion of sense. The death-wish is theologically un-Christian. We are supposed to make the best of our lives, to find enjoyment in doing our best. Even for a martyr to wish martyrdom is a temptation to be resisted – Eliot makes that point, not wholly satisfactorily, à propos of Thomas à Becket. (I suspect, as a historian, that Becket wished for martyrdom at the end.)

The confessional is the stuffy boxlike coffin in which 'men bury their uncleanness with their priest'. The priest himself asks, 'What was the good of confession when you loved the result of your crime?' Common sense replies, what indeed? A more Protestant view would be, then why not do something about it? It was a Lutheran invention, we are told, that cleanliness comes next to godliness – 'cleanliness', he repeats, 'not purity'. Why not go in for it then? Or, at least, try. It is suggested that piety can have a falsity like successful crime, or politics. Sometimes 'pious men die in brothels unabsolved'. Well, if they believe that sort of thing they should not take the risk; or perhaps not be caught there.

The Holy Office in Rome, which we used to know as the Inquisition, took objection to this book on account of its morals, which it described as 'paradoxical'. I am bound to own that my sympathies are with the Holy Office: 'paradoxical' was only a kinder word for perverse. Catholic authority, in old-fashioned but straight-forward language, condemned 'violent and immoral books cloaked in the glitter of aesthetics'. The Cardinal in charge wanted a score of passages changed; Greene avoided that, somewhat casuistically, by saying that the matter rested with the publishers. The Pope himself, Paul VI, was more sympathetic – he was described in Rome as having something of a Hamlet in him. And, with a wry smile: 'That was Cardinal Pizzardo. There are bound to be some things in your books which offend some Catholics; but you needn't worry.'

It is no business of mine to worry over nonsense problems. All I need say is that I couldn't bear the book. In England it was awarded the Hawthornden Prize.

The other eminent Catholic novelist, Waugh, was no more at ease with the moral confusion – to use no worse word – of his colleague's work. He described Greene's play, *The Potting Shed*, in writing to him as 'enthralling', but in writing to his wife, Laura Waugh, 'the play is great nonsense theologically'. Well, if these people set themselves nonsense problems, they can expect to get into inextricable tangles – like C.S. Lewis on the Problem of Pain, or the 'booby-traps' which Graham says he has set himself in his own life (he also applies his own word 'infidelities'). Favourite reading with him is theology, and Waugh describes him as 'deep in a condemned book by an Italian theologian who holds that mankind was created to redeem the Devil'. We see what superfluous nonsense they involve themselves in.

Of the play, *The Living Room*, Waugh wrote to Graham that he was 'dazzled by your mastery of your new art. The play held me breathless. . . . A first-class play.' For himself he wrote his real opinion: 'I felt the tone was false, the piety of the old Catholic ladies wasn't piety. The tragic love of the heroine wasn't tragic.' Of *The Quiet American*, it is 'a masterly but base work'. (I find *my* comment on the book, when read going through Wyoming: 'it's comic, the solemnity with which all this stuff is treated as a revelation of life, when its revelation is only fantasy. Result: the ethical problems are unreal, because his world is unreal – melodrama'.) Of another novel about Greeneland, in this case Africa, Waugh expressed 'admiration for your superb description of the leper village and for the brilliance with which you handle the problems of dialogue in four languages'. Fair enough, for he is an accomplished technician. But the content? To a fellow Catholic, Lady Longford, he called it 'a most distressing book', and to another, Christopher Sykes, 'M. Grisjambon Vert has written a very sorrowful novel.' Eventually he comes clean with Greene himself: 'I cannot wish your book success. God forbid I should pry into the secrets of your soul. It is simply your public performance which grieves me.' Like the Holy Office, Waugh thought that Greene did not set a good Catholic example.

To be fair, having said that I neither like nor respect (except technically) his serious novels, I ought to say what it is in his work that I do like and can admire. There are two categories that I appreciate, his short stories and the light-hearted comic books that he calls 'entertainments'. I regard him as a short story writer with entire admiration, immensely more so than, say, Kingsley Amis, with whom I agree politically, not with Graham. But, then, in criticism one must discount one's bias to achieve justice of mind. Graham himself holds that four or five of his short stories are among his best work, and I am happy to agree with him. 'May We Borrow Your Husband?' is a masterly rendering of ambivalent sex life on the Riviera, acutely observed, not shared: altogether not his line, as he makes clear himself. In the second category, *Travels With My Aunt* is wholly enjoyable: no perverse moralising or inversion of good sense. I recall that Father Gervase, Graham's spiritual adviser, and our common friend, preferred the light entertainments to the gloom of the serious novels. Even the short stories, however, are described as 'Tales of Innocence and Corruption'.

Let us look at the most masterly of them, 'The Destructors'. Waugh wrote, 'I wish you didn't think "destruction is

a sort of creation".' Perversity again, for it is *not*. The theme
is the destruction, by a gang of young vandals, of a beautiful
Wren house still left standing after the Blitz. '"What do you
mean – a beautiful house?" Blackie asked with scorn. It was
the word "beautiful" that worried him – that belonged to a
class world that you could still see parodied at the Wormsley
Common Empire. "We'll pull it down," he said. "We'll
destroy it."' This they proceed to do bit by bit, meticulously,
devotedly. It is our degraded society all right, young vandals
at work in every town – in the absence of the birch which
the police know they need. What is the good of a psychological talking-to for such types? They are simply out of hand.

The scene is set in the usual squalor. 'The lav was a
wooden shed at the bottom of the narrow garden, with a
star-shaped hole in the door: it had escaped the blast which
had smashed the house next door and sucked out the
window-frames of No. 3.' Spring in London means spar-
rows in the dust, and we read of the 'dreary waste of
Bayswater'. In another story we are introduced to the squalor
of the Edgware Road. Waugh comments on 'the inimitable
Clapham drabness' of *The End of the Affair*. This adds another
epithet to the familiar characteristics of Greeneland, the
seedy, the squalid, the drab. Even Oxford is described in
these terms: 'the peevish noise of innumerable bicycles, the
gas works, the prison, and the grey spires'. And why should
our 'baseless optimism' be 'more *appalling* than our despair'?
It may be sillier; even so, we need not despair; when one is
'unhappy about a girl' one 'can simply go and buy another
one'.

I fear that in much of his work the cult of squalor is top-
dressing for sentimentality beneath. Or his view of the world
is an extrapolation from inner misery – it is not exactly
fantasy but latches on to its complement in the outer world,
actively seeks it. In *Ways of Escape* we learn that he journeyed
to all those horrible places to escape – what? From himself?
Or just boredom, to which he has been subject all his life –
like Waugh going to the local cinema three or four times a
week. Or both of them taking refuge in drink. What about

the beauty of nature, art, the visual world there to refresh the soul?

Let us look into a lighter, later work, *Monsignor Quixote*. I found it a charming book, really a fable or parable, and the innocent Monsignor an engaging character. The story is delightful, but the thinking in it! – the argumentation slithery and disingenuous, confused as usual in trying to bring Catholicism and Communism together, Marx and Jesus Christ and all. Karl Marx wrote, 'Religion is the Opium of the People.' He did not write that to recommend either religion or opium. Greene attempts to explain that away by making the Monsignor say that in the 19th century opium was not an evil drug, just a tranquilliser for the well-to-do, which the poor could not afford. 'Religion is the Valium of the poor – that was all he meant.' This is not true: it is *not* what Marx meant. Marx hated religion, as strictly Communism does – one has only to look at its record everywhere. We know from his autobiography that Graham likes opium; the argument is not only disingenuous but intellectually second-rate.

So too with the demonstration of the Trinity. 'Two bottles equal in size. The wine they contained was of the same substance and it was born at the same time. There you have God the Father and God the Son, and there, in the half-bottle, God the Holy Ghost. Same substance. Same birth. They're inseparable. Whoever partakes of one partakes of all three.' The friend comments, 'very ingenious'. I think it infantile.

And what's all this muddled argument comparing Stalin and the Inquisitor Torquemada favourably, excusing them both: 'Torquemada at least thought he was leading his victims towards eternal happiness.' 'And Stalin too, perhaps.' Neither statement is true. Torquemada thought that heretics were doomed to eternal perdition, not eternal happiness. And Stalin certainly did not believe in the latter. The excuse for their crimes against mankind follows. 'A few million dead and Communism is established over half the world. A small price.' Then, 'A few hundred dead and Spain remains a Catholic country. An even smaller price.'

The facts themselves speak out against this deplorable nonsense. Belief in Communism is on its way out in the world: the facts have shown that it does not work. As for Spain – is it a Catholic country today? What an intelligent observer sees is not the Marxist illusion, the 'withering away of the state', but the withering away of these fanatical beliefs. As of other transcendental nostrums, we may say. The dead, we are told, need our prayers; then, a few pages later, 'I never pity the dead. I envy them.' This looks like a contradiction – why pray for them then? Still more, it looks like the death-wish expressed before, in a new guise.

We are presented with the usual Marxist jargon familiar to me from my undergraduate days. 'The capitalist state is a machine invented and used by the capitalists to keep the working class in subjection.' We can see for ourselves today how free from subjection the workers have been in Soviet Russia. Once more an excuse for it is put forward. 'Men will always have to choose a lesser evil and the lesser evil may mean the state, the prison camp, yes, if you like to say it, the psychiatric hospital. . . . But when we arrive at Communism, the state will wither away.' Some hopes! Nowhere is the oppression of the state more riveted upon the necks of the people than under Communism.

I am going to intervene with a moral of my own: it is people's beliefs, their fanaticisms, that not only make fools of them but render them ruthless and cruel, lead them on to the crimes against mankind such as those of Torquemada and Stalin.

Greene has always been partial to Communism, ready to defend the indefensible whether in Soviet Russia or Cuba. I challenged him on this a few years ago, in a letter to *The Times*, when he stated publicly that if he had to choose between living in Soviet Russia or in the United States, of course he would choose Soviet Russia. I asked, did he really mean this? If so, did he know what he was saying? Had he thought out the consequences? Whatever criticisms one may make of the United States, it is a free society. It does not hold its people in subjection, rule by persecution, prison camps, or by psychiatric hospitals, let alone the murder of millions. The anti-Americanism of Greene and Waugh is unworthy of them.

This did not prevent him from writing a Foreword recommending *My Silent War*, the account of his spying for Soviet Russia for thirty years, by Philby, described as 'the master spy of the 20th century'. I find my note says, 'Read with disgust and horror, New York, March 1969'. I do not want to go into the story of this heartless man, responsible for the deaths of other human beings, other agents, in the course of his services to Soviet Russia. It was certainly an exceptional achievement, to live a double life all that time, gaining access to secret information and handing it on, unsuspected by his colleagues and comrades in the British Secret Service. That was a well-known case of the Old School Tie racket!

In the Thirties Graham edited a book, under this title, from various contributors. There they all are – Wystan Auden and Stephen Spender, Harold Nicolson and Anthony Powell, William Plomer, Calder-Marshall; Eton and Harrow, Winchester, Wellington, St Paul's, Rugby, and of course Graham's Berkhamsted. But Kim Philby is not there – he had not yet surfaced. They could not, or would not, believe that one of them was capable of such things. I gather Philby's public school was Westminster; I note the usual self-deprecation, the newspapers' 'gratifying exaggeration of my own talents'. His services to Soviet Russia, and his disservice to his own country, could not be exaggerated. Suppose it had been me, not protected by the Old School Tie: I should not have been given the benefit of the doubt. He obviously hates his country, and the Establishment. I have no reason to love the Establishment, but that does not lead me into treason.

Philby tells us that he made his decision to become a Communist and serve Russia as the result of 1931. I have always regarded that year as a decisive turning-point, when the upper classes in this country ganged up to do down the Labour Movement, with the disastrous consequences that led straight to the war at the end of their rule throughout the

Thirties. I had more reason than Philby to resent what happened, for I was caught as a Labour candidate in the fraud of the Election in 1931 and continued the struggle in Opposition throughout that hopeless decade.

Philby tells us, 'the politics of the Baldwin–Chamberlain era struck me then, as they strike me now, as much more than the politics of folly. The folly was evil.' These men were wrong, but they were *not* evil. They did not rule by mass-murder. And in the end they fought against the evil thing, declared war against Hitler and all his works, while Communist Russia co-operated with him and helped Nazi Germany for two whole years, 1939–41, until attacked. Baldwin and Chamberlain, whatever we think of them, did *not* make a pact with Nazi Germany like the Molotov–Ribbentrop Pact which triggered the war.

I do not wish to go into the appalling personality revealed by his book, the heartlessness of it – obviously the long-time double-life killed any heart in the man, as with his comrades in the Russian Secret Service, always ready to abduct and kill. I merely note my comment on the portrait on his book: 'It gives him the look of a snake, a very male snake (five wives), the inhuman pitiless look of a snake, the concentration of a poisonous snake's head – and, I suppose, the fascination.'

I was shocked at Graham introducing such a man's book to the public. He recommends it as 'an honest one, well written, often amusing'. It does not amuse me, it appals me. 'The end, of course, in his eyes is held to justify the means. But this is a view taken, perhaps less openly, by most men involved in politics, if we are to judge them by their actions, whether the politician be a Disraeli or a Wilson.' Disingenuous again, or simply confused? – All we need say is that their actions do not include murder. Graham goes on: ' "He betrayed his country" – yes, perhaps he did; but who among us has not committed treason to something or someone more important than a country?' We recognise what he is referring to – his religion and his own personal life: we will not pry into that, though he has himself spoken of his 'infidelities', and his work has the constant refrain of 'guilt'.

All I am concerned with is the intellectual confusion, the second-rate thinking, the sentimental *suggestio falsi*: it is not true that all men are guilty of treason, either to country or individual. There is such a thing as loyalty to the one, fidelity to the other.

I will go no further. Graham acquits this evil man: 'He was serving a cause and not himself, and so my old liking for him comes back, as I remember those long Sunday lunches at St Albans when the whole sub-section relaxed under his leadership for a few hours of heavy drinking. . . . After thirty years in the underground surely he had earned his right to a rest.' My comment on that reads, 'Yes, to a traitor's grave. You ass, Graham!' Perhaps a more charitable comment is that of a member of his family – 'He is a goose about politics.'

In *Ways of Escape* his plea is: 'A writer who is a Catholic cannot help having a certain sympathy for any faith which is sincerely held.' Here again is the missing link in the argument, a missing link intellectually – for one's sympathy must depend on the character of the faith. No doubt the religious belief of Thuggee in India was sincerely held, but it led to the strangling of thousands of victims. A few pages further on we read of a Scottish planter and his wife in Malaya who drove into Kuala Lumpur for dinner. Chinese Communists took advantage of their absence to shoot their two-year-old daughter point-blank. 'The Party has resolved the question of love.'

In *The Ministry of Fear* we are told that 'Pity is cruel. Pity destroys. Love isn't safe when pity's prowling round.' Once more this is perverse, the inversion of ordinary human sense. One could construct a whole anthology of such perversity. Perhaps the Holy Office has done so. Waugh did not in the end approve, and he questioned the moral issue of Scobie's fate in *The Heart of the Matter*. Greene explains that 'suicide was Scobie's inevitable end; the particular motive of his suicide, to save even God from himself, was the final twist of the screw of his inordinate pride.' I have no desire to intervene in the discussion between these two experts in the casuistry of moral nonsense. I find such a resounding phrase

as 'the appalling strangeness of the mercy of God'
meaningless.

I am better equipped to take up his comment that Mexico
saw 'the fiercest persecution of religion anywhere since the
reign of Elizabeth'. This is an untruth with both Greene and
Waugh, and the mistake occurs again in the Foreword to the
autobiography of the Elizabethan Jesuit, Gerard, edited by
my former pupil, Father Philip Caraman, S.J. One can more
truthfully point to the far fiercer persecution of the Spanish
Inquisition, which burnt out all opposition to Catholicism in
Spain, while it happily survived in Elizabethan England. Or
one might point to Louis XIV's *dragonnades* which smoked
out Protestants in thousands, and drove them abroad to
become France's most enduring enemies. When it comes to
history these people make no effort to state the truth, they
merely repeat their bias. The intelligent are not taken in.

Nor by the exaggeration implicit in the question, 'Sometimes I wonder how all those who do not write, compose or
paint can manage to escape the madness, the melancholia,
the panic fear which is inherent in the human situation.' This
also is a very biased view; it applies only to a marginal
minority of abnormal persons who are no examples, let
alone mentors, for the rest of us. Nor again are 'years of
guilt' necessary 'to clear the haze of dreams and hopes and
false ambitions'. A Protestant would say, then behave yourself, or at least try to, and certainly not take refuge in the
death-wish. 'I had always thought war would bring death as
a solution in one form or another' – a solution for what? one
may ask – 'but here I was alive, the carrier of unhappiness to
people I loved, taking up the old profession of brothel-child.'

It is not for me to say whether there is any harm in
brothels. This one was in horrid Haiti: 'One night the three
of us braved the dark to visit the brothel I have described as
Mère Catherine's.' Apparently Waugh disapproved. He
describes a party given at Rheims to visit the champagne
houses, when Graham arrived in the bus with a bottle of
whisky which he 'swigged for comfort' all through the *vin
d'honneur* and the banquet given them. At the end Graham
'wanted to find a brothel, and wouldn't believe that they

were all closed'. Next morning he lurched out of the lift with bloodshot eyes – he had sat up to 4 a.m. drinking whisky. Drinking certainly plays an enormous part in the books, all those 'long evenings of solitary drinking'. I must say that, for someone who 'had always assumed before, as a matter of course, that death was desirable', he has managed to survive very well.

Opium plays its part too. He says in his autobiography: 'Of those four winters which I passed in Indo-China opium has left the happiest memory.' In horrible Hanoi 'I was smoking then a little opium two or three times a week.' There he graduated to two pipes as an *apéritif*, and after dinner 'returned and smoked five more'. Next day 'dinner with French friends and afterwards smoked six pipes'. A week later, in Phnom Penh, 'I had eight pipes'.

I fear that this is very unlike the domestic life at All Souls which I enjoyed. But Graham says that he was grateful for the experience of being drunk one whole term at Oxford, from breakfast to bed, for it gave him a good head for drink. He certainly seems to have had no reason to complain about his health, as I had in all those years.

Contacts with him were few, naturally enough, since he was so much abroad in those awful places, while I was buried in historical research, in the Public Record Office and British Museum, with dear Richard Pares. For a short time Graham was Literary Editor of the *Spectator*, for which I wrote occasionally, a breather from heavy research (my form of drink). Graham had over him as Editor a West Country Nonconformist humbug, one Wilson Harris, who attacked *A Cornish Childhood*. Graham was amused by this righteous type's way of coming into the book room, snooping any that had any salacious or pornographic promise – such as an international report on the White Slave traffic – then, covering it with some respectable League of Nations literature or piece of high-mindedness, marching out. Richard Pares used to call him 'a man of asbestos'.

In 1955, after finishing *The Quiet American*, the 'mood of escape' took Graham no further than to Monte Carlo, 'to live luxuriously for a few weeks in the Hôtel de Paris (chargeable as an expense to my income tax), to work long hours at the Casino tables (my losses I considered might be fairly chargeable too)'. In 1966 he decided to leave the country for good and settle abroad. He was made a Companion of Honour. Or, as Waugh put it, 'Graham Greene has fled the country with the CH and a work of Communist propaganda.' I do not know which book this refers to.

The last time I saw Graham I was rather surprised to run into him in the street in London. So I hailed him with, 'I thought you were not supposed to be here.' He blushed a little, and explained hesitantly, 'Oh, I'm allowed ninety days.' I can sympathise with writers – a whole string of them – who leave the country to evade punitive British taxation, which penalises those who work for the benefit of those who have no intention of doing so, and for other causes which I detest. But I have no sympathy for those who, safely ensconced in Paris or Antibes, write back to the papers approving of the squalid society which we have to put up with here.

And now, *pour comble de tout*, he has been awarded an OM. I do not know what Evelyn would say about that, but long may M. Grisjambon Vert enjoy it at Antibes!

Daphne du Maurier: Fortune and Romance

Everybody has urged me to write about my neighbour and friend of many years, Daphne du Maurier, and at length I have capitulated. Why not? Well, I know some of my limitations; one is that I have never been familiar with the world of the theatre, though I love it; another is that I am no authority on modern novels, and do not spend much time reading them. However, I have read a good many, though apt to be choosy; in another word, I am discriminating, not easy to please.

On the other hand is the historian, and the fact that I have known this extremely reticent, reserved writer, hard to know, and not easy to understand for all her world-wide popularity. Few know the real woman. And then there is Cornwall . . . As the Duc d'Aumale said on a famous occasion – Marshal Bazaine's surrender of Metz to the Germans: 'Il y avait la France.' There is indeed Cornwall – which we share in a way, looking out over the same beautiful bay: Daphne from her eyrie up above the eastern peninsula leading to the Gribben, which she has celebrated in her books; I at the neck of the western end of the bay, the cone of Black Head, with its prehistoric cliff-fort, and the wonderful view down to the cove at Trenarren, more sheltered, less extensive and wild than hers from Kilmarth.

We sometimes say that we could signal to each other across the intervening blue space of water. We are both a bit psychic and do exchange signals, conducting a good deal of our correspondence by telepathy. Though there are letters, exchanges of photographs, cards, books.

The historian is naturally fascinated by her fabulous historical background, the brilliantly gifted and variegated Anglo-French family from which she comes. Every good fairy seems to have stood in at her christening, including the clergyman who performed the ceremony – a Reverend Bernard Shaw.

Daphne herself looks back to her grandfather George du Maurier (1834–1896) as the creator of the family, the source of its distinction. For he was a man of genius, with an extraordinary range of talents. Half-French, half-English, he was at ease in both languages and wrote light verse in both. His chief fame came from his cartoons and drawings in *Punch*, recognised in his own time as an authentic visual register of the Victorian age. His main line here was to score, not too unkindly, the ubiquitous snobbishness of the age, as Thackeray, his mentor, did in literature. Du Maurier had other artistic talents; he was a good portraitist and illustrator of books. He illustrated Mrs Gaskell's *Sylvia's Lovers*, after whom he called one of his daughters. He knew the circle of Pre-Raphaelite artists, and was a success in society, for in addition to charm and humour, he had a beautiful tenor voice and was a good amateur actor.

On top of all this he won a second fame as a writer, with three novels, two of which may be regarded as Victorian classics – *Peter Ibbetson, The Martian, Trilby.* Everybody knew the name of Trilby when I was young, for it caught on and set the fashion: there were 'trilby hats' and costumes, I don't know what-all. The novel had prodigious success, and not only as a novel: made into a play, it took both London and New York by storm, and must have made a packet in those days when one could hold on to one's own earnings and not have them confiscated for objects of which one disapproves.

George du Maurier was careful about money, as his famous son Gerald, Daphne's father, was not. Daphne has spoken to me of her 'French peasant' inflexion, though the background was much more varied and interesting. There was a Breton element in the stock; the grandfather had a Breton motto the family quoted and adhered to: Abret-ag-Araog, First and Foremost. Perhaps that counted for something in Daphne's make-up, the absolute fixation she came to have on Cornwall. It was like a coming-home to her, she did not really find herself until she found Cornwall. Then, and only then, she began to fulfil herself. It is really rather queer.

But she believes in luck, as I do. (She has had all the luck, *Ich nicht.*) She told me once that her grandfather, her real precursor and preceptor, wrote the plots of his novels into a black book, into which she writes the plots of hers, for *luck.* She certainly has had luck with her all the way (*my* grandparents were illiterate – perhaps I have rather over-compensated for that).

The French side of the family did not go back to peasants, but to the *petite-noblesse* of the *Ancien Régime* with a château and all, before the disaster of the French Revolution. They had, as a matter of privilege, an interest in a glass-blowing factory. Daphne has taken this into her novel *The Glass Blowers*, making provident use of everything that has come her way by experience or reading and observation – as that prudent, careful man, William Shakespeare did in his work.

There came into the record and the tradition a figure of even more interest to the historian. Daphne's great-great-grandmother was the notorious Mary Anne Clarke, mistress of George III's soldier son, the Duke of York, about whom there exploded a tremendous Regency scandal. Not over the sex affair: all respectable George III's sons were very sexy and several of them had illegitimate families. That was all in the day's work in Regency society: Lady Oxford's children were known as the Harleian Miscellany, all by different fathers.

The Duke of York and Mary Anne made a public scandal for her little habit of selling commissions in the Army (of which he was the head), or at least taking money on them. Daphne has had the courage and candour to write the life of her ancestress in *Mary Anne* novelistically: needs must, for there was not all that material to go upon biographically.

In the biography she is sympathetic enough; in the family history, *The du Mauriers*, she is rather hard on her. I don't have much fault to find with Mary Anne, except for her extravagance: she had only one thing to sell, and she sold it. When the scandal broke she was paid off with an annuity, for her life and that of her daughter Ellen. So the family had *that* to go upon in two generations; it gave Ellen's son, George du Maurier, a start in life.

Was there anything else? Daphne says modestly that nobody knows who Ellen's father was, 'duke or dustman'. Perhaps Mary Anne herself did not know, as is often the case; naturally she would prefer to have it the Duke's. I have sometimes wondered where those beautiful blue eyes of Daphne's came from, periwinkle blue or lavender blue. That remarkable colour is a noticeable feature in all the members of the Hanoverian Royal family, from George III downwards.

I must say this for Mary Anne, apart from her good looks: she had spirit and courage, determination to hold on, in spite of starting from nothing. Daphne allows that she had fighting qualities. She fought for her children and saw them through. The determination did not come from the du Maurier side, into which Ellen married. It may be that the gifts came thence; for Ellen's husband was a clever inventor, though he had no practical success.

What a rich plum-pudding it all makes – gifts, talents, looks in every direction; then too spirit, courage, determination. One sees all these in Daphne's make-up and achievement; one notices, in addition to the beauty – those eyes! – the determined set of the chin.

Then there is her father, another famous figure, the actor, producer and theatre-manager, Gerald du Maurier. He too had luck with him all the way: he never knew what failure was. When he first went to New York as a very young man, all doors were open to him as his father's son. Still, though everything came to him easily, almost casually, he deserved his success. Not just for his fabulous charm – he had a charming generous nature – for which women swooned; he had a devoted personal following, crowds recognised and followed him. I am no historian of the theatre, but I can discern two elements in his achievement worthy of historical record. After the exaggerated rhetorical style of Victorian acting – of which the Cornish Henry Irving (really Brodribb) was the prime exponent – du Maurier brought in a more natural, easy style: none of the old pomposity, over-acting. Secondly, he had good standards, with his father's literary background. He had a wide range, and was very successful with Edgar Wallace's thrillers. But his real fame in the theatre came along with his partnership with Barrie, from whose plays du Maurier was inseparable: he created his parts in them and directed others, he produced them, *The Admirable Crichton, Dear Brutus*, the seemingly indestructible *Peter Pan*, the lot. A Barrie play was a du Maurier play too; overlooked, under-estimated in this cruel age for their sentiment, they are nevertheless a part not only of the history of drama but of literature.

How does Daphne stand in this colourful concatenation of genius and talent, character and temperament?

She was much closer to her father than to her mother, whose profession was also acting before her growing family came to take first place, along with her quasi-maternal care of Gerald, who – moody, temperamental, extravagant – needed it. So there was theatre on both sides. Yet the young Daphne was not enamoured of the stage, let alone glamourised by it: she even speaks of sitting in their box 'glowering' sullenly at the stalls. She took it for granted as the work-a-day background of their family life. She speaks of herself as a 'loner', disliking company and preferring solitude. Clearly she was odd-man-out in that family.

This is significant for her future. It explains the fact that she did not take to writing for the theatre. In all the large body of her work there are only two unimportant plays. A dramatist needs to be geared to society, at least easy with it, if not necessarily a sociable sort of fellow. Daphne never was: her nature was that of the born novelist. Henry James held that, for that vocation, one needed to be half in life and half outside: enough in life to know what it is about, and enough outside to observe what is going on in the aquarium.

Here again she was fortunate: her not easy nature, her *difference*, was right for her vocation from the start – once she got over the difficulties of beginning, which she did with that characteristic determination. Hers was a stronger character than Gerald's. He had a marked feminine streak, though a conventional man, easily shockable. His daughter not; she had a masculine independence of mind. Independence is a clue to her nature; she was determined to go her own way. We must not say that she is a 'throw-back' to her grandfather – as Elizabeth I was to hers: George du Maurier was a genial, very sociable fellow. Yet Daphne's genius has more in common with him than with her father. Where did that spirit of independence, that fighting courage, come from?

We must probe a little more deeply. Psychological ambivalence has enormous advantages, especially for artist or writer: it doubles the sensibilities and the responses to life. William Shakespeare, Flaubert, Proust, Henry James, even Tolstoy – almost all the great artists have it, in greater or lesser degree. This does not necessitate *physical* ambivalence: this is where people go wrong about William Shakespeare. (Henry James: 'Nobody ever understands *any*thing.') Physically no one could be more feminine than Daphne: pretty as a girl, growing into a beautiful woman, that lithe and graceful figure – then graduating at the proper time to the fulfilment of marriage and normal family life. But beneath this delicate, beguiling exterior I detect an element of masculine steel and stoic courage.

She always wanted to be a boy, disliked being a girl and the business that goes with it. She wanted above all things to be free and independent: the very reverse of the 'clinging' woman – one cannot imagine her as such. As she has said to me, 'I have always been the bread-winner.' She not only thought of herself as a boy, but it is a clue, little spotted by the great heart of her public, to her work. No less than five of her novels tell the story in the first person as a male character. With her world bestseller, *Rebecca*, the story is seen through the eyes of a woman – as with *Jane Eyre*. Daphne has had the best of both worlds. What luck again!

We need not pause over her education, merely observe that she did not go to the university – unlike those whiskered academic ladies so much occupied with lit. crit. that they cannot even see common sense about the Dark Lady. A writer's education is primarily self-education. Daphne did have something more than a spell of finishing school in Paris. Here was another advantage of that bilingual background. She had a natural instinct for France, and a special feeling for Paris – like her grandfather's nostalgia for the Rue du Bac. (One recalls the little Prince Imperial's sigh, in exile: if only he could see the omnibus debouching from the Rue du Bac – as of course he would have seen it from the Tuileries.)

This Paris background came in handy for her second novel, with the youthful title *I'll Never Be Young Again*. An emancipated young lady of the Twenties, this book rather shocked her *bourgeois* father, still more the very Victorian Q., who was mentor to us both, the tutelary deity of Fowey. He carpeted her at The Haven: 'My dear Daphne, people don't say such things,' the old innocent reproved her. The young lady, who *knew*, replied, 'But, Sir Arthur, they *do*.' The dear old boy couldn't face the thought, especially with his old-fashioned gallantry about women, and wondered whether this made suitable company for daughter Foy and her friend Lady Vyvyan of Trelowarren.

That happy group of young females were more free-spirited and adventurous than he knew – not only in man-handling boats, but in ranging the moors on their ponies, tramping miles across heath and bog in all winds and weathers. The eastern side of Bodmin Moor is rather unknown and treacherous country, no roads, but bogs. One autumn night Foy and Daphne got lost there – as John Wesley had lost his way a couple of centuries before. The girls ultimately glimpsed a light: Jamaica Inn at Bolventor.

Here was the seed of a subsequent bestseller, *Jamaica Inn*, which also made the fortune of that granite-raw establishment by the wayside. Today coach-loads of tourists draw up there – luck again: it must help to keep that exciting melodrama fresh and green – as with another romantic novel, *Frenchman's Creek*, snaffled for the name of a café-restaurant on the town quay at Fowey. I am reminded of Byron and Tom Moore out on the Thames one evening, when they heard one of the river-men singing a popular Irish Melody of Moore's. 'There is *real* fame for you,' said Byron.

What brought Daphne to the riverside at Fowey in the first place?

It was by accident that the family happened upon the curious, idiosyncratic house beside Bodinnick Ferry opposite the town of Fowey. The place was odd enough to suit Daphne and the whole ambience to excite her imagination. Odder still, she had the strange feeling of 'coming home' at last – unaccountable, and perhaps psychic, when after all she was not Cornish and did not, in our phrase, 'belong'. (A few, rather chosen, people have had that sensation too – perhaps the place chooses the person, as with me at Trenarren.)

'Ferryside', as it became, is a peculiar, very recognisable building. The ground floor was a store and workshop, the only habitable part up above, cliff at the back, but the front facing the river, harbour, estuary and magnificent view out to the open sea. Daphne's mother made a habitable house out of it; her father, geared to London and Hampstead, did not like it. It was Daphne who adopted it and found it propitious for writing: this made it her own. Not only for writing: she took like a duck to the water, learned to handle boats and to sail, eventually had her own sailing craft built to her own specifications.

Independence at last! She was not happy in London, or with conventional social life, moody and difficult. More important, that was not conducive to her writing. She had begun, as we all do, with poems and short stories. Not much luck with the poems, though they are authentic enough: they also show talent, unlike much of the formless uncooked verse going without effort into print today. But for her stories there was an uncle standing by ready to publish them, as editor, in *The Bystander*. Thus she was launched; but the strange and really fascinating thing is that it was only in coming to Cornwall that she found herself.

Here she found inspiration. Out of it came, in 1931, her first novel, *The Loving Spirit*. Plyn of course is Fowey. There is an ancient place Pelyn, near Lostwithiel, up above the river. Stranded between there and Fowey was the old hulk of a sailing vessel that had belonged to a family called Slade. The young writer ferreted out all she could find about the family. There was the grave of old Jane Slade up the hillside in the lovely churchyard of Lanteglos; a descendant was alive and active still at nearby Polruan.

In the book they are called Coombe, after the name of the Rashleigh farm above Menabilly. It is a romantic family story of three generations through the 19th century – perhaps the sense of her own family coming through, if unconsciously, translated into Cornwall. Still more is it a translation of place: ships and sailing, the sense of wind and sea blows through it, along with (of course) the love element.

We can sleuth the young woman in her book as she sleuthed the Slades to create it. The epigraph is from Emily Brontë, and her famous poem is quoted: 'No coward soul is mine'. That has remained true for Daphne throughout her life: she thus early recognised a kindred spirit. It is no less a portent: she was to write, years later, about the half-Cornish Brontës.

We find her regular signature tune, the girl wanting to be a man, half-a-dozen times over. Perhaps we may quote only one sentence: 'He was her second self, he was to do all the things that had been denied her because of her sex; he loved the sea and the ships with the same passion that she did, and because he was a man he would become a sailor, and she would see through his eyes all those dreams she had imagined when she was alone.'

A revealing sentence tells us that she had a way of hiding her loneliness so that she appeared 'willing and cheerful in face of others'. This is said of the heroine, but it is true of her creator: I have always found Daphne cheerful and willing, but I must add to that her kindness, a generous spirit for all her careful reserve.

An historian naturally notices her acute sense of time, time as a dimension. Her heroine (really Jane Slade) had travelled 'half a century, out of the world into space, into another time'. Again, of her son, 'she knew him to belong to the future, when she was dead and in her grave'. Time Present leading to Time Future and back into Time Past. This almost psychically points forward to the most original of her later novels, *The House on the Strand*, which operates with practised skill on two levels of time. On a more familiar level it points to her continuing interest in history as such, which inspires several of her books. We see that her remarkably varied body of work is all of a piece.

Walking the cliffs on the western side of the estuary towards the Gribben headland, with its tower for seamark, Daphne and her sister spied the old manor house of Menabilly in a clearing of its woods. Later they set out to find it from what had been the entrance, with lodge, at Four Turnings along the main road. They found the long drive completely overgrown, almost impassable, and were forced to turn back in the dark. At a second attempt from an entrance nearer the headland, across the park, they found the house. Deserted, forlorn, overgrown with ivy, atmospherical, waiting . . .

It was the home of the Rashleighs, a Devon family that had come to Fowey in the Elizabethan age and prospered there. Something of their town house remains in the Ship Inn at Fowey, a panelled great-chamber upstairs, and their tombs in the church behind. John Rashleigh sailed his ship, the *Francis*, up to Plymouth to serve under Drake against the Armada in '88.

I possess the fine Dutch print of Drake that came from Menabilly, also a few pieces of its furniture, including a unique decorated wardrobe. My great-grandfather, a Lanyon, was the estate carpenter there in early Victorian days.

Doctor Rashleigh, the late Victorian owner, deserted it – apparently he had unhappy memories of his lonely childhood there with a repressive grandfather. Daphne penetrated by a window into the back of the house and explored the historic mansion, deep in dust and dry rot, yet beautiful in its unloved state: Queen Anne staircase, panelled walls, wood-work, family portraits. All crying out to be loved, and brought back to life again.

The place possessed her imagination, salted away in a corner of her mind, till it took wing as Manderley in *Rebecca*. That was some years later. Meanwhile the house slept, or dreamed on, with its ghosts: a Sleeping Princess lost in its woods, like the house in Alain-Fournier's *Le Grand Meaulnes*, that fairy-tale book, one of the half-dozen modern books I should most like to have written.

Daphne told me that, in the years between, she would occasionally peer in through the shutters at the front: there was the dark panelled dining-room with the family portraits on the walls. I had a similar obsession with Trenarren, home of the ancient Hexts, also deserted for a house in Devon. I used to sit on the roadside wall, looking into the shelving garden, flowering away to nobody at all, and wonder 'Why am I not living in that lovely place?' I too kept a secret corner for it in my imagination – to flower, not in a novel, but in many poems.

Paradoxically, Daphne's novel *The Loving Spirit*, in which the theme of the girl who wishes to be a man is celebrated, led to her marriage. The book was read and admired by an heroic young officer, who had won a DSO and Croix de Guerre in the 1914–18 war, a professional soldier who came to be known as 'Boy' Browning, since he was thought the youngest Major in the Army.

The courtship was swift and romantic. He brought his boat down to Fowey and cruised up and down the river, occasionally catching sight of the fair writer within, and not unobserved by those interested blue eyes. As luck would have it, their families had been acquainted in the previous generation, so the siege was established in due form.

Not until next year, 1932, did Daphne capitulate. It would seem to have been a cool and rational decision on her part, certainly a courageous one; for, marrying a professional soldier meant a departure from her chosen way of life, an upheaval from beloved Bodinnick and accompanying him around to headquarters camp-life, at any rate part of the time. She may not have realised that the Germans were heading for a renewal of the war, with all the dangers that would involve for a growing family. In the Second German War, 'Boy' Browning bore an heroic part as Commander of airborne troops, in the terrible shambles at Arnhem, etc. In all this Daphne's courage never failed her.

She made the decision, as she says, for a 'fuller life'. She had been in love before, for some years, with a cousin more than a decade older; then there was her love for her father, who greeted the news of her engagement with, 'It isn't fair!' Daphne was now twenty-five, not just of an age to know her own mind – she had always known that; the gallant Major was again ten years older – it seems that she was impelled to reserve her love for an older man.

No nonsense about a fashionable London wedding: this remarkable woman, who had such reason to be proud of her historic background, has always been above any kind of snobbishness – her grandfather's chief target. The wedding was kept secret: only a couple of neighbourly witnesses, and early in the morning up the hill to Lanteglos church, by Jane Slade's grave. I find it touching.

When they came back to set off for their honeymoon, all the riverside turned out to give them a send-off. The Couches – dear Q., with wife and daughter – were there in their rowing boat to hail them with a bottle of home-made sloe-gin. And so off, out at harbour mouth, passing the Gribben and down the coast to the Helford River and therein Frenchman's Creek, the future drawing ever onwards, opening out.

In 1938 Daphne hit the jackpot with *Rebecca*: it became not only a bestseller but a world bestseller – films of it, stage-plays, television. Its good fortune is not my subject, but one must pay tribute to the undying vitality of the book that has kept its place in the forefront – Abret-ag-Araog – for half a century.

Here we are concerned to locate the author in it. The background is the house that had for so long appealed to her imagination, and which the success of the book – what a stroke of fortune! – was to enable her to occupy. It is all so recognisable – the cove, the headland with its beacon, and there *was* the hulk of a wreck on the beach below, the forest of rhododendrons and camellias. The house in the book is rather larger and grander: something of Milton of the Fitzwilliams in Northamptonshire, where Daphne stayed as a girl, is added with its grand staircase.

Here one recognises the author: 'My father was a lovely and unusual person'; again, 'I remembered my father and his scorn of superficial snobbery.' There is the girl who wants to be a boy and has never possessed a brother. We recognise the pattering feet of a couple of dogs, as always. From the back wing of the house one cannot hear the sea – that Victorian excrescence was happily pulled down when Daphne came to live there. I assume a little credit for encouraging her to get rid of the plate-glass from the front and restore the proper small panes.

The heroine – a kind of Jane Eyre – confesses that nerves make it difficult for her to face people outright. Here is Daphne's exceptional shyness, that has enabled her to keep the world at bay and concentrate on her work. In those days I hardly knew her, but a wartime friend who was also something of a bestseller, Phyllis Bottome, was anxious to meet her and, rather temerariously, I took her over. Phyllis was a good old war-horse, rather masculine, half-American, ready to tackle anybody.

When we arrived I caught a glimpse of Daphne wriggling with shyness round the corner of the house, willing herself to confront the unknown. At tea old Phyllis took charge. 'Ever been to the United States?' I think that once Daphne had had to go over to confront a ludicrous charge of plagiarism from some silly woman who had also written a book in which someone falls in love with someone else. 'Couldn't you come and give some lectures?' 'Oh, no!' – I saw the look of horror in those eyes at the thought.

As I watched those two famed ladies fencing with each other I thought that it had been a mistake to obtrude the warhorse upon the shy colt, and that they would hate each other. Not a bit of it: the mere man observing the scene was quite wrong. Those two women became good friends and started a correspondence. I mention this as an aspect of Daphne of which the public may be unaware: she is a thorough good sport – as that first book has it, covering her lonely spirit with willingness and cheerfulness.

When I re-read *Rebecca* now I see it as the triumph it is, perfect *in its own terms* as both romance and detective thriller worked out with the sheer cleverness and ingenious skill that was to become characteristic. It deserved all its success – and she was only thirty when she achieved it. I confess that at the time, all unknown, I was jealous. The Thirties were a miserable time for me, held up in my work by years of illness. It made me criticise, with the irritability of a member of the duodenal club: Max de Winter for name of a Cornish-man of family, pure Hollywood! It should have been Car-minow, or Godolphin or Penhallow. The sinister Mrs Danvers? – one wouldn't have kept her on as housekeeper for a fortnight, etc. Irrelevant in the book's own terms.

However, I was somewhat consoled when my own bestseller, *A Cornish Childhood*, came out, and Daphne's lawyer at Fowey commented, 'This is the real thing.' Actually, as her increasingly impressive body of work unrolled I came to appreciate it more, not only the later books, which I rate more highly, but the earlier too, remark-able for so young a writer. An odd stroke of fate happened to *Rebecca* – to be taken by Neville Chamberlain to Berchtes-gaden as light relief from Hitler!

Daphne was a soldier's wife, and Browning was heavily engaged in training troops for the eventual come-back. They were together at times in the danger-area of Southern England, at Hythe in Kent then in Hertfordshire. There were now the worries of a young family to cope with, two girls and a boy about to appear. Nothing daunted, Daphne took up war-work along with it, as gas-decontaminator in a First Aid unit, all with spirit and good humour. When a lone raider dropped bombs on the farm nearby, it was 'Damn that man! I hope he hasn't hit the cows.' The south coast was the constant target of these hit-and-run raids, apart from

major blitzes on London and the cities. Bombs fell round the
harbour at Fowey, at Bodinnick and Polruan. There the
sisters Angela and Jeanne were land-girls 'digging for Victory', breaking in soil and growing food up at Pont, while
U-boats nearly strangled the country at sea.

It was wonderful what brave women accomplished to
keep the country going in those appalling years. So many of
the Brownings' friends in the Army were killed. It is
noteworthy that the women of the *Herrenvolk* were not
called out, conscripted in this way: the Germans simply
enslaved other peoples, and killed them off in millions.
Daphne was reading Churchill's account of the years after
the first German war, and sharing his generous regret at the
continuance of the blockade that had brought the Kaiser's
Germany down at last. *Ich nicht*: I knew the German record
too well. Even Daphne was impressed by Eden's reminder
that Germany had forced war on Europe *five times* in the past
eighty years.

In the midst of all these anxieties she was reading her
grandfather's *Peter Ibbetson* and writing her own *Frenchman's
Creek*. This is not a favourite with her: she refers to it
disparagingly as 'more or less Jeffery Farnol'. He has been
long forgotten: this book not, it has gone on selling ever
since, for it has life in it. It is a favourite with me: I find it a
combination of romance and adventure, more in the vein of
Q., whom we both admire.

When I look back over the marginal comments I made at
the time they all appear appreciative. Scenes are 'well-set',
dialogue 'couldn't be bettered', etc. Here is the place to
notice her specific gift for dialogue, always natural and easy,
unforced, effective. The book is very atmospherical, the
inspiration, I noted, nostalgia. The action concentrates on
the Helford river, below her friend Clara Vyvyan's 17th-
century Trelowarren. (The colonnade of trees in *Rebecca*, by
the way, is the avenue of over-arching ilexes there, like a
cathedral aisle.) One notes a few specifically Cornish touches
– the servant laughing at the lady secretly, 'as if behind his
eyes'. The Cornish have an odd sense of humour: that is the
way we sometimes regard 'foreigners', not giving ourselves

away. As for the lady, she sometimes uses the boy's voice she employs in addressing servants.

If we look for the author, she is not far to seek. 'I wish I were a man,' says the lady; then 'I too would find my ship, and go forth, a law unto myself.' There is the longing to be free, no longer hampered by petticoats: 'At last she was playing the part of a boy, which as a child she had so often longed to be.' There are things that a man and a woman would not admit to each other, the reserve imposed by sex. Is there an anti-male fleck – at least flick of the wrist – in the female concern for the male (which Barbara Pym described as 'universal'), when the lady of Daphne's novel sees the man, without illusions, growing fat and unattractive, 'making some woman miserable'?

Marriages are denominated monotonous, not merely for the alliteration, I fancy; a writer's life is certainly not, for all the necessary drudgery – one lives in the imagination, the ideal 'to be cool, aloof, utterly detached'. 'I would be alone,' says the heroine at the beginning of the story. It ends in a flurry of action: 'exciting', says my comment, and 'high melodrama'. Why not? It is a recognised literary genre, and I enjoy the romance. Take it on its own terms, as I take Q. and Robert Louis Stevenson.

I did not enjoy the next book, *The King's General*, about Sir Richard Grenville and the Civil War in Cornwall, partly owing to a defect in me, no doubt. This is a straight historical novel, and I hardly ever like historical novels. For a pro-fessional historian, unprofessionals never seem to get it quite right. Even the great Walter Scott, for example. Those historical novels of his that are good are the ones that deal with the recent past which he knew thoroughly – some half-a-dozen, like *Redgauntlet, Waverley, The Heart of Midlothian.* Stories like *Ivanhoe* are tushery for children, and I could not bear to read *Kenilworth* today – with its nonsense about Leicester and Amy Robsart – any more than I can *Westward Ho!*

When the centenary of Kingsley's book came about – I had enjoyed it as a boy, of course – I was asked to write a new Preface for it. I re-read the novel, and replied that I did

not like it. The publishers rejoined – would I write a Preface
then saying why I did not like it? So I read it again, and
found that I could not bear it. Kingsley's 'muscular Christianity' is so Victorian, so untrue to the Elizabethan age. I
suppose there was an element of that, approximately, in
Drake and Hawkins; but the atmosphere, a much more
subtle matter, is all wrong: Victorian, not Elizabethan.

So I did not respond to *The King's General*, though I had
had a small hand in suggesting sources for reading. A straight
history of the Civil War in Cornwall, like Mary Coate's, is
more my cup of tea, don that I am. Actually she had made
extensive use of the Vyvyan archives at Trelowarren, before
she suggested their transfer to Exeter – for safety – where
they were destroyed, along with a great deal of historical
material, West Country records, in the German Blitz on the
city. These were the so-called Baedeker Raids, in which the
civilised *Herrenvolk* concentrated on historic cities, Canterbury, York, Bath etc.

At last, from Christmas 1943 Daphne was able, from her
years of work, to move into her dream house, where she
remained ensconced, hardly ever leaving it, for the next
quarter of a century. There she called the sleeping princess
deep in the woods alive, brought the house back to life,
restored it, looked after the gardens, walked the cliffs,
regularly swam in the cove. And worked: it provided further
stimulus to the imagination.

It became a family home, at least for the children, sealed
off from the outside world. (Daphne had had enough of it –
as I had had, once I withdrew within the walls of Trenarren.)
'Boy' Browning – 'Tommy' to the family – received the
reward of his outstanding services in the war by being
appointed Comptroller of Princess Elizabeth's Household,
and, when she became Queen, Treasurer to the Duke of
Edinburgh's. This meant life in London. Daphne did not
share it: she remained firmly within the paradise she had
attained. Anyone of conventional outlook would have made
the most of these grand opportunities in London. Not a bit
of it: no snobbery in this quarter; she preferred her own

fairy-tale world, and would make the concession of leaving it only once a year for a Royal party.

Neighbours at home were mystified by this addiction to solitude: we have seen that it was her true nature all along. Now she could indulge it and live in her fantasy world. The Menabilly peninsula is indeed a magical place. Neighbours, who were not invited to penetrate, used to have a joke, I don't know how true. Daphne was supposed to have set up wigwams in the woods for the kids – her idea of childhood happiness – until Tessa said, 'Why can't we go to school, and be like other girls?' In that remark, if true or something like it, is all the difference between genius and ordinary humanity.

In 1951 came another Cornish romance, *My Cousin Rachel*, which has always been a favourite of mine, except possibly for the rather melodramatic ending. But this naturally appeals to film-producers, since it opens up visual effects, and this novel has been quite recently televised, as *Rebecca* has been. *Rebecca* was filmed with Caerhays Castle standing for Manderley: the most beautiful of Nash's country mansions, looking down appropriately upon its cove. *My Cousin Rachel* was fortunate to have for a background an historic house in North Cornwall, looking across into Devon, going back to George Grenville, cousin of Sir Richard of the *Revenge*, in Elizabethan days.

In 1960 came one of her most remarkable books, though overlooked, overladen by the novels: *The Infernal World of Branwell Brontë*. This is a *tour de force*, to have brought alive and rehabilitated that submerged character among his three famous sisters. For poor Branwell was gifted, but died young without fulfilling himself as they did. This book calls our attention to another gift of Daphne's – her nose for research, her growing interest in it, and the industry she was prepared to put into it. The sources for the astonishing, the virtually unique writings of the Brontë children are many and various, but also extremely difficult to work out and interpret. Daphne has done this with devotion and complete sympathy – and converted me in the process. This is a beautiful book.

Everything shows that it is authentically hers. To begin

with, it is the story of a boy: he was apt to look down on his sisters for being 'incomplete', he was their leader, the creator of the extraordinary inventions in their fantasy world, the Kingdoms of Angria and Gondal. He invented the dialect, a mixture of Yorkshire with Latin and Greek, which kept their secrets to themselves, and the minute handwriting no one else in the family could read. He was ambidextrous, and could write with both hands at the same time. His poetry shows talent and vividly expresses his personality. So too his gift for painting: almost all his paintings have disappeared, but one can never forget those haunting profiles of his sisters.

He was their leader: all the hopes of the family rested on him. Yet he failed them. These young people of genius had no encouragement. Branwell wrote to Wordsworth: no reply; Charlotte to Southey: no reply. They read and hoped to contribute to famous *Blackwood's* (to which I used to contribute in its last days). Not until Charlotte wrote *Jane Eyre* did they break through – too late for Branwell.

When he gave up, through failure and drink (with which I have no sympathy), possibly drugs too, Charlotte, to whom he had been closest, seems to have turned away. I shared her attitude. I hate weakness of character, and blamed him, the male among them, for leaving all the burden to Charlotte, who battled through to fame. I fear I was wanting in sympathy: Daphne had compassion for the poor young fellow, her comprehension of humanity altogether wider than mine. Her aim was 'understanding for a figure long maligned, neglected and despised', to rehabilitate him and give him his proper place where he belonged – and now, through her understanding of him, belongs. I need not say with what sympathy she renders the atmosphere of that raw Haworth parsonage, with so much youthful genius cooped up in it; nor elaborate on the fact that the Brontës had been an inspiration from the first – the title, *The Loving Spirit*, came from a poem of Emily's.

Daphne gave me my belated copy, with an inscription of which I am proud: 'A.L. from his student, with love.' But that came later, after my conversion.

I may have been some help when came the crisis of her

leaving Menabilly: here was a situation I could well understand and even enter into. The old family to whom it
belonged wanted to come back and resume residence after a
lapse of two generations. This meant a terrible wrench for
the imaginative writer who had so identified herself with it
and made it famous, while keeping it mercifully private. I
knew it would be a heartache, and deliberately set myself to
be consoling.

She was to move a mile or so up the road to Kilmarth,
another Rashleigh house higher up the peninsula, with a
splendid view south and west all over St Austell bay and out
to sea. A slate-hung, Queen Anne house it was atmospherical
enough in its own right. I knew it well during its occupation
by Charles Singer, historian of science, of a rationalism to
banish any ghosts. All the same, it was as numinous as
Menabilly, and Daphne made it even more psychic when she
came to write about it. For, I consoled her, the move would
give her a new inspiration, as it did.

That same year, 1967, came her illustrated book, *Vanishing
Cornwall*. Naturally we both view the overlaying of the
country with modern structures, factories, housing estates,
caravan sites, popular resorts, Butlin camps, with alarm and
despondency – and I regard the increase of population with
utter horror: responsible people, especially scientists, know
that the population explosion of our time is the gravest
danger to the human race, and in my view accounts for
much of the troubles around the world.

Still, Daphne's approach to the subject is not the same as
mine. She is interested in the visual appearances, the surfaces
of things – the sea and ships, cliffs, rocks, waves; hill and
heath and moor. She is well qualified to write about them:
has she not ascended our mountain, Brown Willy – geologi-
cally of the most ancient in Britain? This I have not done.
The interest of the historian is solely with the past, and with
the present only so far as the bones of the past peep through
the skin. In short, Cornwall to me is a country of the mind,
a construct of the historical imagination in which I live – not
in the hideous time into which we have survived, the slack
society around us . . . I avert my eyes, am even more

withdrawn than Daphne: she has at least given hostages to fortune, as I never would. She has had more confidence in life, and produced a family.

She collaborated over this book with her son, a gifted photographer, who contributed the characteristic illustrations. What gifts that stock has brought out! Her elder sister, Angela, who succeeded to the home at Bodinnick, is a reputable novelist, and has given us a less reticent autobiography in *It's Only the Sister*. The youngest sister, Jeanne, is a painter: and I detect artistic talent again in the book-jacket of a daughter for a collection of her mother's short stories. One is almost inclined to repeat Gerald's exclamation on his daughter's engagement, 'It isn't fair!'

Kilmarth bore fruit in perhaps the most original and ingenious of all her books, *The House on the Strand*. That is the meaning of Ty-war-dreath, the parish in which Kilmarth stands – the 'house' being the vanished priory, which dominated the life around our bay in the Middle Ages. This was a new field of exploration, and the student did her research conscientiously into the 14th century, when the noble bishop Grandisson ruled the diocese from Exeter. Here are the vanished people of that age, Champernownes, Carminows, Bodrugans.

The tenant of Kilmarth is once more a scientist, who has developed an hallucinogenic drug which takes him on trips into that past. I cannot here go into the complex, double and parallel plot, merely note that it is another *tour de force*, so skilfully interwoven as to carry a strange sort of conviction. Anyway, what more real than the world of imagination in which one lives? When I go round Cornwall I often know who were living in the 16th century in the places I pass, and quite a lot about them, when I have no idea who the occupants are today.

But we are pursuing the author. We recognise her in the 'intolerable strain' of waiting for the arrival of unwelcome guests . . . anticipating the 'dire moment' of a car coming down the drive. (I can only say that she has never been other than welcoming to me – far more than I deserve.) And we gather that it is easier to entertain, 'albeit unwillingly', out

of doors. We must not make too direct a transcript from life
to the text, as with any author – William Shakespeare, for
example – though all fiction depends on autobiography.
(The modernist slogan in criticism, 'the Death of the
Author', is already out of date and was always nonsense.)

However, we do encounter the ups and downs of married
life, that can be 'precious, exasperating, monotonous and
dear'. As for the fantasy world that is so exciting, it holds a
fascination which is lacking in the world of today; 'The
trouble is that day dreams, like hallucinogenic drugs, become
addictive; the more we indulge, the deeper we plunge. . . .'

Research can become an addiction – and also a resource
when the imaginative scope of a novelist reaches its term.
Daphne has spoken of that to me, with her usual common
sense – remarkably, that has always gone in tandem with her
fantasy life, kept a good balance. The 1970s saw her venturing into the Elizabethan age, with two books about the
brothers Anthony and Francis Bacon – a curious choice.
Why?

For Anthony it had this advantage, for a writer with an
Anglo-French background, that he spent so many years in
France, the twelve years 1580–92. As the brother of Francis
and nephew of Elizabeth I's chief minister, the great Lord
Burghley, Anthony Bacon is well known to us Elizabethan
scholars. He was Essex's right-hand man, his intelligence
agent and director of his foreign correspondence. During his
years in France he was closely in touch with Henry of
Navarre, to become Henri IV, and the leaders of the
Huguenot party.

Both Anthony and Francis were known in their time to be
homosexuals. But Daphne's exploration of the Montauban
archives brought to light something hitherto unknown about
Anthony. He had a narrow escape, in that Huguenot ambience, from charges of sodomy with his pages. It needed all
Henry of Navarre's authority to weigh in and rescue him.
Similar charges were threatened against Francis later and
partly account for his climbing down at the time of his fall
as Lord Chancellor, when he was expected to put up a fight.

All this is quite well known about Francis, but no one had

known the new facts about Anthony. So I gave the book a warm welcome in my review of it. I could not do the same for the second volume about Francis Bacon. It was altogether too difficult a subject – all that expertise required about the law and jurisprudence, Bacon's technical work as Lord Chancellor, his no less technical work in philosophy and science. He was of course a genius *in these fields*.

Why then did Daphne think to tackle him? – Because she wanted to connect him with William Shakespeare, with whom Bacon had no known connection: their paths were wide apart, their genius totally different, the one all for poetry and the theatre, the other for prose, law, science, high politics. When Daphne asked me whether Bacon might not have had at least a hand in Shakespeare's plays, I replied shortly, 'Bloody rubbish!' She took this with her usual sportsmanship. Bacon no more wrote Shakespeare's plays than I wrote Daphne's novels, or than she wrote my books.

It is extraordinary that people should want to think that anybody but William Shakespeare wrote his own works. Nobody thought such nonsense in his own time, they knew quite well the most popular dramatist of the time who wrote the plays, as Ben Jonson did his – nobody has thought up such rubbish about him, though we know much less about his early life than we know about Shakespeare's, about which we know quite enough.[1]

Still, one lot of crackpots favour Bacon as the author of Shakespeare's plays. Another lot of loonies would like to think that the light-weight Earl of Oxford wrote them. I wonder that there is not a third school of thought devoted to the notion that Queen Elizabeth I wrote them under an assumed name. Others would *like* to think that Richard III did not commit his murders. One does not discuss these matters with people who have nothing to discuss with. One tells them; and if they then cannot follow, what does it matter whether *they* get it right or wrong?

The plain fact is that ordinary people do not know how to *think*, strictly speaking: they may get it wrong, they may

---

[1] v. my *Shakespeare the Man*, and *Shakespeare's Self-Portrait*.

even get it right, they cannot tell which. That's the joke on them, though it is rather a wry one. All great writers know this fact about humans – no one better than William Shakespeare himself. Good politicians know it quite well, perhaps especially those most given to democratic humbug. Franklin Roosevelt once said, but privately, 'the public never understands'. He did not dare to say it out loud; but it is a duty of the historian to speak the truth, perhaps especially in democratic society. (Only the elect *know*.)

At last in 1977 Daphne produced an autobiography, or a fragment of one up to her marriage in 1932; so she entitled it *Growing Pains*, and subtitled it, *The Shaping of a Writer*. That is the accent of the book, and indeed what is most important to her. As with Barbara Pym, writing is all in all, though their fortunes were so very different. (And as with me, too, though no novelist.) Daphne inscribed the book for me: as such: 'For A.L., my Professor and dear friend, Madame Non-Non, otherwise Daphne.'

That refers to the game we play since she came to Kilmarth. When her old senior makes suggestions – for example, that she should write a book about her Dogs, as I have done about my Cats – and she will not do it, then she is Madame Non-Non. She always knows her own mind, and it is usually Non. Very occasionally it is Yes, then she becomes Madame Oui-Oui.

For all the times she has generously asked me over to lunch, I have never once persuaded her to break the bounds and visit Trenarren. When she entertains me, always alone, it is a delicious lunch and wine is always offered. We neither of us take it, we stick to water. (I cannot bear to read another word about the drinking, the appalling private life of Hemingway or Scott Fitzgerald, such adolescents – and so boring. Henry James and Eliot, Edith Wharton and Willa Cather for me.)

An utterly honest and candid autobiography – it ends with her marriage in 1932 – it still maintains a reserve natural to her. The essence of that nature is to be *free*. When still quite young, hardly more than a girl, 'I'm rapidly coming to the conclusion that freedom is the only thing that matters to me at all.' Above all, freedom to write. And about that, the essential thing, she tells us concisely how it comes about, wells up in the mind of a born writer.

> The seed of an idea might take some five-and-twenty years or more to germinate and come to the surface, fusing with later observations – these observations in their turn blending with characters from long-forgotten books; but finally a story or a novel would emerge, and neither the model nor the writer would be aware of the transformation or of its origins.

That tells us all that need be said of the mysterious process.

It is a mistake to probe into it – as so much contemporary criticism does – to expose the seed-bed from which creation comes to the blaring light of day, or tearing up the roots to see how they are getting on. In fact a curious thing happened, she told me, after writing this book. Hitherto she had always projected herself into the character she was writing about and became that person, woman or man. She feels that writing about herself directly 'did something' to her, inhibited the creative process from operating. She never wrote another novel.

All along she had been inspired by the past. Here again we join hands – it is the same for me. 'Always the past, just out of reach, waiting to be recaptured.' And she asks the searching question, Why? I suspect because so much of the inspiration in all the arts comes from nostalgia – think of Poussin or Claude, Debussy or Duparc or Elgar.

It is curious that we had so much in common without ever knowing each other in those years – the whole of Cornwall, for one thing; and, in especial, the leading Cornish writer, Q., whom we all look up to as our head. Daphne was a close friend of the family – I was not up to that – a sailing, riding, walking comrade for Foy, Q.'s daughter. Moreover, his great friend, Barrie, so famous and successful then in the theatre, was Uncle Jim to Daphne.

It was after what she considers this psychological 'block'

that I made the suggestion, to be helpful, of a book about her dogs. After all, they have been important, closest of companions all her life, and must have interesting characters. But Non-Non: she needs to project herself into another persona.

She may have written a few more short stories since then – I recall her going on a cruise to collect ideas: the sea has always been suggestive to her. Think of *Rebecca*: there was the hulk of a wreck in the cove below the hut, away from the household, at Menabilly where she wrote. Altogether there must be a score of short stories, as authentic as the novels. No space to write about them here, but I remember the same characteristics, transcripts and characters from our local life. They evince too her sensibility for the psychic, the rendering of fear, the sinister side of fantasy, as in 'The Birds', which also lent itself to a Hitchcock horror film.

In these last years she has put together scraps from the workshop, given us the original draft of *Rebecca*, what she calls with her usual candour 'scraping the barrel'. Her courage amounts to stoicism about life. She tells us no more. I do not feel at liberty to go any further into her convictions and beliefs, or the one venture we had into the question of survival after death. This was after her soldier husband's death at Menabilly, the pathos of all his schoolboy possessions in his room upstairs.

We exchange tokens, photographs, Christmas cards, presents of books, messages, even brief letters, much more since her coming to Kilmarth. We are both hoarders. When I think of the archives mounting up, the undisturbed *Nachlass* of manuscripts, books and papers at both Kilmarth and Trenarren – somebody is going to have a great deal of fun (or work) in the next century.

And what a body of work she has accomplished in this! Who could have foreseen, from those early days at Bodinnick, what it would mount up to? I am sure that Q. did not, though he did say that the critics would never forgive her for the success of *Rebecca*. It has all been a wonderful success story, and more: a triumph of fulfilment in work (my gospel), for which we Cornish folk in particular can be grateful for what she has brought to life for people all round the world.

A Buried Love: Flecker and Beazley

Oxford – and in particular the Ashmolean Museum, to which Sir John Beazley left his wonderful collection of Greek *objets d'art*, painted vases, figurines, gems, sherds, fragments of 'the glory that was Greece' – brought together an exhibition for the centenary of her greatest scholar in this century and of all time in his chosen field. For consider: he not only put the vast subject of Greek vase-painting on a firm scientific and aesthetic basis, but virtually rounded it up and completed it in his own lifetime.

His obituary in the British Academy *Proceedings* tells us that:

> The master plan was nothing less than the identification of all the painters of Attic red-figured vases, great and humble alike. To that and to the parallel study of painters using the black-figured technique Beazley devoted his whole life; although he found time for other fields and produced there enough to have been the life work of any other scholar.

His achievement is indeed hardly credible. The second edition of his *Attic Red-Figure Vase-Painters* dealt with more than 700 painters he had identified. His parallel work on the black-figured identified 500 potters and painters, of some 10,000 vases from collections all over the world. Coincidentally he made Oxford the world centre for the study of Greek art, while his collections there continue the work.

He had a unique combination of scholarship with aesthetic sensibility which enabled him to recognise and piece together a work of craftsmanship from sherds in half-a-dozen places. His linguistic ability was phenomenal – he knew about fifteen languages, and regarded learning a new one as recreation. Behind the single-minded devotion and determination there was something stranger: he gave his life to his work, he sacrificed the living of life to it – as his friend, the poet Flecker, observed that he was going to do.

In this he was like A.E. Housman, inspiration and mentor to them both. The public thinks of Housman as our prime classical scholar, as I dare say he was as a Latinist. He is even more widely known as a poet, while his sardonic personality has come across in a number of biographies; even his well-concealed private life has at last become public.

Housman had comparable figures in his field of scholarship; not so Beazley, who had no equal in his, and – it is fair to say – never will have. Nor is Beazley's personality known to the public: no less withdrawn than Housman's, Beazley was much more successful in concealing it, and destroyed as much of the evidence of his early life as he could lay hands on.

In my old age I am probably the last person to have been in touch with something of it; and I owe this man of genius a great debt, for it was he who elected me in my working-class youth to a scholarship in English Literature at Christ Church. Thus it was that I learned of his relationship with Flecker, buried with Flecker's early death at thirty; but the inner nature of that relationship, I have only recently realised, is only fully revealed in Flecker's poetry.

The external story is well told in John Sherwood's sympathetic biography of Flecker, *No Golden Journey*. He describes the relationship as 'a highly charged emotional friendship' – which it was, and more. Though it has not been told from Beazley's point of view, Flecker's poetry reveals its nature in the way poets have of blurting out the truth, for in verse one can say anything, most people will not understand what is being said.

What is stranger than the fact of sexual love is the degree

of intellectual interpenetration. For Beazley too began as a poet. Though he destroyed as much as he could get hold of later, from what is left we see that he had more ideas and images than Flecker; they worked so closely together that often Flecker would take up an idea of Beazley's and rework it into a poem of his own. Beazley's scholarly idea of a 'frieze of the gods' appears in Flecker's poem 'Heaven'; or a stanza from a poem by Jack will be re-worded by his friend.

I know nothing so intimate in the history of literature – I don't think that even Verlaine rewrote Rimbaud's verse. Nor is it that Flecker's early poetry is superior to his friend's; Flecker's is more personal and revealing, Beazley's more impersonal and scholarly. From this unparalleled co-operation Flecker saved from destruction a score or so of Beazley's poems – some of them transferred and re-worked – while I have tracked down only three, all that were published, in the *English Review*, in which Flecker's early verse appears too.

Beazley gives nothing away; by this time, 1911, it is:

> I have made myself the master of the horse Desire,

as Housman never did. Or,

> The secret of happy days –
> Would you know it?
> Suck the juice out of things, then away, and forget them.
> Who sips and never is drunken, wise is he:
> Though I fade, and my eyes are sunken, look at me.

Still, we have:

> A rose-wreath for your rustling hair,
>   The trembling rubies for your ears.
> But since the faces of the gods
>   Are shadowy now as long ago,
> Let's cover up, and hide away
>   All knowledge and desire to know.

He managed to cover up very well in that long lifetime of
eighty-five years, world renown in his sphere, a closed,
walled-up heart. Until now, when Flecker's poems give us
the key.

Beazley, a year younger and scholar of Balliol, winning all
the classical pots and prizes, was intellectually more mature
than Flecker next door at Trinity. Jack was already the critic,
going through Flecker's poems line by line, with detailed
criticisms of words and images. He was sure that Flecker had
genius – which meant everything to him, constantly criticised and questioned by his conventional parents, the Headmaster of Dean Close School at Cheltenham and his
formidable wife, who wanted a safe, scholastic career for
their wayward, passionate son.

Jack saw that scholarship was not for Roy, with his Second
and Third in the Schools – even the Newdigate did not come
his way, though he expected it. Beazley's intuition told him
that one day Flecker would make a *dramatic* poet, as he did
with *Hassan*, a stage success – after his death, alas. Meanwhile
the two shared everything, including Nellie, the Carfax tart
– though Jack had to pretend that she was a boy to get any
enjoyment out of it.

It is clear that the bisexual Flecker was the masculine
partner, Jack the feminine. When young he had a markedly
feminine beauty – as Flecker wrote: 'he reminds me of
Shelley, especially when he lies on the hearth-rug, with his
long light hair, slight frame and pensive face. Indeed such a
fellow is not often to be met with outside of a novel or
romance.' Certainly the friendship, with its Greek overtones,
was the romance, and the inspiration, of Flecker's all-too-
short life. Jack remained youthful-looking so long that it
became 'embarrassing', says Mr Sherwood: 'tired of being a
bloody Peter Pan', he wrote. I well remember those shy,
retiring looks, the dust-gold hair and exclusive expression as
a don at Christ Church; he retained those looks into old age.

Absorbed in the Greek view of life, Jack already had no
conventional religious belief; and shortly we find Flecker
writing, 'I have at length definitely become an agnostic', and
he wrote a one-act, anti-religious play. This was anathema

at Dean Close School – so appropriately named – where Flecker's parents were all the more strenuously Christian for being Jewish converts. So the friendship was deeply disapproved, and Flecker forbidden to bring Beazley home to the house. Flecker's mother was a dragon, and later did everything she could to suppress the story of the relationship and keep Beazley's name out of her son's biography.

The parents were unable to keep them apart; together in Oxford, we find them together on cross-country jaunts in Wales, in Italy, sharing a room in Paris or Bonn – Flecker learning the languages for the Consular service, while Beazley pursued his addiction to Greek pots wherever he went. Here they are in Venice:

> The town whose quiet veins are dark green sea,
> The town whose flowers and forests are bright stone:
> There it was the God came to you and me
> In the signless depth of summer. All alone
> We lay . . .

There was a good deal of lying about, not only on the hearth-rug but out of doors, to judge from the few photographs that remain. They had 'too good a time in Italy', but – 'Curse it, father heard Jack was with me.' Then

> Life stood still a moment, mists came swinging
> Blindly before us: suddenly we passed
> The boundaries of joy: our hearts were ringing
> True to the trembling world: we stood at last
> Beyond the golden gate,
> And knew the tune that sun and stars were singing.

And again:

> We that were friends tonight have found
>   A fear, a secret, and a shame:
> I am on fire with that soft sound
>   You make, in uttering my name.

This was years before Auden popularised such affairs:

> Lay your sleeping head, my love,
> Human on my faithless arm . . .

but the relation between Flecker and Beazley over the years was far from casual, unlike many of Auden's.

We know little of those lyrical jaunts all over northern Italy, except that once the couple were stranded penniless in Florence. Jack's circumstances were even more straitened than his friend's, while Flecker was dependent upon the conditional doles he received from his parents. Beazley gives nothing away in his verses. T.E. Lawrence, who was one of the circle, had a perhaps exaggerated opinion of them: 'Beazley is a very wonderful fellow, who has written almost the best poems that ever came out of Oxford; but his shell was always hard, and with time he seems to curl himself tighter and tighter into it.'

This was what Flecker found, as the early ardour cooled off, though as late as 1911 we find him writing excitedly from abroad: 'If Beazley's poems are in the *English Review do* send me a copy.' While Lawrence wrote later, it was not possible 'to discover how much he had written or why he had abandoned it', I think it is clear that he had decided that his vocation was for scholarship, not poetry – or, rather, the decision was made for him by his passion for pots, which survived everything. This is the theme of one of Flecker's best-known poems, 'Invitation to a Young but Learned Friend to abandon Archaeology and play once more with his neglected Muse':

> Has Fancy died? The Morning Star gone cold?
> Why are you silent? Have we grown so old? . . .
> May summer keep his maids and meadows glad:
> They hear no more the pipe of the Shropshire Lad!

Here is something of what Housman meant to this esoteric circle, himself buried in scholarship until overwhelmed by the experience – death of his early friend – that led to his *Last Poems*. Flecker reproached his friend:

> Lover of Greece, is this the richest store
> You bring us – withered leaves and dusty lore,
> And broken vases widowed of their wine,
> To brand you pedant, while you stand divine? . . .

He can have had no idea of the summit of world renown his friend would ultimately reach in his chosen field:

> You who would ever strive to pierce beyond
> Love's ecstasy, Life's vision, is it well
> We should not know the tales you have to tell?

Beazley was never to tell them, he resolved to keep silent all his life – and to put his *life* into his scholarship. That was where his genius lay. There were few people at Oxford at that time who realised what lay behind Flecker's poems, and in those benighted days would have disapproved if they had.

In fact Flecker and Beazley were leading rather *risqué* lives, if less openly and less audaciously than the Cambridge Apostles whom they knew. There was a good deal of coming and going between them. Maynard Keynes came over to see Beazley, and found him 'quite unspoilt'. In 1908 Flecker moved to Cambridge to prepare for the Consular service; Beazley, visiting him there, found Strachey and Keynes the cleverest men he had ever met. Keynes had a typically supercilious view of Flecker, who for his part was not much impressed by Rupert Brooke's poetry. (Actually, before 1914, Flecker and Brooke were regarded as the rising hopes of English poetry: next year both were dead.)

In January 1910 Flecker and Beazley were sharing a cheap room in Paris together, while Jack was studying Greek vases in the Louvre. Here the previously athletic Flecker – given to the sport of roof-climbing at Oxford – developed the throat trouble which announced the tuberculosis (hence his feverish activity) which killed him in a few years. When writing his verse play, *Don Juan*, he returned to Oxford for

Jack's judgment. It was rather cool, and this cast its shadow. Herbert Trench of All Souls, who was at this time managing the Haymarket theatre, was distinctly encouraging; he believed in Flecker's future as a dramatic poet – to be justified, if all too briefly, by the subsequent theatrical success of *Hassan*.

Posted abroad to Constantinople, the ambivalent Flecker found himself a devoted wife in the Greek world to look after him in his recurring illnesses. Beazley had now found himself a niche as a young classics don at Christ Church. How bored he must have been teaching Honour Moderations to recurring undergraduates! When Flecker invited himself to stay, Beazley replied with a drawing of himself as an effigy on a tomb in the cathedral, and 'I shall be delighted to see you. I will put you up in a neighbouring tomb!' In a way, this gives a clue to Beazley's later life: he gave up *life* for scholarship – a reason why his scholarship was so wonderful. The visit was not a success, the old glad days were over: Flecker found Jack plunged in melancholy – as indeed I found him later, something wraith-like about him, an absorbed ghost.

From the Middle East, in 'Gravis Dulcis Immutabilis', it is still:

> Come, let me kiss your wistful face
> Where sorrow curves her bow of pain,
> And live sweet days and bitter days
> With you, or wanting you again . . .

There had evidently been ups and downs between them, as usual in such intense relationships.

> And listen, while that slow and grave
> Immutable sweet voice of yours
> Rises and falls, as falls a wave
> In summer on forsaken shores.

Those shores were now of Asia Minor, where Rupert Brooke was to find a grave. In 1910 Flecker wrote from Constantinople, where

There lies a photograph of you
  Deep in a box of broken things.
This was the face I loved and knew
  Five years ago, when life had wings:

Five years ago, when through a town
  Of bright and soft and shadowy bowers
We walked and talked and trailed our gown
  Regardless of the cinctured hours.

Now I go East and you stay West
  And when between us Europe lies
I shall forget what I loved best,
  Away from lips and hands and eyes.

There was only one more encounter. Flecker and his wife
were in Paris at the turn of the year 1912–13. Beazley was
there independently, using the Christmas vacation to work
at the Louvre. Flecker's wife wrote coolly: 'My husband was
glad to see him again, and to live once more in his company
the old life of a student in the Latin Quarter.' How much did
she know of it?

Flecker would still be writing up a poem, in 'The Oak and
the Olive', on a theme from Jack's old black Notebook –
that of their nostalgia for Greece, and Flecker's home-
sickness for England now that he was abroad. Then, ill in a
sanatorium in Switzerland, he was dying for news of
Oxford; 'Is Jack in his coffin yet?' is his last word.

This was the Beazley whom I knew – if that is the word
for it – in my young years at Oxford.

Flecker died in 1915. J.C. Squire, in editing his poetry,
wrote, 'I cannot help remembering that I first heard the news
over the telephone, and that the voice which spoke was
Rupert Brooke's.'

Beazley did not marry until after Flecker's death, when
again he made a Jewish choice. Marie Bloomfield, whose
husband had been killed by the Germans in their war – so
that, a gifted linguist, she would never speak German – was

a remarkable woman, a talented photographer whose slides were a great help to Beazley's work. She built up a record of the thousands of pots and pieces, vases, figurines, sherds, intaglios, gems from the many countries they visited together. She subordinated herself to serving him in every way, guarding him with maternal possessiveness – 'my Jacky' constantly on her lips.

She made an exotic figure against the ecclesiastical desert of Tom Quad, not much appreciated by the staid Dean and Canons. Regarding herself as some kind of classical goddess, she had a tame goose that waddled after her, recognising her by her unmistakably loud check skirt.

Jack's colleague in teaching Mods was the Latin scholar, S.G. Owen, whose chief interest in life was the food and drink at high table. We called him DT; and 'You've no idea of the horrors of the war – had to eat potatoes in their skins.' 'You had better go and hear Gilbert Murray weep over the *Medea*,' he would say – and true it was that the eminent man had a lachrymose voice.

No love was lost between Beazley and Owen, who, purple-faced and with a curious pine-shaped head like William IV, had no sense of beauty or the distinction of his junior. However, he got his come-uppance from Housman, when he dared to produce an edition of Juvenal: Housman wondered where he got his certainty from, until he turned to the title page and saw *Dominus illuminatio mea*. (Motto of the Oxford University Press.)

One weekend, while Jacky was away at Cambridge, the pet goose ate the *Daily Mail*, and died of it. Owen teased Beazley with 'So Goosey's dead'; to this he replied glumly, 'Yes – and many worse men are alive.'

Marie had a daughter by her first husband, Marie Ezra, first wife of Louis MacNeice. I used to see that enthusiastic hetero pursuing the schoolgirl still in pigtails about the quad. Her mother was much against her daughter eventually marrying the son of a bishop; in a way she was right, for the marriage did not last. But that was another story.

I found Marie Beazley extremely flirtatious – I don't think she got much change out of her Jacky, I always thought it a *mariage blanche.* A Spanish refugee artist who drew Oxford figures with their speaking characteristics – Gerald Berners, for instance, fondling a lobster (he lunched off lobster every day) – drew a good likeness of Beazley, with a beautiful Greek youth in the background. Has that portrait ever been reproduced?

Marie took particular notice of me, and would ask me to a light lunch in their rooms – Jacky silent as ever, and the moment lunch was over he vanished into his inner sanctum. In St Giles's they shared the exquisite Judge's Lodgings – built as a town house for the Marlboroughs – with a fellow exotic, 'Wee Pricie'. One evening when I was bidden up to dinner, Marie appeared extremely *décolletée*, black velvet with a yard of beautiful old lace. Her daughter let the cat out of the bag with 'O Mummy, you told us not to dress!'

That evening after dinner there turned up one of Jacky's men friends from Flecker days. They disappeared into another room – a distinct *gêne* in the atmosphere; Marie was out of it, put out, and I left early. Her attitude to me expressed itself in: 'I know what would get under your defences – a young Greek girl.' Did she fancy herself in the rôle? I decided not. Unlike the young man in Ronald Firbank's novel, I was not fascinated by her little schoolboy moustache.

When I got to All Souls – where Marie first met her Jacky, at lunch with T.E. Lawrence – I found a faith for myself in Marxism. I became a fanatic, though not a Communist – and asked Marie to lunch alone to tell her that here was my vocation, and gave her her *congé*. She must have found that comic and told of it, for I afterwards heard of it from a mutual friend.

But that is part of my story; and now they are all dead, and I an old man.